SCIENCE AND TECHNOLOGY EDUCATION AND FUTURE
HUMAN NEEDS

Volume 6

Food,
Agriculture and Education

Science and Technology Education and Future Human Needs

General Editor: JOHN LEWIS
Malvern College, United Kingdom

Related Pergamon Journal

INTERNATIONAL JOURNAL OF EDUCATIONAL
DEVELOPMENT*

Editor: PHILIP TAYLOR

Throughout the world educational developments are taking place: developments in literacy, programmes in vocational education, in curriculum and teaching, in the economics of education and in educational administration.

It is the purpose of the *International Journal of Educational Development* to bring these developments to the attention of professionals in the field of education, with particular focus upon issues and problems of concern to those in the Third World. Concrete information, of interest to planners, practitioners and researchers, is presented in the form of articles, case studies and research reports.

*Free specimen copies available on request.

Food,
Agriculture and
Education

Edited by

A. N. RAO
National University of Singapore

Published for the

ICSU PRESS

by

PERGAMON PRESS

OXFORD · NEW YORK · BEIJING · FRANKFURT
SÃO PAULO · SYDNEY · TOKYO · TORONTO

U.K.	Pergamon Press, Headington Hill Hall, Oxford OX3 0BW, England
U.S.A.	Pergamon Press, Maxwell House, Fairview Park, Elmsford, New York 10523, U.S.A.
PEOPLE'S REPUBLIC OF CHINA	Pergamon Press, Room 4037, Qianmen Hotel, Beijing, People's Republic of China
FEDERAL REPUBLIC OF GERMANY	Pergamon Press, Hammerweg 6, D-6242 Kronberg, Federal Republic of Germany
BRAZIL	Pergamon Editora, Rua Eça de Queiros, 346, CEP 04011, Paraiso, São Paulo, Brazil
AUSTRALIA	Pergamon Press Australia, P.O. Box 544, Potts Point, N.S.W. 2011, Australia
JAPAN	Pergamon Press, 8th Floor, Matsuoka Central Building, 1-7-1 Nishishinjuku, Shinjuku-ku, Tokyo 160, Japan
CANADA	Pergamon Press Canada, Suite No. 271, 253 College Street, Toronto, Ontario, Canada M5T 1R5

Foreword

The Bangalore Conference on "Science and Technology Education and Future Human Needs" was the result of extensive work over several years by the Committee on the Teaching of Science of the International Council of Scientific Unions. The Committee received considerable support from Unesco and the United Nations University, as well as a number of generous funding agencies.

Educational conferences have often concentrated on particular disciplines. The starting point at this Conference was those topics already identified as the most significant for development, namely health; food and agriculture; energy; land, water and mineral resources; industry and technology; the environment; information transfer. Teams worked on each of these, examining the implications for education at all levels (primary, secondary, tertiary, adult and community education). The emphasis was on identifying techniques and resource material to give practical help to teachers in all countries in order to raise standards of education in those topics essential for development. As well as the topics listed above, there is also one concerned with the educational aspects of ethics and social responsibility. The outcome of the Conference is this series of books, which can be used for follow-up meetings in each of the regions of the world and which can provide the basis for further development.

JOHN L. LEWIS
Secretary, ICSU-CTS

Contents

B. Case Studies

C. Discussion of Issues

Introduction

1

Food, Agriculture and Education

A. N. RAO
National University of Singapore

It is more than a coincidence that the conference which formed the basis for this book met in the beautiful city of Bangalore, which is a good example of an Indian city reflecting all the cultural, ethnic, religious and educational diversities of India. Bangalore is also well known for its various national scientific institutions and industries.

For food and agriculture, the word "Bangalore" has special significance. Literally, the word means *cooked beans* or *steamed beans* with plenty of protein and nourishment. For the majority of Indians, food is God (*Annam Brahma*), because they recognized from the time of Vedas that there is an intimate relationship between *Sun–Plants–Food*, the fundamental chain relationship and the basis for all food production. They also declared that food is the life-giving and sustaining principle and hence it was considered as part of God and a gift of God. Annapurna, the consort of Lord Shiva, is the goddess of food.

Education is regarded as part and parcel of the overall social economic system of any society and the principle role of education is to promote and improve the knowledge and value system of a given society. The development of the society depends on the educational system that it follows. Education is also a lifelong process through which knowledge, ideas and skills of an individual develop either in a formal or informal manner. When proper values are absorbed, the individual becomes a useful member of the society and the society flourishes. Therefore the medium of education can always be properly utilized to bring improvements either at individual, society or national levels.

When we look at food and agriculture problems from the point of view of education, it becomes very clear that at present very little is done in schools and colleges to improve the understanding of the children or students to prepare them to appreciate and solve the problems involved. In fact this was one of the main reasons to have had a conference of this

3

nature and to have produced this book in order to redefine our goals and to improve teaching curricula and methods.

Under the title Food and Agriculture we can identify five major topics: (1) food production, (2) food consumption, (3) preservation and storage, (4) biotechnology, (5) technology transfer. In what follows I shall outline key information about each topic. The educational implications will then be discussed.

Food production and food consumption

The total food production of the world today is about 3.8 billion metric tonnes. Of this, 98% is produced on land, while the other 2% is from marine and aquatic sources. Cereals, root crops, vegetables are the major products. Highest production of cereals is in North America, Asia and East European regions. Almost 50% of the root crops is produced in Asia (215 million tonnes compared with world production of 526 million tonnes). Farm animal distribution is more or less uniform throughout the world, though there is a wider variety of animals in the tropical regions.

More arable land per worker is available in North America (29 hectares) than in Asia (1.8 hectares). The percentage of irrigated land is highest in China (40%) by comparison with Africa or Europe. About 60% of the population is engaged in agriculture in Africa and Asia, while in developed countries it is 5–15%.

Production levels vary between developed and developing countries (for maize, 22 tonnes per hectare against 2 tonnes per hectare; for wheat and rice, 14 against 2 tonnes per hectare). Nearly 40% of the cereals are fed to animals to produce meat.

The total available land worldwide is 13 billion hectares. Of this the grazing area is about 3 billion hectares and agricultural land area is about 1.5 billion. The percentage of forest land when compared to grazing land is twice as much in South, Central and North America; in Africa it is about the same; it is less in South Asia and Australasia. Only in South-East Asia is the forest area about twice as much when compared with cultivated land and grazing land put together (57% against 22%). Land availability for the extension of agriculture is highest in South America (81%), whereas in Asia almost 72% of available land is already utilized. Any further increase will decrease the forest areas.

Soil resources are being depleted and nearly 11 million hectares of arable land are lost every year. Erosion, desertification, soil toxicity and crop land converted to other uses are the main reasons. The annual soil loss is about 100 billion tonnes and nearly 75% of this is in South-East Asia and Africa. Soil conservation methods are most important and different types of soil need different conservation methods.

Of the total water available, 97% is salty and only 3% is fresh, 12% of the cultivated land is irrigated, producing 20% of the global harvest. Better use of water resources could improve production in developing countries.

At present the knowledge available in developing countries on fertilizer use is insufficient. Farmers tend to use fertilizers based on trial-and-error methods. When organic fertilizers are used it is on the basis that the more the dung or organic waste used as manure the greater will be the yield. Most of such manures are domestic or farm waste products, accumulated over a period of time and then transferred to the fields. When the same principle is applied to the use of chemical fertilizers, the results can be, and sometimes are, disastrous. Well-informed scientists are needed to educate the farmers. Leaching is a particular problem. Sometimes as much as 50–80% of the fertilizers applied are washed out of the soil and not absorbed by the plants. Fertilizer input per kg per hectare is highest in Japan, followed by UK, China and USA. Fertilizer used is particularly low in countries such as India and in Africa.

Plants grow in intimate contact with a variety of insects and micro-organisms; some are useful, many are harmful if the plants do not have the necessary resistance to withstand them. Crop plants also need to compete successfully with weeds. Application of pesticides and herbicides offer partial relief. Work on the genetic production of plants that can withstand different kinds of disease and damage is in progress and many types of biological control methods are being used. More well-trained analytical chemists are required to build up scientific expertise, especially in developing countries.

Food experts in different countries seem to agree in recognizing two major problems in food production. First, to grow the required quantity of food where it is needed by the people and to grow the right kind of food that is accepted by the majority of the people. Secondly, to be able to distribute the food to places where it is needed. Food supply from one country to another involves the cost of the food (unless it is a gift) and cost of transportation.

Viewing from the global level, it becomes clear that there is enough food production in the world, adequate to feed all the people. But there are millions of people in the world who suffer from hunger and starvation. The tragedies in certain parts of Africa are glaring examples. More technologi-cal skills and economic support are needed to improve productivity. Economic implications play an even greater role than technical and scientific ones. Poor people can ill afford to grow enough food and much less to buy it, even if available in the local market. Food aid, however, is not the best answer and improving the economic conditions of the people is the only solution. Education has a great role to play in this.

In fertile lands, the following agronomic practices are suggested: (1) methods involving multiple use, crop rotation and interplanting several crops at a time should be employed; (2) maximum irrigation facilities should be provided, despite the cost; (3) organic manures, crop residues and green manures should be used more than synthetic ones; (4) garden farms should be encouraged as these can involve growing many types of crop on small areas of land. In dry lands of intermediate fertility: (1) a concentration on crops that can grow in almost rainless conditions, such as millet, sorghum, amaranth, beans, maize, etc.; (2) soil cover crops which prevent soil erosion should be used and legumes are recommended. In marginal lands, next to deserts: (1) grow shrubs and bushes which act as barriers to wind erosion; (2) cover soil with grasses which grow well in dry soil; (3) Plant trees (*Prosopis*, *Casuarina* and *Leucaena* are recommended) and legumes.

The world average intake of food is 2600 calories per person per day. In developed countries the average is 3250, while in developing countries it is 1500–2200. Malnutrition results when the daily intake falls below 1500 calories. Hunger is a debilitating, devastating and intensely painful human experience. Hunger incapacitates an individual from doing any physical work or thinking efficiently. Almost 1 billion people in the world are under-nourished and around 20 million people die each year due to hunger: 41,000 every day, 28 persons every minute, including 21 children. Nearly 75% of poor people live in rural areas in developing countries where the infant mortality rate is very high. Present methods for supplying food or giving food aid do not eliminate poverty. Social and political problems are frequently the reason for this.

The Chinese example is a good one to study, since China has eliminated malnutrition and the food produced is shared among all the population. The agricultural system is based on ecological principles where practically nothing is wasted and all the residues, agricultural, human and animal wastes, are efficiently recycled. China has the largest irrigation system in the world and produces more than one-third of the world's rice. China also produces nearly one-third of the world's freshwater fish. Human labour is available in plenty. The integrated and decentralized administration helps to achieve a high degree of self-reliance.

In some countries starvation is not due to lack of food production, but because food is either not available or people cannot afford to buy it. Distribution and supply, and increasing the buying power of the people, are mostly political and economic problems.

However, whatever the cause of starvation, it is expected that in the next 30 years the world human population will increase to 8 billion from the present 5 billion. Thus the demand for food will increase rapidly. Increasing production and making the food widely available is a problem of considerable urgency. Because not all countries can become self-sufficient for food, the problem will need to be solved internationally, but in every country education, and in particular science education, can play an important part.

One other topic which should be mentioned is cash crops. Crops like coffee, tea, cocoa and peanuts are grown in developing countries in the tropical regions and are major sources for earning badly needed foreign exchange. Their capacity for earning money means that they are sometimes given priority over agricultural development. If cash crops fail in any particular year, then the country, as well as its people, will be poor and they will not be able to import food from other countries. Another problem is that commodities fluctuate in price: a quantity of sugar one year may buy eight barrels of oil, but the same quantity a year or so later may only buy one barrel. Policies might be changed and more food produced to meet local needs instead of importing food.

Food preservation and storage

Efforts being made to augment food production will only be successful if efforts are also made to prevent food losses after harvest. In general, the post-harvest loss in developing countries is very significant. The loss of staple foods, such as root tubers, vegetables and fruit, averages 30% of total production. The kind of losses include: reduction in food value as a result of physical loss; reduction in weight — quantitative loss; reduction in ingredients — quality loss; nutritional and germinative loss. Deterioration, contamination and changes in the composition of the nutrients are inevitable. An understanding of such aspects as transportation and refrigeration or cold storage facilities, as well as understanding of rural and urban markets, is also very important.

Over the last 15 years some research has been developing into the post-harvest physiology of fruits and seeds, considering the possibilities of extending the ripening process and reducing respiratory losses. Such work may be helpful in the development of simple techniques which could be applied in developing countries to help maintain both the quality and quantity of food after harvesting. But basic research on storage of crops produced in developing countries is rare. This aspect should be taught as part of plant physiology under the title "Post-harvest physiology of crop plants and the extension of their shelf-life".

Biotechnology

Biotechnology is the application of scientific and engineering principles to living cells to produce goods on a commercial scale. The modern methods of biotechnology that are directly relevant to agriculture and food production are (1) plant and cell tissue culture; (2) recombinant DNA technology; (3) bioprocess technology; (4) biological nitrogen fixation; (5) vaccine production. Many international meetings have been convened in the last 5 or 6 years and the discussions in almost all of them have emphasized the need to incorporate the various topics as part of science teaching for manpower improvement. Many of the methods listed above were started as simple laboratory techniques to understand growth and biochemical reactions at cellular or molecular level. But today each one of these areas has grown into an independent, multi-disciplinary subject that draws two or three science subjects. Knowledge is increasing and the benefits to be derived are immense and will meet the basic needs of the people. Therefore, they should form part of the curriculum at secondary school, college and university levels.

Biotechnological methods are already well used and increasingly contribute to the market value of agricultural, food and beverage products. Some idea of potential increases in yields is demonstrated in the following table.

TABLE 1. *Current and Potential Yields of Selected Agricultural Products as a Result of Biotechnology*

Product	Current yield	Potential yield
	tonnes per hectare	tonnes per hectare
Sugarcane	70–90	150–200
Cassava	15–20	60–100
Tomato	20–40	60–100
Oil palm	2–5	10–12
Peanuts	1.6	4
Castor oil	0.6	2.5
Tropical hardwood	10–20	40–60
Tropical conifer	12–20	40–60
Bamboo	25	100
Guinea grass	25	50

The following is a list of tissue culture topics related to the time when they are likely to be of benefit.

TABLE 2

Short term	Medium term (3–8 years)	Long term
Vegetative propagation of plants	Embryo rescue	Somatic hybridization
Disease elimination	*In vitro* fertilization	Hybrids, mutant cell lines
Germplasm exchange and storage	Somaclonal variation	Organelle transfer
	Gametoclonal variation	Chromosome transfer
	Anther culture and haploidy	Gene transfer
		Secondary metabolites

Some of the above topics can easily be incorporated into cell and molecular biology teaching. Many of the methods can be taught in an informal manner to the public and to agriculturalists who can use the methods as a routine to improve or increase plant production. Many horticulturists are already practising these methods.

Biotechnology can help animal producers in the breeding of animals and improve their health and nutrition. Important topics are monoclonal antibody production, embryo splitting, cloning and sexing of gametes, genetic engineering, and the transfer of embryos and semen between different countries to improve the quality of livestock. Many of these topics should be included in teaching, especially at tertiary level as part of physiology, genetics and molecular biology.

Isolation of identified genetic materials and transferring them into other cells to produce new characters has offered a tremendous opportunity to improve crop plants through biotechnological processes. The improvements envisaged in the quality of crop plants are several. New genetically modified plants can be introduced into the field in a very short time in contrast to traditional genetic methods. Many combinations of desirable characteristics can be mixed so that the newly synthesized plant will be superior in production and provide resistance to pests and diseases.

At present there are major limitations in identifying the genetic characters at the molecular level and regulating the gene expression. But in course of time, and with improved instrumentation and techniques, major successes should result. All the major growth characteristics of plants, including the increase in size, ratio between vegetative and reproductive parts, defoliation or fruit drop can be successfully controlled. Suitable plants which will grow in adverse or limited conditions will also be produced.

Because of the advances in genetic engineering, there is an urgent need to protect relevant habitats to preserve gene pool materials now that we have the technology to use such material more effectively than ever before. Yet again training and education at college level is necessary.

The production levels of rice, wheat and maize have already been considerably increased due to improved genetic varieties and many countries have benefited. The improved varieties can yield about seven times more than traditional varieties. The results of this so-called green revolution, obtained by earlier genetic techniques, can be further improved by the new developments in biotechnology used in association with sound ecological and physiological understanding of agriculture.

Technology transfer

Many experts believe that most of the food deficiencies experienced in developing countries can be met by transfer of technology from developed to developing countries (with appropriate modifications wherever necessary) provided the necessary manpower to receive and adapt the technology is available. Such manpower can be found only through science education.

However, it is necessary to remember that soil and other biological parameters are much more variable in the developing countries of the tropical and subtropical zones than in the developed countries of the temperate zones. Thus agricultural methods used in developed countries may not be suitable for direct transfer. Many modifications may have to be made with regard to methods and technologies. Many contradictory reports and results are not uncommon in the published literature when methods suitable in one area were applied in another country or region without studying the local variations. Even within a given country, most of the information is available in and around laboratories and agricultural centres. The information is either totally unavailable or not adequately passed on to the growers in distant places in the country. Uneven distribution of trained manpower and scientists also causes problems. Remedial measures cannot be undertaken unless the problems are studied on the spot by well-trained scientists, who can communicate directly with farmers and the public. Some of the major educational centres and research institutes should be moved to rural areas, even if remote from the capital.

Educational aspects of food and agriculture

Food is an essential component of all our lives. Food and agriculture is therefore important in every country. Some of the problems with which they are concerned are deeply involved in political and economic issues. Our concern here is specifically with those which can be solved through science education by removing the ignorance of the public and increasing and improving scientific manpower.

The system of science education which many countries have today is suitable for teaching basic sciences, but we rarely teach how this body of knowledge can be employed to solve the problems of society. In fact both are necessary. Science education should be relevant to day-to-day needs and it should give training in the scientific skills and methods essential for finding solutions to everyday problems.

In the past, educational systems have usually been concerned with producing specialists. Society has waited long for these students to solve the problems. Today we realize that the system is far from satisfactory because the size of the problems is far too great to be solved by the small number of specialists. We need many more specialists to work together in teams in co-operation with practitioners such as farmers, well-informed administrators and others, including the general public. The basic problems of food and agriculture should have a much larger place within the curriculum in schools and colleges in order to achieve two improvements: first, to make more people aware of the magnitude and variety of the problems involved, and secondly, to encourage more young people to take on careers towards solving those problems. It is not the object of science teaching to turn all science students into farmers, but all of them should be able to appreciate the problems of farmers and to help others to solve problems in an appropriate manner.

A change in the quality of education can only come about when the advantages of a new system are demonstrated and this will take time. But the barriers between academic knowledge and applications need to be broken down. A body of knowledge which is not useful is of no value. The problem areas should therefore have a central position in the curriculum whether they concern food and agriculture or any other topic. This does not mean that all existing science courses should be totally redesigned, but that there should be greater emphasis on practical applications and the acquisition of the necessary scientific skills for problem solving.

Awareness of food and agriculture is important at primary level, for we should not forget that in many developing countries children may have no education beyond the primary school. At that level scientific laws and principles are far less important than encouraging pupils to think for themselves. At the secondary level, the emphasis should be on teaching problem-solving, and at the tertiary level plant and animal productivity and all other factors that contribute to these topics are important and should be correlated with one another. An emphasis should be put on the ecology of agriculture, including both the theoretical and applied aspects of the subject.

Given that educational change takes time, a strategy for gradual development should be employed. The following are suggested as stages in that development.

Immediate needs

(a) Relationships should be established between basic concepts and their applications. Crop plants and farm animals should be used as examples whenever possible.
(b) Research students in biology should devote more attention to the improvement of plants and animals which are of economic importance.

Mid-term planning

(a) There should be greater emphasis on interdisciplinary teaching.

(b) The limiting factors between present yields and possible yields should be identified.

(c) Favourable and unfavourable conditions for the growth of crop plants should be defined.

(d) Available information on pest control and plant diseases should be disseminated as widely as possible through both formal and informal education.

(e) Knowledge of diseases of farm animals, their cure, prevention and economic implications in local and regional contexts should be provided.

(f) The scientific principles which help to understand and improve storage and preservation methods for food in the home and at national level should be taught.

Long-term planning

The following topics should be included, mainly at the tertiary level: molecular basis of reproductive growth; plant growth under stress conditions; nutritional and preservation processes; development of less expensive and more cost-effective nitrogen fertilizers; oxidative nitrogen fixation; production of hydrogen from water using solar radiation; controlled release of fertilizers; plant and animal growth regulators.

General

In addition to the above, mass media, short courses and other adult education methods should be used for informal and continuing education. In these the relationship between economic, sociological and the scientific aspects of food and agriculture should be stressed and their roles in solving various problems clearly defined.

Society will function well when the basic needs of life are met, and of these food is the most important. Education can help to meet these needs and all efforts should be made to improve the education and knowledge of the people in order to promote a better quality of life.

A. General Section

2

Children and Agriculture

JOS ELSTGEEST
Middelburg, The Netherlands

This is not the first chapter written about agriculture and elementary education. Far away from the fields and the hoeing we have cultivated many a fertile thought on children and agriculture. Although our intention as writers is good, it is sad that our influence in this world, which suffers so much hunger and starvation, has been so little. Of course, we realize that writing alone is not sufficient to alleviate the wrongs in this world, so we have not confined ourselves to writing papers and articles. We have made regulations that "agriculture" should be included as a subject to be taught in our systems of education. We have drawn up syllabuses, composed texts and devised methods for our teachers and pupils. Schools have been provided with agricultural implements, and "school gardens" made part of the school compounds. Yet, it looks as if we have not written enough. Or should we say that we have not thought enough? Perhaps we have not done enough.

Syllabus teaching and agriculture

Imagine that we find ourselves one day in some remote village. This is our own village. We are poor and we have little money. We live in a self-made mudhouse and possess some pots, a hoe, a bucket for water, some clothes, a bed, and some other less important things. There is water in a not too distant river. Around us there is plenty of land, but most of it is of a poor quality and requires back-breaking work in order to cultivate it. We are poor. So are our neighbours. There is no employment around our village and going to town to look for work brings no relief. There are too many like us who are looking for work.

This sketches the situation which millions of children in our world face. It is the reality of life for many who finish some form of elementary or primary education. And I refer here to almost "normal" circumstances where neither the curse of drought, nor war or other man-induced calamity has led to the extreme disaster of mass starvation or other suffering.

It is legitimate to ask what can be done about this state of affairs. There are poverty and drudgery in many such villages. The houses are dilapidated, or makeshift shelters. The plots of land are hard to cultivate. The food is poor, sometimes insufficient, at best monotonous. In short: life is hard and there is no prospect of escaping from it. But should there be a way of facing it? Could there be a will to challenge it? And is that will accompanied by the necessary knowledge and insight to accomplish anything? In a search for an answer to these questions we turn to education.

Rightly so, for it is the task of the elders to take the young ones by the hand and put them on their own feet. The question remaining is whether the elders asked themselves such questions as those above. Traditional family and tribal educators probably had little time to sit down and ponder these questions: there was work to be done in order to survive, and in the process of surviving they educated the young because they are still surviving. School educators, those who educate in a regular manner within a regulated system of education, approach these problems not from the necessity of survival within, but from directions given by an authority without. Well meant as these directions are, they have the inherent danger that the teachings do not penetrate into the daily lives of the children being educated.

One undesirable outcome has been that the school is regarded as a possible way out of the need for subsistence farming rather than a way into more fertile fields. Since the word "primary" implies the word "secondary", the expectation of many was that school would eventually lead to paid employment. Even where "agriculture" was a compulsory subject, it was reasoned that the better your marks in this subject, the better your chances became of never having to depend on farming for your livelihood. And so the best farming pupils got qualified out of the fields. School education has often caused a negative attitude towards living off the land. Many a syllabus on agriculture has aimed high, but scored low. This, too, is a reality which we have to face.

Of course, we all have seen, or heard about, worthy examples of good agricultural education in exceptional schools led by gifted teachers, and where the scores were considerably higher, at least within the school. Alas, these examples are few and, in some cases, they have been praised out of existence. Left and right of us we encounter the ordinary village schools of less accomplishing allure. They are far from achieving what we envisage and they need our support and good counsel.

Good counselling does not consist of urging teachers "to tell the children about modern methods of agriculture". Such counsel is based on the magic belief in the power of the word (our own). Another semi-political slogan: "Teach them agriculture, the backbone of our economy!" is equally bad advice which has often led to a ritual hour of work each week in the field, and every child detested it. No child has yet been well educated by wishful thinking, nor by phraseology, political or otherwise. Which child of the age between 6 and 12 cares about an abstract backbone, anyway?.

Perhaps it would be well briefly to reflect on our still vaguely worded problem of the teaching of agriculture in primary schools.

When referring to "agriculture" we often use the word "farming", and two kinds come to mind immediately:

1. Subsistence farming: (a) for yourself and your family to survive, or (b) growing sufficient food for the nation as a whole.

2. Industrial farming: (a) on a small scale, cashcrops for sale, (b) on a large scale, specialized production of world commodities.

When people talk about "education" they are inclined to think of a whole educational career comparable to the one they themselves have followed. It is a little difficult to realize that for very many children primary education is all they get. Their educational career is nothing but primary.

The complexities of industrial farming are too far from their experience to make much sense. They live close to homefarming for subsistence. However, if ever an agricultural problem presents itself to young children, it will be in their food-bowl. The foresight and insight required to value a real agricultural problem is of such complexity, even at the simplest level, that our primary children cannot oversee nor grasp it. I refer here to the problem as an adult grasps it, and it is through an adult formulation that these problems find their way into syllabuses. Yet components of these complexities belong to the world of children and can be handled by them. They need time and opportunity to gather experiences, to build upon these, to find relationships and, within themselves, to develop knowledge and insight, so they gradually learn to make sense of this complexity of experiences and their interrelationships. This spells out the task of primary education: provide and use experiences and exercise (process) skills which enhance the growth of understanding.

Good counselling to primary schools acknowledges this reality of childhood. Running an agricultural policy to improve the economy of a country is not a children's problem. A child's task is learning to interact with the land and the things of the land, so that he can begin to become a good farmer, knowledgeable and skilful. Saddling children with our adult policy problems and forcing verbal solutions upon them, is clearly starting at the wrong end. By the time they need these teachings they will have forgotten all about them. Teaching children to face problems with confidence does belong to the reality of childhood, and therefore to the realm of primary education, provided the children are faced with problems which *they can handle*. This should be our point of departure in the teaching of "agriculture" in the primary school. The problems which children can handle, which they can manage, must be placed into their hands, literally. These problems must be found in the real, concrete objects, taken from their own surroundings, and which they manipulate. So, we shall now consider how to deal with the following.

Children and the things of the land

Soils, growing plants, flowers of many kinds and shapes, fruits and (germinating) seeds, seedlings, water, rain, air and sunshine, and animals big and small that dig and tunnel, eat and scratch, bore and scrape. These are the "things of the land" that children encounter, with which they can interact directly and in which they can discern form and structure and the force of life in its many manifestations. These "things of the land" can be placed into the hand of the children, so they can explore and investigate and search and compare and experiment. They can direct many "what-happens-if" questions straight to the objects under study by placing them in such situations that they respond through their natural behaviour. Thus "asking the things" is bound to give the children valid and valuable answers. By asking the right question in the right way the children obtain a right answer, and with it the confidence and the joy to carry on.

For this they need the guidance of their teacher who asks, thinks, puzzles and sees for them and with them, and who prods them by helping them to clarify their queries, or by giving them the question they could not yet formulate. This approach (of asking the things themselves as a scientist does) helps to create in the children an attitude of mind, a sense of curiosity, a spirit of inquiry. It induces the children to develop and use skills and abilities required to satisfy this spirit of inquiry. This is the way to understand things and events and their inter-relationships, which leads to understanding the greater complexities of man's agricultural interaction with nature.

Allow me now to illustrate my point by looking into a few classrooms.

I bypass work (although I regard this as extremely valuable) done by very young children who watch a bean and a pea grow in their own jampot with awe and enthusiasm, and who show this with great pride to their parents as if they have moulded the young shoots themselves.

I shall only mention the little boy who wanted to know whether a bean would germinate on spittle. He planted his seed in a tin and dutifully spat on it three times a day. Great was his surprise when the bean did germinate, but it grew in a stunted way and eventually wilted. "It died because of the poison in my saliva," he recorded in his science workbook. However doubtful his achievement may look at first sight, he did establish a relationship between the growth of his plant and an outside influence.

I give a fuller record of the work done by a fifth class in Kigurunyembe, Tanzania, where the children studied soils. They started by collecting a number of different soils taken from the forest, the fields, the riverbed, the riverbank, the roadside, a hilltop, a valley and from the cultivated garden at the back of their school. First they "analysed" their soils and found "big sand" and "small sand"; they found small sticks, straw, bits of leaves and other (organic) rubbish, but all in quite different proportions according to the origin of their soils. They found different rocks in their soils, and a different colour each time they made a wet smear of their soil on white paper. They began to understand that "soil" is many things; that one soil can be very different from another and (most revealing) that the neat division of soils into sand, clay and loam, found in their textbooks, did not make much sense.

Soon they started discussing what would make a good soil and what a bad soil. They were allowed to test their guesses by planting seeds in their different soils, keeping records of their daily growth. Naturally this did not make them much wiser at this stage as the experiments were highly inconclusive. In what they suspected to be poor soils the seeds thrived, while "rich soils" showed very disappointing results. However, reflecting on these unexpected results established the suspicion that obtaining information from experimenting with such complex things as soils and living plants is no simple matter. But the interest was there, and they continued eagerly to follow up all sorts of ideas.

They learned how to use a balance effectively. Although their balances were simple and home-made, they were accurate enough for their purpose. They weighed equal amounts of soil for comparison, using washers and nuts as units of weight. They translated their findings into a picture, which was a graph. They found the simple way of establishing the amount of water retained by a sample of their soil by weighing their samples dry and wet. They measured (and timed with the help of a tick-tock pendulum) the amount and flow of water through given samples of the different soils. They measured and graphed the "speed" at which water is "taken up" by different soils. They also established the percentage of air in each soil and began to understand that even air is a component of soil. They compared and discussed, appreciating the information obtained from their graphs, and fairly well deduced the comparative quality of their soils.

They collected a variety of little animals creeping out of their soils and they had lots of fun watching their structures and movements through hand-lenses.

In another school teacher Hamisi took his class four out to collect all kinds of seeds, and the children had been busy sorting and classifying these. Some had broken open seeds to look inside and they had identified obvious parts which they described in vernacular terms. The children had started a number of investigations when, one day, a problem arose which captured the interest of the whole class. One boy had brought a big cob of maize, and somebody asked:"How many seeds are there in one cob?" Wild guessing led to a lot of disagreement until they decided to count all the seeds in this cob. There were four hundred and seventeen grains in this cob, which surprised some of the children who still had a vague idea of large numbers.

Then teacher Hamisi presented an interesting problem: "Would all the seeds on this cob, big and small, grow if you plant them?" The class felt sure that all the seeds should germinate and grow. "They are all seeds, aren't they?" was their argument. "Fine," agreed teacher Hamisi, "that is what you think, but how do you know whether the maize seeds think the same?" There was no alternative but to try and see. The children prepared ten seedbeds and counted carefully how many seeds went into each bed. They watered the plots and placed hay on top so the soil would not dry too fast in the burning sun. Then they forgot to add water regularly.

Teacher Hamisi did not correct this error, but he just waited. Only a few seeds in each bed germinated and grew. "How come?" inquired the teacher a few days later. "You were so sure the other day. Now look what happened." The children admitted: "We did not give them enough water." They blamed themselves for they were still convinced that a seed is a seed, and so it ought to germinate. However, a few of them began to think of other possible reasons: "Perhaps some of the seeds were not planted deep enough?" (This became a problem for further investigation later.) "Perhaps some seeds were no good and therefore rotted." Teacher Hamisi only added: "What can you do now to make sure? For you have not solved the problem yet."

They took a new cob and counted the seeds, planted them very carefully at equal depth, and this time they took pains to keep the plots well watered. More seeds germinated and grew, but not all, which surprised the children for their belief in "they are seeds, aren't they?" was very strong. "Then," they decided, "something else must be wrong." "Would insects eat our maize?" "Would somebody have dug them up?" While pondering over various possibilities they unearthed the seeds and found that quite a few were rotting. Others showed no sign of germination nor of being eaten by insects. Finally they agreed that not all seeds in a cob are good enough to grow and they changed their problem into: "Can we make it so that all the seeds we plant do grow?"

They planned their new experiment very carefully. They chose only what they considered good, healthy seeds: big ones with no hole or blemish of any kind. They took every precaution they could think of when they planted their seeds, and then they waited. Two days later an excited boy announced that he had counted all the seedlings the night before, and the number was exactly the same as the number of seeds they had sown. Triumph! "Let us go and make sure," suggested teacher Hamisi. But when the class arrived at the plot they found a goat happily munching away at their seedlings. Never had a goat run so fast for its life for the children were furious. But the experiment was inconclusive. They built a fence and started all over again. They were determined to check their ability "to make all the seeds we sow grow".

While the whole class was engaged in the common problem just described, groups of children filled the waiting time with other activities. Some tried to grow seeds without soil, others planted seeds that had been cut in half. One group investigated how the depth of planting influences germination and growth. A few children wanted to know if "crowded seeds" have a chance to live. They made holes in the ground and filled these up with a handful of seeds all at once, after which they watered the soil as usual, awaiting the surprising results. One boy planted half a cob of maize: "Would the seeds sticking in the cob sprout?" It was a very busy class.

In all their perfect imperfection these examples are but snapshots, momentary slices of school life. However, if an approach as illustrated here does not lay a firm foundation for thoughtful agriculture, I would not know what does. Throughout these, and many other experiences and experiments which are not described here, the children develop an insight which is, perhaps, the most valuable one for an agricultural career, however humble it may be.

By manipulating real living things such as seeds, plants or insects, and by letting these respond to being placed in situations which the children themselves create and control (for instance, by watering the soil, pruning the tips, turning pots upside down, making it dark) they gradually become aware that living things show a pattern in their responding behaviour. The children become conscious of the fact that by manipulating and controlling the environment, they can influence and control the response and behaviour of living things in certain ways. And is this not the basis of all agriculture?

A question often expressed is the following: should children not be given more specific agricultural instruction which they can apply in later life to improve farming and so to raise their standard of living?

I would like to leave this question open. Many like me are inclined to say "of course!" But we shall start to disagree, perhaps, when we discuss just how to accomplish this in such a way that children in later life do remember our instructions, and do apply them in their own situation.

To the extent that children grow older and wiser (also at school) and are given, or assume, greater responsibility to act (to cultivate), they will need and ask for more specific instruction on how to do things well. Whenever they ask a question which arises from the activities at hand, or from the needs of the moment, there will be a willingness to learn. To ask means to want to know. Besides, if we help the children to develop an inquiring mind, we are preparing fertile ground in which to sow the seeds of practical imaginative and creative knowledge.

3

Agricultural Science Education for Development

ABRAHAM BLUM

The Hebrew University of Jerusalem, Rehovot, Israel

The sad state of the art

Thirty-eight countries with a population of 1300 million people are termed low-income countries. Their average gross national product is 200 US $ a year (World Development Report, 1980). They are spread over most continents, but have many things in common: above all, they are poor and agrarian but have not enough food. Three out of four people work in agriculture, but they produce today less food *per capita* than 10 years ago — in spite of the Green Revolution. Over 450 million are undernourished and every year millions of children die of hunger, starve or suffer from malnutrition.

The only hope for a long-range improvement of the economic situation of these countries is appropriate rural development. Even in countries where oil or important mineral deposits have been discovered, the rural sector — the majority of the people — remain poor and often under-nourished, and the social gap has widened.

Much has been written about the Green Revolution (Dahlberg, 1979) and the development of high-yielding varieties of rice, wheat, maize and other major crops. This development in itself has been one of the major achievements of applied science and genetic technology. The potential of these new varieties is high, and some of the most populated countries on earth have raised their yields dramatically. But as with all assumed panaceas, backlashes occurred and basic problems became obvious. To justify their name, the high-yielding varieties demand intensive cultivation methods; for example, the use of fertilizers and more knowledge. Both capital and modern know-how are not easily available to the majority of rural dwellers in developing countries. Even if governments, development banks and co-operatives provide loans and the necesary infrastructures, the crucial point remains: more knowledge is needed, especially skills in applying new, science-based, rural technologies.

23

Who is going to teach hundreds of millions of youngsters, who will have to grow food for their families of tomorrow the science and technology they need to fulfill their prime task in life? It would appear as obvious that this should be one of the main challenges of school, using the powerful tool of science education. Yet, schools in many developing countries go on teaching science for the very small percentage who will take up a scientific career and neglect the vast majority of pupils who need appropriate knowledge in science and technology, applicable to agriculture. They adapt science curricula from highly industrialized nations who have become curriculum powers, and adapt even culturally foreign examinations. Often these new science curricula contain very little about the scientific and technological problems which most pupils will encounter in their life, namely in agriculture. They usually stress Man on the Moon, instead of Man in his Field.

Secondary schools in many of the developing countries train gifted village boys for future life in the city, and drain the villages of their best potential for local leadership. Only a few educational policy-makers seek a non-alienation of rural youth towards the villagization concept, like the Solomon Island Educational Policy Review Committee (1973) did, trying to maintain their way of life. Most school systems in developing countries *adopt* rather than *adapt* science programmes from the industrialized West.

Part of the problem lies in the separation between pure or "conventional" science teaching and agricultural education. Unesco recommended that pupils should be assured of the equivalence of agricultural and general science courses (*Education in a Rural Environment*, 1974), but in reality "in many cases, agricultural education makes for social segregation" (Malassis, 1975).

No wonder that many leading development experts have written off or doubt the effectiveness of the school as partner in rural development in developing nations, and put their money into extension services and other forms of "non-formal" education (Coombs *et al.*, 1973). True enough, the latter have offered some very encouraging breakthroughs, for instance, the training and visit extension system (Benor and Harrison, 1977) in South-East Asia. Yet schools still have their advantages: they reach into areas which are not served by extension systems, they have prestige, and if teachers get the right kind of training and support, including suitable curriculum materials, they can do a great job.

Many science curricula in developing countries have not taken up this challenge. They were strongly influenced by major American and British science curriculum projects. Even those who did a remarkably good job in the adaptation of a European science curriculum to the conditions of developing countries, for example the Scottish integrated science adaptations in the West Indies and in Swaziland, neglected the agricultural potential for science teaching. Still more regrettably, even where science curricula with agricultural themes and development attitudes have been introduced, the needed teacher retraining has mostly been neglected.

Different approaches

It has been suggested that science and agricultural teachers "ought to meet regularly to discuss and adjust the cross-references of their respective subjects. Problems encountered in the agricultural course will be studied in the science course . . ." (*Education in a Rural Environment*, 1974). This meeting between two teachers who teach separate curricula, but are supposed constantly to co-ordinate their lesson planning, is a beautiful dream, far from reality. Unless the two subjects, agriculture and science, are correlated at the curriculum level, the gap will not be bridged.

One approach is illustrated by G. H. Owen's *Agricultural Science* in Zambia. From the first chapter onward simple agricultural experiments are introduced. The author states: "The study of this subject is not just for the rural dweller, but is important for all the citizens of a country. The knowledge can be passed on to the people in the villages to help them improve their methods." As in most agricultural science courses, practical issues are emphasized at the cost of other science issues. Apparently, quite unco-ordinated, a more prestigious "pure" science course is taught in Zambian schools and overshadows the applied, technological approach.

An integrated approach with agriculture as the central theme is adopted in the life and agricultural science curriculum developed in Israel. It treats the whole range of biology, but is based on an agricultural approach (where feasible and practical) and includes interwoven chapters on economics (Ministry of Education and Culture, 1980). It is an alternative to the BSCS-based high school biology curriculum. In order to ensure an equivalent status, parallel examination status was sought and achieved. The Inter-University Board on Student Admission accepted it as one of the science options (besides physics, chemistry, and biology) which would fulfil their minimum science requirements for university entrance. Such a recognition is important; it gives the new program (and approach) the prestige needed to be able to compete with more traditional science courses. Since in Israel science curriculum projects are heavily involved in the writing of the examination papers, the chances that the examinations reflect the spirit of the new curriculum are good.

Another approach is to have an agricultural option (module) in a science program. An example of an agricultural chapter in a modular-science course is "The Influence of Agricultural Activities on Soil Erosion" of CENAMEC (1979), the curriculum of the National Science Teaching Centre in Venezuela. The student manual starts with an explanation why soil erosion is such an important topic in some of the agrarian states of Venezuela, and why the problem should be studied from the point of view of various disciplines: climatology, geology, soil science and ecology. Accordingly, the learning and teaching materials are divided into four modules, each of which centres around one of the four disciplines. The need to sensitize students to the problem by involving them in the planning aspects is emphasized in the teacher's manual.

In Fiji, agricultural science is taken seriously, in a system which features elements of both the combined science approach (with agricultural chapters) and the approach of co-ordinating two parallel and interlocking curricula. Besides "basic studies", which include basic science, "modern studies" were also introduced (Ram, 1972). The basic science course was developed by the University of the South Pacific and is used also in other Pacific islands. Although the project leaders state in the introduction to the science readers that they are concerned with key areas of South Pacific resources, technology and agriculture, only few agricultural references can be found. Even in the booklet on plant products which emphasizes essential oils, spices and dyestuffs, not much is said about the cultivation of these plants. This approach is counterbalanced by the parallel modern studies units, for example, The Coconut, Growing Meat Chickens, Profit from Plant Nurseries, produced by the Curriculum Development Unit of the Department of Education. The modern studies units were successful in integrating principles of modern, scientific agriculture with techniques of production and involving pupils in practical project work, based on sound economic lines.

Probably the most established agricultural science curriculum with a wider focus on developmental, science and society issues is the agriculture as environmental science (1978) curriculum in Israel which is co-ordinated with the biology and the physical sciences curricula of junior high schools (Blum, 1973). Some of the uits, e.g. those on the world hunger problem or on plant protection (featuring the DDT controversy), appear as options in both the agriculture and the "pure" biology curricula of 9th grade, as well as in senior high school environmental studies curriculum. The agriculture as environmental science curriculum took into account the fast urbanization of large parts of the country and the fact that the biology curricula of the last decades tended to keep students inside, in the laboratory. Urban youth, more than their rural peers, need to be educated towards an appreciation of plant life and especially of ornamental plants and beautification of the environment. When the coordinated agricultural science curriculum project started in 1966, it was considered a revolutionary change in comparison to the good, old "rural studies type" of gardening. But in time it achieved scientific respectability and changed pupils' attitudes towards the problematic school subject of agriculture. This change in respectability was founded on the agreement that agricultural science is in no way less scientific, but certainly more relevant to social and developmental issues, when compared to conventional science courses. Thus, the stage was set for the full integration of agriculture and biology in the life and agricultural science curriculum for senior high schools.

SUCCESSFUL TECHNIQUES

Various techniques can be used to let pupils experience how agricultural knowledge is created and used for rural development. All of them were used, for example, by the agriculture as environmental science project.

1. Field experiments are the most important technique. They can be simple and very meaningful. They start with common crops which are used in subsistence agriculture and with simple improvements which cost nothing or very little, but can improve the yields. For instance, where row planting is still uncommon, its advantages can easily be demonstrated by simple, comparative field experiments. Other simple topics are the use of compost or fertilizers, discovering the optimal spacing between root crops, comparisons between varieties, etc.

One can start with qualitative experiments and training in observation skills and then go over to quantitative field trials which demand more measurements. One can even try bifactorial designs, if interactions between two factors are to be studied. Some of the latter experiments have been devised for schools, without the need for statistics.

Probably in most school field experiments one would use controls or comparison plots. Then the idea of repetitions (which are made concurrently, in field experiments) is introduced to show how one can overcome experimental design problems like unequal soils and related factors. To learn how to sample can be fun. Sampling is usually connected with drawing lots and similar "games".

Improvements in existing subsistence crops which are demonstrated in school plots and which can be seen by parents and neighbours have the best chances of affecting rural development. Yet, socio-cultural factors can be a hindrance. In many developing agrarian countries, subsistence farming is left to the women. Men do some of the physically more demanding jobs, they are in charge of marketing and, if they grow crops, these are usually the cash or export crops. In order to attract boys to agricultural science, the latter crops (coffee, cocoa, tea, rubber, oil palm, etc.) should also be kept on the school farm and be subject to experimentation. Since most of these crops are perennials, serious problems of space and investments arise (Bergmann, 1978).

What has been said about plant experiments is in principle also true for experiments with domestic or marine animals, but experiments with animals are more difficult to handle, are more apt to be invalidated by unplanned interferences from the outside and sometimes pose moral problems, if the experiment comes close to cruelty. Keeping animals in school poses specific maintenance problems, but their being "alive" and moving attracts many pupils more than plants.

2. Field experiments should be supplemented by related laboratory or classroom experiments. The most widely used are soil and germination experiments; but also issues in plant protection, breeding, growth hormone effects, and many other relevant topics which are basic for agricultural development have been investigated in classroom experiments. These experiments are quite close to experiments done in "regular" science teaching and I shall therefore not go into more details here.

3. Games are often used in science education when more complex and especially social and cultural problems, which cannot be investigated experimentally, are dealt with. While learning games can be as effective in agricultural science as in science teaching generally (Blum, 1976, 1979b), games are especially appropriate to stimulate developmental issues. The most appropriate variations are role plays and simulation games, through which students learn to understand how different interests clash. These games create an atmosphere of interaction: the same is true for planning games, in which an optimal solution has to be worked out by students.

4. The involvement of pupils in rural development reaches its peak when they actually take part in a real development project. In some countries the idea of education for self-reliance and the need for pupils' help in financing their school by raising agricultural crops has been widely accepted. Yet, often pupils and parents get the feeling that they are "exploited" if self-reliance is enforced and if the educational message does not reach the audience. In other cases pupils co-operated, but remained passive.

After pupils in the higher forms have studied the principles of scientific investigation and have discussed the problems of agricultural development, they should be challenged to apply the knowledge gained in a field experiment to solve a real local problem (even if it is a small one). This can be done in the form of a small, local project — first as proposal on paper, and then in reality, after having secured the co-operation of those in the community who have to sanction the project or can help in its implementations.

5. Popular scientific and technical literature is a resource which is often neglected. If schools really want to prepare pupils to be able to acquire new and useful knowledge in their adult life, they must give them the skill to do so. In a farming, developing community this means that school leavers must be skilled to read simple pamphlets published by the advisory services and farming magazines. Scientific literacy is a problem even in developed countries, and recently a concentrated effort has been made to deal with this issue by involving science teachers (*Language in Science*, 1980). The question how to teach pupils to read texts which use technical and popular-scientific terms, and how to motivate them to do so, still needs serious

study, but some more attempts have been made (Blum, 1982). No doubt, this is another challenge to science teachers.

Conclusions

Two main obstacles prevent science teachers, as a whole, from taking a more active part in rural development education. firstly, their primary allegiance is directed towards their own group and not towards the needs of the vast majority of pupils. Secondly, appropriate curriculum materials are not abundant. Yet, as more and more relevant approaches and techniques in the field of science education for rural development emerge, are tested and become available, the arsenal of adaptable curricula and learning–teaching materials grows.

Four things are needed to give this movement momentum: (1) More backing by the educational and political leadership in developing, agrarian countries for changes in goals and priorities, in favour of an agriculturally based science curriculum. (2) Close co-operation between schools and development agencies. (3) More international dissemation of rural–agricultural science education curricula, units and evaluation reports, perhaps with the help of a specialized clearinghouse, which so far does not exist. (4) More study, knowledge and training in the art of adapting existing approaches, techniques and units to different ecological and socio-cultural conditions.

References

Agriculture as Environmental Science (1978) A Curriculum Project. Jerusalem: State of Israel, Ministry of Education and Culture.

Benor, D. and Harrison, J. Q. (1977) *Agricultural Extension, The Training and Visit System.* The World Bank: New York.

Bergmann, H. (1978) Agricultural instruction in primary schools — a contribution to rural development? *Development and Cooperation* 2/78: 9–11.

Blum, A. (1973) Towards a rationale for integrated science teaching. In: *New Trends in Integrated Science Teaching*, Vol. 11. Paris: Unesco, pp. 29–51.

Blum, A. (1976) A game to teach the life cycles of fungi. *J. Biol. Educ.* **10**: 203–207.

Blum, A. (1979a) Curriculum adaptation in science education — why and how. *Sci. Educ.* **63**: 693–704.

Blum, A. (1979b) The remedial effect of a biological learning game. *J. Res. Sci. Teach.* **16**: 333–338.

Blum, A. (1982) The rose detective — a strategy to train pupils in reading bio-technical texts. *J. Biol. Educ.* **16**: 201–204.

CENAMEC (1979) *Influencia de las Actividades Agricolas en los Procesos Erosivos del Suelo.* Unidad modular. Version experimental. Caracas: Centro Nacional para el Mejoramiento de la Ensenanza de la Ciencia.

Coombs, P. H. with Prosser, R. C. and Ahmed, M. (1973) *New Paths to Learning for Rural Children and Youth.* New York: International Council for Educational Development.

Education in a Rural Environment (1974) Paris: Unesco

Kelly, P. J. and Wray, J. D. (1971) The educational use of living organisms. *J. Biol. Educ.* **5**: 213–218.

30   A. BLUM

Language in Science (1980) Study Series No. 16. Hatfield, Herts: Association for Science Education.
Malassis, L. (1975) Agriculture and the development process. *Tentative Guidelines for Teaching*. Paris: Unesco Press.
Ministry of Education and Culture (1980) *Life and Agricultural Sciences Curriculum*, Jerusalem (Hebrew).
Owen, G. H. (1973) *Agricultural Science*. Lusaka: Longman Zambia.
Ram, H. (1972) *Directives on Curriculum Development*, 1.1.72. Suva: Ministry of Education, Youth and Sport.
Solomon Islands Education Policy Review Committee (1973) Education for What? Honiara: Solomon Islands Government Press.

4

Agriculture and Biology Education

WILLIAM V. MAYER

Biological Sciences Curriculum Study, Colorado Springs, USA

Of all the sciences, biology is the one intimately concerned with the daily lives of humans. It has something to say on almost every aspect of human existence. It deals with water, food, health, reproduction, heredity, and the physical and biological environment in which humans exist. To cover all of the topics to which biology contributes would take a veritable encyclopaedia. For the purposes of this chapter then, only one topic, agriculture, will be considered. While students in biology courses have a vague understanding that plants provide food, they are given little knowledge of what is actually involved in producing a single pound of food. While biology courses can be faulted for this gross omission, it must also be pointed out that a significant amount of agriculture is conducted without any knowledge of the biological principles involved. Biology offers explanations for the phenomena being experienced in farmers' fields. But farming, by-and-large, does not profit from these explanations because it is largely conducted on an empirical and traditional basis using methods that have proven effective and failing to experiment to find if there is some better way to reduce labour and costs and increase yields. There is a symbiosis between agriculture and biology on which neither has capitalized and from whose exercise both would profit.

How should one orientate a biology course to provide application of what is learned in the classroom to what is experienced in life? Without turning all biology students into farmers, how can we give them an appreciation of what goes into placing food on their table and providing a balanced diet? Almost all the necessary content is currently present in biology courses, but it is the way it is presented and the emphasis given that makes the difference. To understand the role of biology in agriculture does not mean complete realignment of existing biology courses, but, rather, relatively minor changes in content and emphasis to turn an academic presentation into a practical one. It does not take a great shift to encourage

31

students to see that what they are learning has value beyond the classroom. One approach to using biology to understand agriculture is to begin with the biology currently presented and see how it can, with relatively little effort, be focused on an area so important that without it life would not exist.

Begin with sunlight. For all practical purposes we can say that the energy for living activities is derived solely from the sun. Not only does sunlight provide the energy required for photosynthesis, it also maintains the environment of the planet at a temperature optimum for life. In addition, solar energy has been stored by being trapped in such fossil fuels as coal, oil, or natural gas. It is used as the engine by which evaporation of water occurs to be deposited as rain to result in the energy of flowing water. The sun as our energy source focuses our attention on its importance in maintaining life upon this planet.

Plants are selective in their use of sunlight. While we are conscious of that part of the electromagnetic spectrum extending from the short ultraviolet to the long infrared rays and visible to our eyes, plants perform best in the blue and red ends of the visible spectrum with green largely reflected to give plants their characteristic color.

The sun radiates its energy in all directions and from the sun the Earth is only a dot in space. Thus, the Earth receives only a tiny fraction of the tremendous solar energy released when hydrogen forms helium. Reduce this amount further by the observation that only half of the Earth is illuminated at any one time. The theoretical amount of light approaching the Earth is about 5,250,000 kcal per square meter per year. But, because of being dissipated as heat and reduced further by clouds and dust, the actual amount that falls on a square meter is between 20 and 40% of the theoretical amount. Thus, life on earth exists upon a tiny fraction of total solar energy.

To exemplify how solar radiation is converted to food energy, trace for the student what happens to light when absorbed by one of the most efficient captors of energy among the food plants, corn. Go beyond the formula for photosynthesis to question how many kcal of light energy are required to produce a kcal of corn plant for human food.

In the good farmlands of the world one acre may produce 100 bushels of corn which, when air dried, will consist of 5600 pounds of shelled corn, 5200 pounds of roots and stubble, 1400 pounds of cobs and 4000 pounds of stalk. Of the total 16,200 pounds, the shelled corn available for human nutrition represents but 35%. On the basis of these data a student can see that a far greater volume of plant material is produced than is directly usable by humans for food.

But what does it take to produce a hundred bushels of corn? The answer is as follows: water, 5,000,000 pounds; oxygen, 6800 pounds; carbon dioxide, 1900 pounds; nitrogen, 130 pounds; phosphorus, 22 pounds;

potassium, 110 pounds; sulfur, 22 pounds; magnesium, 33 pounds; calcium, 37 pounds; iron, 2 pounds; manganese, 0.3 pounds; boron, 0.06 pound. In addition, minute quantities of other elements such as chlorine, iodine, zinc, copper and molybdenum are necessary. What a tremendous amount of many chemicals are necessary if light is to form them into human food! This view of plant production is far more realistic than simply indicating that CO_2 + H_2O produce carbohydrates in the presence of sunlight.

Frequently textbooks list elements essential for life and indicate that oxygen, hydrogen and carbon comprise 99.8% of a plant. However, without nitrogen, potassium, calcium, magnesium, phosphorus and sulfur which add to some 99.975%, plants do not remain viable. It is even interesting to note that the remaining 0.25%, which seems almost insignificant, is also essential even though each component of this fraction occurs in less than one-thousandth of a percent. Chlorine, zinc, iron, copper, manganese, molybdenum and boron are essential trace elements in this category. In addition, some plants require traces of such elements as silicon, cobalt, sodium and selenium. The consequences of the absence of such tiny percentages of chemicals is humbling and shows the need for further understanding of elements essential for the growth and well being of green plants. Does the average biology course even mention trace elements? If not, how will the average citizen understand plant nutrition and the importance of chemical balance of soils? It is unrealistic to leave students with the notion that oxygen, carbon, hydrogen and nitrogen alone can form a living entity. To do so means we have simplified our presentation to the point of error.

Are we teaching practical lessons in our biology classes? Are we providing students with a realistic understanding of what it takes to feed the human population? Are we including these basics of agriculture in our biology classes or are we slighting them because such application indicates they are unlikely to be subects for ladies and gentlemen to pursue?

Because of the quantities of mineral resources required to produce a hundred bushels of corn, students soon come to the conclusion that the earth will be depleted of these resources in a relatively short order. This is the time to introduce the concept of cycling for none of these minerals are permanently bound within the corn. The cycles for water, oxygen, carbon dioxide and nitrogen can be easily documented as well as the fate of other elements required for the hundred bushels of corn. The concept of cycling is a critical one for the maintenance of life on this planet and is particularly well illustrated by the agricultural practice of replacing chemicals removed from the soil if corn production is to continue. This brings up the question of distribution of resources, for the chemicals bound in a food product such as corn normally are not returned to their point of origin but may be shipped and consumed thousands of miles from the place of growth. In essence, shipment of food stuffs involves exporting the basic, not naturally renewable elements that were required for their production. This is not critical for water, oxygen or carbon dioxide, but may become a limiting factor for future food production for elements such as soil nitrogen, phosphorus, potassium and others. Thus, we introduce the concept of soil fertility and the necessity of its maintenance with either natural or chemical reintroduction of elements removed at harvest time. With such a comprehension, fields may be kept fertile for generations if their essential elements are not permanently removed. Fields have been cultivated for centuries when properly maintained. Without comprehension of the necessity of maintenance of mineral levels one is faced with the return to nomadic agriculture wherein forests are burned and crops planted until yield becomes minimal, at which time the nomadic farmer moves on to burn and plant still more forests without the knowledge that proper husbanding of the initial fields would allow continued yields of food.

From just a simple list of plant requirements a student can be led to understand why corn cannot be effectively grown in the drier regions of the world and why soils deficient in nitrogen, phosphorus or potassium are unlikely to produce good corn crops unless these elements are supplied by fertilization, and even then, with all the raw materials present except for a minute quantity of a given trace element, the crop might still be considered a failure.

The requirements for plant growth and development are not largely known. Students can begin to develop an understanding of the great demands on raw materials that are made by the production of human food. As societies become more complex and populations increase we continue to augment demands on our land and raw materials to produce still more food. But, without some kind of management program, our lands will become exhausted, our crops depleted, and available food reduced to the point where ignorance could lead to starvation.

Normally, we do not inform our students that 5,026,157 pounds of raw materials are required to produce 5600 pounds of shelled corn or about 900 pounds of raw materials for every pound of shelled corn which can serve as human food. Even though cattle may eat the stalks and other plant parts and ultimately be consumed by humans, it must be emphasized that trophic levels make this an acceptable practice only if the initial food materials, such as grass, cannot serve as human food.

One can cite the practical application of the second law of thermodynamics which essentially states that when energy flows from one species to another, some is always lost as heat. Such energy eventually returns to the environment with only a slight fraction having been used in the process of living. Only the constant influx of solar energy permits the maintenance of life for, if energy available on earth were finite, there would be a breakdown of complex molecular structures and ultimately life would end.

With plants utilizing less than 1% of the light energy that reaches them they constitute the basic trophic level, that of autotrophs. The first level heterotrophs that feed on the plants are primary consumers and the carnivores that feed on the herbivores are secondary consumers which, in turn, may be consumed by tertiary, quaternary, and so on consumers. Students must understand that as food energy moves from one trophic level to another, only somewhere between 10 to 20% is available to produce the organisms of the next higher trophic level. Ten thousand pounds of grain will produce a thousand pounds of cattle, which, in turn, can only produce a hundred pounds of human beings. Thus, the lower the trophic level on which organisms exist, the more efficient is their energy utilization. In the overall scheme of things, meat eating is justified only in those cases where a first order consumer utilizes those food sources not directly utilizable by human beings. One might wish to introduce the role of enzymes at this time, pointing out that grass eating herbivores possess enzymes that allow them to convert grass into animal proteins. These enzymes are lacking in humans and a human eating grass is consuming only bulk but not obtaining nutrition from it. Emphasis on processes such as these focus the students' attention on the practicality of biology and its applicability to understanding the limitation to life on earth.

The relationship between humans and their environment is dramatically expressed when students understand that only 0.1% of the raw materials in the corn example are converted to human food. Students can be asked to compare yields in the wild with yields under cultivation and asked to account for the differences when managed raw materials are made available to the cultivated plants. The situation becomes further complicated by not only having the raw materials available, but available in a form usable by plants. Iron, for example, is an essential for plant growth and many soils are iron rich with over 45,000 kilograms of iron per hectare. However, in neutral or alkaline soils the iron compounds are insoluble and almost unavailable to green plants so that a new dimension, not just of presence, but of presence in a usable form is added. The role of pH can now be considered.

Couple the raw material required with the observation that between 2 and 4 billion kcal of light energy are received by an acre per year. When one calculates that 1.79 kilograms of dry weight corn plant is produced per meter and that each gram of corn plant contains about 3.8 kcal, the square meter will have produced 6,802 kcal of food for the year which is only 0.13% of the 5,250,000 kcal of light that would reach the Earth each year in the absence of clouds, dust, etc. In fact, only about one half to one million kcal would actually reach the corn plants to produce those 6802 kcal of food so that only between 0.68 and 1.36% of the available light energy is captured. Since the shelled corn represents 35% of the plant material, only 0.24 to 0.48% of the energy of sunlight finally becomes the energy of human food. What a profligate waste of energy! Are there suggestions as how more effectively to use solar energy in the production of food? Is this not a problem of major importance for the entire human race?

Figures like these, readily available in the scientific literature, seldom find their way into the biology classroom because they are not part of the "academic" work of the year. Therefore, our citizens seldom have a concept of how much energy and raw materials are required to provide plant food for one human being. The conversions, as seen by the above figures that convert the energy of sunlight to shelled corn, show a process that is not efficient and postulate limits on the amount of energy and raw materials available for food production. Note also that these figures are optimal. Less effective farming measures, less rich soil, fewer available raw materials, and fluctuations in temperature or sunlight will all serve to reduce this predicted yield.

Using quantitative data to interpret biological phenomena gives data that the average person usually accepts without question. However, because of the great number of variables involved in dealing with biological systems, all such figures can be only approximations and food production figures serve to elicit student questions as to the validity of forecasting made on them. This is a scientific problem that very seldom finds its way into the classroom. Instead students are taught that facts are facts and figures are accurate interpretations of them, when, in reality, facts are subject to change and figures are influenced by a great variety of factors within the natural world. Let us briefly look at some of the factors which impact on calculated figures for food production.

Animal and insect pests consume large quantities of food originally destined for human consumption. But such ravages are not necessarily dependent upon human food crops. In parts of India, rat populations fluctuate in relation to blossoming of bamboo. During this period there is almost an unlimited quantity of food for rats which, with their short generation time, multiply very rapidly. When the bamboo fruits are gone, this enlarged rat population is free to consume those crops meant for humans. Thus, agricultural production may be adversely affected by the flowering of the bamboo, a situation not normally factored into crop production figures.

Data dealt with so far indicate the importance of light and students will normally assume that the more light the better and conclude that more intense, longer light periods will lead to greater food production. However, the situation is not that simple. Do we, in our biology classes when discussing the photoperiod, discuss its effect on food plants? Normally, when discussing the reactions of photosynthesis, the biology teacher mentions reactions that take place in the light and dark. But seldom, if ever, is the importance of the dark period discussed. The growth cycle of many plants is dependent on the length of the dark period.

Frequently one reads in the literature of "long day" and "short day" plants, but almost never are the terms "short night" and "long night" plants used. Some soybeans, for eaxmple, are long night plants while others are short night plants. What does this interpretation of photoperiod say to students about the production of food crops, for example?

We frequently talk, in our biology classes, about symbiosis. But how frequently is the association of fungi with green plants mentioned? We now know that the formation of mycorrhizae, occasioned by the symbiotic relationship of fungus with a higher plant, is absolutely essential for the growth and well-being of certain higher plants. All cereals, legumes, fruit trees, cotton, as well as other agricultural plants develop mycorrhizae. Where such symbiosis does not exist, some higher plants do not do well.

In the seventeenth century North American Indians planted corn and beans together. Can a biology student answer the question as to why? How do we relate, essentially what is an abstraction, namely nitrogen fixation, to the practicalities of agriculture? Do our students really understand the role of the bean in providing nitrogen to the corn plant? It is just such illustration as this that tie academic biology to the practical world. While the Indians could not explain what was happening in biological terms, empirically they knew that corn grew better when planted with beans. We can now provide the answer as to why, but in so doing, have sacrificed the practical example as practiced by the Indians.

One of the values of a biological theory is prediction. But in our biology classes we seldom look to the future. Certain predictions can be made with a fair degree of accuracy. Among these is population increase. Today, the world's population stands at 4.47 billion with a doubling time of 39 years. Thus, by the year 2000 we can expect some 6.35 billion people on earth. Currently food consumption already exceeds food production. *Per capita* grain production is 4145 kilograms, but per capita grain consumption is 4203 kilograms. By the year 1990 *per capita* grain production is expected to reach 4897 kilos, but consumption will have risen to 6723 kilos. What do these figures tell us about quality of life in the future?

What about the chemicals that enter into the production of food? By the year 2000 it is projected that the human population will use some 2800 trillion meters of water with severe regional deficiences projected, especially in those lands with low rainfall and rapid population growth. At the present time about 70% of our water supply is used for irrigation. By the year 2000 this number is expected to fall to some 51%, but, at the same time, water used in industry and mining will increase from 22 to 41% of the total. Water recycles and is a renewable resource, but one deals not only with water quantity, but also water quality. Polluted water is not drinkable by humans and certain pollutants will actually poison the plants upon which our life depends. Student investigations of water quality and quantity, currently and projected into the future, may give a realistic, if frightening, picture of the status of this essential for life.

While agriculture depends on solar energy, it also depends on chemical energy for fertilizers, for petroleum to run pumps and farm machinery, to provide transportation and to resist insect pests. But chemical energy resources, too, are finite and rising costs of chemicals may make it impractical to fertilize, to run farm machinery, or spray for pests, which, in turn, will have a deleterious effect on yield. While mineral resources should remain adequate, it is obvious that they are nonrenewable resources and are not equally distributed over the face of the planet. A look into the future dictates that prudent practice should initiate mineral recycling *now* rather than waiting until a crisis develops.

Not only the quality of water, but the quality of air has been deteriorating and air pollutants have had a significant negative effect on agricultural crops. Industrialization has led to the change in pH rainfall. The analysis of the deep ice of Greenland glaciers and Antarctica provides data that, prior to the industrial revolution, the pH of rain was about 6 to 7.6. Today the pH of rainfall in the eastern United States ranges from 3.1 to 6.9, averaging 4.4. The effects of acid deposition are noted almost worldwide resulting from emission of sulphur dioxide and oxides of nitrogen into the atmosphere. To maintain agricultural production at projected rates, these emissions must be brought under control.

Worldwide there is a movement of people from the countryside and small villages into larger cities. Partly this is a result of increases in farming efficiency, partly due to farming inefficiencies. To return to our 100 bushels of corn, in 1800 it required 344 man-hours to raise and harvest 100 bushels of corn in the United States. In 1970, however, it took only 7 man-hours as a result of the application of technology and the introduction of large-scale farms. Farming on a smaller scale takes a disproportionate number of man-hours. But what economies of scale and technology can be predicted for the future? One can't envision a time when no man-hours will be required to raise corn and, while a reduction from 344 to 7 is significant, a reduction from 7 man-hours is unlikely to produce equal farming economies.

The future looks bleak for the ability of agriculture to keep an increasing world population fed in view of negative environmental factors operating on the agricultural establishment. One of these not yet mentioned is the decrease in land availability. Using the United States as an example, the total land mass is 2.2 billion acres of which 1,359 million acres are suitable for agriculture, and of this figure only 413 million acres, or about 30%, can be considered adequate crop land. As other uses, such as mining, industry, roads, cities and towns, occupy more and more land, less and less is available for agriculture as cities, towns and industries usually locate in what, initially, were good farming areas.

Irrigation frequently leads to excessive levels of salt and thus, reduced crops. This is not a problem of the twentieth century, but one of historical record extending back as far as 2000 B.C. when the great cities of Sumeria declined to impoverished villages or were completely abandoned as their irrigated fields become too salty to support productive agriculture. Today, throughout the world, the experience of Sumeria is being repeated in varying degrees.

The encroaching deserts on practically every continent on earth except Antarctica are reducing, by millions of acres annually, productive farmland. Erosion by wind and water is removing productive top soil faster than it can be replaced, further reducing the quality and quantity of productive agricultural land. Couple these observations with quality and quantity of water, acid rain and other air pollutant, reductions in wetlands, and for our increasing population the future poses many problems.

Only by becoming familiar with these problems can a ground swell of concern focus on dealing with them. If people remain ignorant of such data, they are incapable of initiating corrective actions and will ultimately be faced with decisions of catastrophic proportions which should have been avoided if an intelligent citizenry had initiated remedial action early. It seems that future life on this planet should be a concern for everyone living on it and, in terms of educational objectives, should have a high priority.

Biology provides data concerning agriculture and, as agriculture is a primary source of human food, biology plays a very practical part in making us comprehend the impact we have on this planet just to feed ourselves. One could make a case for biology and health, or biology and almost every facet of life on earth, but this paper's focus has been on its applicability to agriculture. It can be readily seen that to emphasize the practical value of biology does not demand restructuring courses completely, but only in changing their focus and emphasis. One can still deal with the biology and chemistry of life, but emphasize the effect on plant life of pollution, erosion, and failing to recycle essential nutrients. One can deal with the importance of water in every cell of every living thing, but also point out how water, indiscriminately applied to soil, can lead to salination and destruction of productive plant life.

Some teachers of biology regard application in the same way they regard manual labor — only as a way to get one's hands dirty. But application not only makes the content more meaningful to students, but application is essential if biology is to contribute to the quality of life on this planet. Unless application is made explicit in biology courses, where will it be made explicit? Biology taught only for its own sake can be a sterile, academic exercise. Taught as a way of understanding our planet and improving the human condition upon it, it can be a major contributing force to the improvement of the quality of life.

Reference

Moore, J. A. (1985) Science as a way of knowing — human ecology. *Amer. Zool.*, **25**:1–55. A scholarly and provocative synthesis as to how biology impacts on the lives of humans.

5

Food and Culture

DOLORES F. HERNANDEZ AND VICTORIA B. BALTAZAR
Institute of Educational Development, University of the Philippines

A major objective of science and technology today is the improvement of the quality of life. It is generally accepted that the biology curriculum has great potential to contribute to this. But does biology teaching actually contribute much to this aim which is so often cited by the political and scientific leaders in the Philippines and other developing countries? The biology curriculum is full of information that is hardly relevant or applicable in this country, considering that the population is mostly rural and the economy still basically agricultural.

An important starting point is to understand people's beliefs and practices relating to plants and animals as sources of food, or for the maintenance of health. If biology teachers expect to bring about changes in the eating and health habits of their students as a result of the knowledge they gain in the study of biology, then they need to be aware of the attendant values, beliefs and social connotations that these things have for the people in their community. Let us take attitudes or beliefs about food. According to the anthropologist Jocano, people seldom think in terms of food nutrients like proteins, minerals and vitamins when they think of food; they think in terms of taste, smell, color and the link between food and culture as illustrated by regional differences in food likes and dislikes, e.g. the Tagalogs' liking for unhatched duck's eggs (balut), the Bicolanos' taste for peppery foods and food cooked in coconut milk, the Cebuanos' preference for corn.

A cultural belief that permeates the Filipino peasant's notions about man's relation to his environment is the concept of "hot" and "cold" which does not refer to degrees of temperature but to certain qualities of elements of nature and to the reactions of the human body to these elements. It is believed that good health is maintained by a proper balance of these elements. Unregulated intake of cold foods could bring about diseases characterized by swelling of joints, muscular pains and stomach discomforts. Similarly, overconsumption of hot foods brings about a general feeling of malaise and one of several types of skin diseases. Thus, food is associated with disease.

Most vegetables except beans and juicy fruits are considered cold; "hot" fruits include: mangoes, some banana species (saba), ripe coconut, pineapple. "Cold" fruits include banana (*bungulan* variety), avocado, sugar apple, lemon, *naranjita,* pomelo, melon, young coconut, *sincamas* and other juicy fruits. Meat is generally considered hot; freshwater fish, cold; but saltwater fish is classified as hot. It has been noted, however, that there are inconsistencies among individuals in classifying "hot" and "cold" foods.

Food prohibitions are associated with certain stages in life: pregnancy, lactation, childhood and infancy. For example, food from the sea, being cold, should not be taken by pregnant and lactating mothers; food taboos for infants include fish, because this causes worms. Folk diet therapy practices are deeply rooted to this day. Many of these practices have been given a scientific explanation, e.g. use of bananas, guava, papaya, starchy foods for individuals suffering from diarrhea. Pectin and starch present in these foods are known demulcents. Also, the pharmacological effects of fruits and vegetables are not being confirmed and their active principles isolated.

Food combinations is another area that needs to be considered because certain beliefs are associated with this. For example, mixing ginger with green vegetables causes dropping of teeth; tubers and green vegetables must be well cooked or they will cause skin eruptions; mung beans must be cooked with green leafy vegetables or mixed with sugar to neutralize their "hot" effect on the body.

Some foods have higher social values than others. For example, meat in general is served during festivities, vegetables are not, especially local ones. Some rice varieties have high social status, for example white rice, but red rice has low social status; corn has low social status in some regions of the country but not in others.

To be effective, nutrition topics should not be too remote from existing beliefs and values. One must integrate the educational approach with the local practices. The anthropologist Jocano recommends that, whenever possible, the lessons should be presented in terms consonant with prevailing beliefs. When making recommendations about diet, the educator should select alternatives which contain food elements that will meet the nutritional needs of the people, and at the same time are acceptable to them. Food taboos, however, can be dangerous if no substitutes are available; in this case the biology teacher will have to discuss the matter carefully in terms of nutritional need, perhaps using local residents who are not bound by the local food prohibitions. Another point to consider is accessibility to food supply. Local food preferences are conditioned not just by beliefs, but by what is available. In fact most of beliefs and practices revolve around locally available foods.

References

Jocano, Felipe Landa (1977) Food beliefs and practices;: starting points in nutrition education. *Nutrisyon*, Vol. 2, No. 2, January–April 1977, 8–15.

Ramos, Alicia C. (1977) Food attitudes and beliefs among selected families in Barrio Ususan, Taguig, Rizal. *Philippine Journal of Nutrition*, Vol. 30, No. 1, January–March, 1977.

6

Food Production and General Education

K. S. KRISHNA SASTRY
University of Agricultural Sciences, Bangalore, India

A feeling that general education has no special relevance to human needs is becoming more and more widespread, particularly in the developing countries. Science education leading to a general science degree traditionally includes subjects like chemistry, biology, mathematics and physics, but a university graduate in science with this background needs further training to be a teacher or to do scientific research. General education up to the secondary level has become even less relevant with a high degree of drop-out. In order to make education more useful to the students and to society, subjects of an inter disciplinary nature, which pertain to human activity and to society, have to be introduced.

The aim of all responsible governments throughout the world is to attain self-sufficiency in food production. In the wake of great achievements in agricultural sciences, it is necessary to integrate into general education a few new facts, thoughts and concepts concerning modern agriculture. Acquisition of knowledge about methods for increasing food production would make education more meaningful. How this could be integrated into education at the primary and secondary levels is discussed in this chapter.

Population growth and food production

The present world population is 4750 million and it will be over 6000 million at the end of the century. During the period 1954–73 the world population growth rate was 2% per annum, while the food production rate was 2.8%, which meant that there was a modest improvement in the availability of food *per capita*. It meant that 3.8 billion people in the world in 1973 had about 20% more food that 2.7 billion people two decades earlier. But to appreciate the acuteness of the problems, it is necessary to separate the developing from the developed countries. In the developing countries, for the period 1965–75, the population growth rate was 2.4%, while food production grew at 1.5%. This was an accumulative deficit of about 1% per annum over the 10-year period.

The know-how necessary in general crop production

The strategy for an increase in food production should involve three major components of equal importance: (a) soil, (b) crop variety, (c) management.

(a) Soil

The wealth of a country depends on the fertility of its soil. The importance of soil as a dynamic system for crop growth, the maintenance of soil structure and fertility should all be emphasized in educational courses. Soil characteristics, plant nutrient availability, the microflora of soils (particularly those which are directly beneficial like free-living N_2-fixers as aspects of soil fertility should be part of general education. Desertification of land caused by neglect where vegetation once flourished should be illustrated so that future generations are aware of the dangers. It is said that the Sahara Desert increases southwards by 100 km a year; that 23 million tonnes of topsoil are lost annually from agricultural land; that the Mississippi carries over 300 million tonnes of soil into the sea every year; that 1.6 billion tonnes of soil goes down the Yellow river in China. In 20 years there could be 10% less land for agriculture. These are hard facts to form part of education.

(b) Crop variety

Variety is the second major component in the strategy for increasing food production. The development of new high-yielding carieties has been a revolutionary achievement. The Green Revolution in wheat production in India is attributable to the new varieties of Mexican wheat bred at CYMMIT in Mexico and subsequently by breeders in India. The average yield of wheat in the entire country of India was 722 kg/ha per annum for the years 1951–4; for the years 1978–81 it was 1551 kg/ha. The average yield of wheat in the Punjab, India, was 2449 kg/ha for the years 1975–8, higher than the yield levels of developed countries like USA, Canada, Australia and the USSR. Similar successes have been achieved in rice production. With the use of new high-yielding varieties, a yield in India of 793 kg/ha during 1951–4 became 1236 kg/ha during 1978–81.

Besides breeding high-yielding varieties, new concepts in energy harvesting by plants and the exploitation of hybrid vigour on a commercial scale has boosted world production: pearl millet hybrids, sorgnum hybrids, cotton hybrids and, more recently, rice hybrids. There is a continual search for newer combinations of parental line for exploiting hybrid vigour and any number of examples can be cited in field crops, horticultural crops and fodder crops. The potential is immense.

Newer methods—tissue culture, genetic engineering—will help to obtain varieties of crop plants suitable for special conditions: those suitable for arid situations, those resistant to frost, those resistant to high temperatures, types suitable for peripheral soils and dry lands, varieties resistant to various diseases and pests.

(c) Crop management

Management includes all the agricultural operations from the preparation of the land to sowing to harvest. A high-yielding variety can only be high-yielding under proper management. Unfortunately aspects of management have been given less research support and consequently the maximum production potential has not been achieved.

Preparation of the land for sowing and subsequent inter-cultural operations are of paramount importance to maintain various soil characteristics, promote root growth, to control weeds and prevent the incidence of pests and diseases.

Water is the most important single input which limits agricultural production. The production of a well-watered crop and that of a drought-stricken one can vary by a factor of 10. The total biomass produced could be reduced to zero under extreme drought. High productivity is therefore linked with irrigation. But over-irrigation can be as dangerous as lack of water: over-irrigation coupled with lack of drainage has resulted in large areas becoming saline-alkaline and thus unfit for raising crops. The need for education in all aspects of water technology is absolute.

The concept of balanced nutrition and the importance of essential elements have to be integrated into management. It is painful to see a farmer adopting all appropriate practices to raise a crop, except for one essential element, a micronutrient needed in small doses, so that yield are reduced (for example, zinc deficiency in India). Education can avoid these losses in yield.

Both education and research are important to solve the problems of plant protection from insect pests, diseases and weeds, all of which cause stupendous losses. Weeds alone can cause anything from 5 to 30% loss in crop yields and insect pests, in severe form, can devastate a crop (for example, locusts and stem borers). Similarly fungal, bacterial or viral diseases can reduce crop yield and often completely kill the plants. This problem has been tackled in developed countries by the use of pesticides, fungicides, etc., but the high cost of this technology is such that it has remained unused in developing countries. Building resistance to these diseases and pests will be real contribution to the developing world.

Post-harvest problems in developing countries can ruin a bountiful harvest. For example, in India untimely rain at the time of the paddy harvest makes it difficult to dry and store it so that the seeds germinate. Proper facilities for drying and storing of the crop have to be developed. It is essential to impress on students the need for proper post-harvest storage.

Animal and fish production

A balanced diet for humans requires use of animal protein to supply essential amino acids. In many developing countries animal and fish production is low and the main constituent of their diet is a cereal. Religious beliefs can prevent meat consumption and another major problem is the availability of fodder. Agricultural byproducts are the major source of animal feed and there is very little chance of increasing the area under fodder. Amongst dairy cattle, a notable improvement has been achieved through artificial insemination and the development of cross-bred cows. In India, the availability of milk increased from 107 g *per capita* per day in 1971 to 131 g in 1981. The potential for the development of poultry, pigs and goats is tremendous. Already the development of inland fisheries is making tremendous strides. Despite all this, there is a need to change the feeding habits of people to accommodate the new trends and this involves education.

Conflicting claims on the use of land

Many countries achieve an increase in food production by increasing the land used for agriculture. This is not always desirable, especially when forests are being indiscriminately cut down. It is estimated that tropical forests are being cut down at the rate of 40 ha per minute, resulting in soil erosion and desertification. There is a need to maintain the present forest area and increase the food yield by increasing productivity. In India, in 1962, 70 million tonnes of cereals were produced in 93 million hectares. In 1980, 113 million tonnes were produced. At the 1962 rate, this would have required 151 million hectares, but instead 104 million hectares were used, saving 47 million hectares.

Greater productivity could release marginal lands now under cultivation for sheep rearing and such other enterprises with greater returns.

Energy and the economics of food production

All the major inputs for increasing food production—tillage, fertilizers, water, plant protection materials, post-harvest processing—are energy-consuming. Intensive food production is so dependent on these inputs that quite often the energy output is less than the energy input. It is said that the energy input/output ratio for a *tin* of cauliflower is 1:0.5, while the ratio for rice production by an Asian farmer is said to be 1:21. These factors are important because of the shortage of energy.

Two billion people in the world depend on draught animal power for ploughing, transportation and other farming operations. 50% of the cropped area in developing countries is cultivated by draught animal, 26% by manual labour and 24% by tractors. Three hundred million draught animals are used to draw 25 million animal-drawn vehicles all over the developing countries. Based on an average of 0.5 hp per draught animal, these animals make available about 150 million hp. Replacement of draught animal power by mechanical and electrical energy would require about $280 billion capital investment and a recurring annual cost of $5 billion—besides quicker depletion of fossil fuel. Animal power, especially in smallholdings in developing countries, has to stay for a while yet.

Agriculture/food production has to be treated as a business and cost–benefit ratios have to be assessed for every crop. Selection and modification of technology has to be done so that ultimately food production is profitable. Governments need to encourage by assuring minimum prices.

These concepts and ideas need to be brought to the attention of students at an early age so that agriculture is well understood as an enterprise basic to human needs.

Education in food production

Because of the urgency for increasing food production as an essential human need, it is necessary to examine how relevant our education is in this endeavour. At the primary and secondary levels agricultural subjects are not dealt with in the science curriculum. At the tertiary level, suitable educational programmes have been started in some developing countries. Any country is in a critical position if it has to rely on food imported from another country. To achieve self-sufficiency a knowledge of agriculture and of food production should be integrated into general education at all levels.

The percentage of students who get some education in agricultural science at the tertiary level is less than 0.01%. Because of the serious problem of drop-outs from schools at different stages in developing countries, the little education they receive should include a component on agriculture and food production.

What basic facts should be included at primary level?

Within the existing framework, a few illustrated facts can detail the uses and importance of soil, water and air for plants, and particularly for crops. The following should be included:

(a) Aspects of the fertility of poor and rich soils in relation to plant growth should be studied.

   (b) Crop plants which serve as food should be mentioned whenever plants are studied.

   (c) Fruits and seeds of various crops should be illustrated as feedstock.

   (d) Plant nutrients should be illustrated.

   (e) The importance of water and air to enable plants and roots to grow should be demonstrated.

What should be included at the secondary level?

At the secondary level, details about agriculture and food production could be included in chemistry, biology, geology and geography courses.

In chemistry, under properties and uses of elements, mention may be made of such elements which are essential for plant growth. For example, when teaching about nitrogen, it may be emphasized that it is an essential element and growth will be poor if it is deficient or absent. Similarly, the importance of phosphorus, potassium, calcium, sulphur, etc., can be mentioned.

Solubility and the chemical nature of salts in relation to their availability to plants may be made part of the work on the properties of salts. The importance of oxygen for respiration and how soil should be loose to allow aeration of roots and the better uptake of plant nutrients should be mentioned.

In geology, soil formation, the importance of maintaining soil fertility, the preservation of topsoil, erosion and its adverse effects may be taught.

In biology, plant specimens taken for study could always be a crop plant, and the following topics might be included:

   (a) role of micro-organisms in soil fertility,

   (b) importance of legumes in N_2 fixation,

   (c) carbon dioxide and its role in plant food synthesis,

   (d) insects as pests and examples of the damage they do,

   (e) fungal diseases, for example rust as a major disease, limiting yields of wheat.

These are a few examples how aspects of food production could be integrated into existing syllabuses.

7

The Need for Continuing Education in Food and Agriculture

G. REX MEYER

School of Education, Macquarie University, Australia

There are two aspects of the food–agriculture interface which make educational programs in this area especially challenging. These are: (i) the dynamic and complex nature of the cycle which proceeds from primary production (agriculture) to processing, to supply storage and distribution, to consumption of food and back to primary production (Fig. 1), and (ii) the fact that all aspects of the cycle are the concern of all citizens at all stages of their lives and are not therefore issues to be addressed by schooling alone.

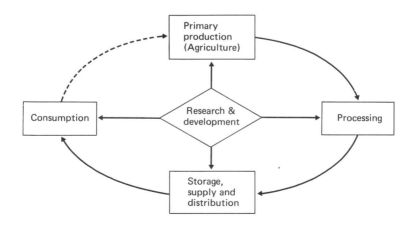

FIG 1. The food–agriculture cycle.

51

The problem — the need for lifelong education

At each point of the food–agriculture cycle problems arise due to a variety of factors, including shifts in socioeconomic balance; population fluctuations; changes in the rural–urban ratio; climatic changes; political factors, and so on. These problems vary from region to region and indeed from country to country and from district to district.

Traditional school courses in agriculture, with their emphasis on farm management, cropping and animal husbandry, have made a very significant contribution to helping communities face, understand and solve these ever-changing problems, but they are not the complete answer and there are several reasons for this. In the first place such courses train only a small cadre of the population. Certainly this is not an inconsequential outcome, since this cadre become key agents for change in the general community and we must look to them for leadership. How this leadership is to be exercised, however, is a central concern of this chapter. Secondly, most of these programs have been concerned mainly, and sometimes entirely, with farming alone — that is with training people to be primary producers. Not all aspects of the agriculture–food cycle have been addressed. Thirdly, traditional agricultural extension courses have tended to mirror this initial pattern of training and so have catered mainly for farmers and not for the community as a whole. Fourthly, by being mainly institutionally based — school, college, or university, dealing only with a restricted age range or with a selected group of students for only a few years — most formal courses of agriculture have tended to see involvement in lifelong learning as something added on — an "extension" service rather than a central concern.

This problem has been aggravated in many systems by fragmentation of responsibility for educating the community about the total cycle. Some aspects are seen to be the province of agriculturalists; others of biologists; others of geographers and still others of economists. Nutritionists and other health educators have a great deal to say about almost all stages of the cycle, but especially about processing and consumption and environmentalists bring their own interpretation to most aspects. Many other specialist groups could be added to this list — chemists; engineers; anthropologists; family planners; social workers and so on.

What is needed to ensure a balanced treatment aiming to equip citizens with basic resources to cope with critical problems and changes in their interaction with food and agriculture are two things: (i) an holistic approach to the cycle and (ii) a stress on continuing education aiming to foster lifelong learning rather than on mere schooling and traditional agricultural extension. The aim should be to create what Unesco has termed a learning society in regard to issues about food and agriculture.

Such an approach is vitally urgent since a learning society, by definition, could do a great deal to solve its own problems in this critical area. No-one, of course, could claim that education alone will solve the food problems of the world or eliminate natural disasters, malnutrition or economic instability, but it adds strong weapons to the armoury for survival and development. If the target becomes the community as a whole; if the main aims are to offer alternatives in the face of change and to help citizens analyse and solve immediate and long-term problems in this whole area; and if the educational processes are systematic and continuing, then at least a community has some hope of surviving and then of adapting and developing and ultimately of improving its quality of life.

I shall attempt to set out here the parameters of an holistic program of continuing (lifelong) education to increase community awareness and to develop appropriate community skills in the area of food and agriculture.

Aims and rationale

At school level, traditional courses of agriculture have tended to focus on preparing students to be farmers or, at least in the upper secondary school, on preparing them for entry into college or university to be trained as agricultural scientists. More recently, however, school courses in agriculture, especially in the junior years of secondary school, have had much more general educational aims. As an example, a new course in Australia, designed for pupils in Queensland in school years 9 and 10 (secondary forms 3 and 4) has the following "global" aims.

"This course in the study of agriculture seeks to provide, to all students (urban as well as rural) a meaningful learning experience to:

(i) develop an awareness and understanding of the inter-relationships and dependencies that exist among plants, animals, man and the farm environment;

(ii) understand the distinctive role of agriculture and thus to enhance the recognition of the dependence of the general community on the rural community;

(iii) understand the processes involved in producing food to service the needs of society;

(iv) assist students to determine for themselves, the nature of their talents, capacities and abilities through the provision of a wide range of concrete experiences in agriculture;

(v) develop an appreciation of the many agricultural pursuits that can contribute to the productive use of leisure time; and

(vi) assist students to develop responsibilities and skills which will enhance their prospects for employment."

Many aspects of such a statement provide a part basis for a holistic community-wide educational program about food and agriculture. These aspects include an emphasis on the following concepts:

— the ecological basis of food production,
— the dependence of the general community on the rural community,
— procedures involved in food production,

and on the following skills and attitudes:

— personal development of general talents, capacities and abilities,
— appreciation of agricultural pursuits which could contribute to the productive use of leisure time,
— development of responsibilities and skills which enhance prospects of employment.

Other aims, however, would need to be added to make such a program less school oriented and more suitable for the community at large. Perhaps, more critically, there is a total absence of a world perspective. A full set of aims for a community program might be expressed as follows:

— understand how food is produced, processed, preserved, marketed, conserved, and managed in terms of the economy;
— appreciate how and why diversity in production of food is important to both the producer and the society at large and take action to increase diversification;
— understand factors influencing the consumption of food including: cultural, historical and religious aspects, over and under-consumption; health and nutritional aspects; maintenance of the quality of food and of diet; the effect of additives; the impact of social and economic factors and so on;
— appreciate that research and development should be encouraged to improve food production; to help with the development and acceptability of new foods; to facilitate distribution and to improve the general quality of nutrition in the local community, national and world community;
— develop skill in identifying and solving community wide and personal problems which may arise from time to time in implementing of the food-agriculture cycle (Fig. 1);
— understand each individual citizen's personal roles and responsibilities in the production, processing, supply, distribution and consumption of food to ensure the welfare (including the wellness) of the individual, the family, the community, the nation, and indeed of the world.

The importance of such a holistic approach should not be underestimated — the world and especially the Third World, is facing a food crisis.

The following figures (Table 1) are from FAO's *Fourth World Food Survey Report (1977)*. They show the deficit in food energy by region in terms of calories and its wheat equivalent, 1972–4.

TABLE 1. *Deficit in Food Energy Supplies 1972–4*
(FAO figures)

Region	Total deficit	
	Thousand million calories/day	Million tons of wheat/year
Africa	73	8.5
Far East	213	24.6
Latin America	14	1.6
Near East	20	2.3
Developing market economies	320	37.0

In recent years the situation of course has become much more serious in countries with developing market economies, especially in sub-Saharan and equatorial Africa where the effects of drought have produced a critical situation. The world economic recession of the late 1970s and early 1980s has further exacerbated the situation. Table 2 shows the world food commodity trade balances for developing and developed countries for the period 1977/79 to 1981. (Figures from FAO *Commodity Review and Outlook 1982–3*).

The inequality of this pattern and the strain on the economics and social fabric of the countries of the Third World is self-evident. Further, data on

TABLE 2. *Food Commodities Trade Balances*
1977/79–81
(excluding fisheries products)
(expressed in million US dollars (FAO figures))

Category	1977/79	1980	1981
Developing countries	−2117	−13,180	−16,535
Developed countries	−8543	−1449	+2457

current world stocks of food from FAO confirm this trend. The report by FAO, *The State of Food and Agriculture 1982,* contains the following statement:

> "Stocks, and particularly those of cereals and dairy products are concentrated in developed countries. For example, developed countries are expected to hold 70% of the world cereal stocks by the end of their 1982/83 season, an increase of 30% over 4 years. Cereal stocks in developing countries have not increased since 1976/77."

And in the same report

> "Accumulating stocks underline the current imbalance in world food supply and demand. Several developed countries are producing food in excess of domestic and export market demand. Some of them have programs that direct food commodities to animal feed or industrial uses. Currently in at least one of them, the United States, programs have been legislated that aim to reduce cereal production. Yet in developing countries there exists a large unsatisfied demand."

Health implications of the food energy deficiency are, of course, highly significant. Recent studies of malnutrition by the World Health Organization (WHO) show an alarming pattern throughout the Third World.[1] Table 3, for example, lists the prevalence of wasting (emaciation) of 1-year-old children in various regions. When it is realized that these data are based on a measure of weight per height and that the table lists percentages of 1-year-olds with weight-per-height measures less than M-2SD of an agreed international reference, the picture is indeed bleak.

The point is that the aims of a holistic program about food and agriculture should take cognizance of these patterns by (i) stressing the development of alternative strategies within developing countries in regard to production, distribution and consumption of food; (ii) indicating to citizens of developed countries the nature and implications of the imbalance in the distribution of food; (iii) indicating how all citizens of the world in effect share the one problem and must co-operate in its solution.

One Australian teacher, Alan Morgan, speaking of agriculture as a school subject at a conference of agricultural educators held in the Australian Capital Territory in 1978 quoted the general aim of a local course as stating:

> ". . . because Agriculture is part of human behaviour and culture, because it is intrinsic to human existence, children should learn to appreciate, understand and feel an empathy for the agricultural process so that they may understand the human condition, the place of

TABLE 3. *Prevalence (Percentage) of Emaciated One-Year-Old Children by Region* (from Keller and Fillmore, WHO, 1983)

	0–10	10–20	20–30	30–40	40–50	50+
Near East & West Asia	Egypt Jordan UNRWA	Yemen	—	Democratic Yemen	—	—
Africa	Cameroon Kenya (rural) Togo Zaire Lesotho Liberia Rwanda (Sth)	Botswana Kenya (urban) Upper Volta Benin Senegal	Mali (Sth) Rwanda Sierra Leone	Ghana (urban) Burundi Togo (1973) Malawi	Mali (Nth)	Somalia (1975)
SE Asia	—	Thailand	Indonesia Nepal Sri Lanka	Burma	Bangladesh	—
Western Pacific	Singapore (Chinese)	Singapore (Malays) Singapore (Indians) Philippines Solomon Is	—	—	—	—
Americas	Brazil Costa Rica Ncaragua El Salvador Honduras Panama Colombia Dominican Rep.	Haiti	—	—	—	—

mankind in the scheme of things and be able to contribute to the future of human existence."

He went on to add: "For its full effect such a philosophy must be protected from being 'schooled' into a curriculum. Such a constraint will sap it of vitality that is its sole justification". If the word "agriculture" in these statements were to be replaced by "the food–agriculture cycle" and if the word "children" were to be replaced by "all citizens in all countries", then Alan Morgan's statements could well provide a general rationale for the continuing education program proposed in this paper.

Who should learn and where they should learn

Since the aim is to influence all citizens at all ages, that is to develop a lifelong program of learning, the program must involve learners in formal (institutional) education; in the non-formal educational sector where adults are engaged in catch-up programs, and in informal education in the community at large.

Schooling as such has an important role to play. Pupils in pre-school and primary school should be given an opportunity to learn key principles and skills in the food–agriculture cycle and since most programs at these levels are based on an integrated curriculum it would be relatively easy to include relevant topics, and to provide an overview of the whole food–agriculture cycle and its implications. In schools with a subject curriculum, as in most secondary schools, appropriate elements of the cycle can be treated in greater depth within the various specialized subjects — agriculture, biology, physical science, health and physical education, mathematics, social studies, geography, economics, industrial arts, domestic science, language-arts and so on. In institutions of higher education a research type orientation or preparation for a teaching role can be emphasized within the various subjects of the over-all curriculum. The point is that the food-agriculture cycle should be seen as a continuing thread through all levels and most aspects of formal education.

In the non-formal sector obvious targets are people engaged in adult basic education such as literacy programs or in catch-up programs designed for those who dropped out of formal education at an early age and now wish to re-enter the formal sector. Many of these non-formal programs are, at present, highly academic and many adults find them irrelevant and so lack motivation and drop out a second time. As many aspects of the food–agriculture cycle are directly relevant to daily life, the cycle provides a rich source of skills and concepts likely to increase motivation. Issues such as family nutrition; home gardening; consumer survey studies; subsistence farming and so on are all relevant, and topics could be selected to interest particular adult groups.

The informal sector provides an open-ended situation for almost unlimited interaction. In the first place the food-agriculture program should slot in to any ongoing national program, especially in developing countries, such as literacy programs; family planning campaigns; campaigns to encourage self-reliance; health and nutrition programs; and extension agriculture programs. In all countries use should be made of community centres; libraries; hospitals and clinics; political centres; recreation centres; sporting clubs; hobby groups and so on by conveying messages about food and agriculture relevant to the interests of these particular groups.

The mass media of course have an important role to play — popular magazines, newspapers; radio and television can convey key ideas, and should be encouraged to co-operate in a community campaign.

In the informal sector the specific target will also vary by age and by social role. Special programs need to be devised for children; for teenagers; for young marrieds; for the nuclear family; for an extended family; for nursing mothers; for businessmen; for the subsistence farmer; for the aged and so on. All these groups have different needs in relation to the food–agriculture cycle, and these needs must be identified and satisfied.

In some countries the most appropriate key target might be the nuclear family. In a developed country such as Australia, city dwellers might be interested in how to maintain family health on a minimal budget and so a focus on consumerism and on organizing the weekly shopping budget may be a good entry point. In a country with a developing market economy and a mainly rural population the most appropriate target could well be an entire village and the entry point may be the exploration of alternative sources of food such as poultry raising, fish farming, bee farming, fruit cropping and so on. Almost certainly in rural areas of many developing countries the most effective starting point would be through traditional practice — sharing knowledge about traditional methods of farming; food storage processes; preservation of food; effective traditional living styles which ensure a balanced diet and so on.

An important classification relates to the producer–consumer continuum. A farmer aiming to produce a surplus of food for sale; a subsistence producer with little or no surplus; and a consumer with no production role at all, clearly have different needs and must be treated in a different way within the program.

What should be learnt and how it could be taught

The content of this type of lifelong continuing education program must therefore change according to the needs of individuals. In particular, location on the producer–consumer continuum is a key factor, as is age, social role, educational level, whether the program is within a developed or developing economy and so on. Nevertheless, some general principles can be identified.

In the first place a great deal of emphasis must be given to the development of flexible attitudes including a willingness to try alternatives; to accept innovations and to appreciate that the quality of life can be improved by positive action on the part of all citizens.

Secondly stress needs to be given to problem-solving, that is to the identification of relevant problems, to ways of seeking a solution and to techniques for implementing positive action.

Thirdly the learning should be participatory so that present skills can be enhanced and new skills developed.

The food–agriculture cycle itself forms the basis of a type of syllabus. Each point of the cycle could provide a wide range of topics for the learning program. One example from each part of the cycle is suggested in Table 4 for a developed and a developing country. Each topic would have to be selected, of course, to satisfy a particular need of the target group.

At school level, of course, the content must be tied in to the formal curriculum and Table 5 lists some suggestions for various subjects of the secondary curriculum.

The methods of teaching should be as varied as possible consistent with the aims and objectives and with the subject matter. Teaching methods within the school sector should be much as for the general curriculum with an emphasis on inquiry learning, participation and

TABLE 4. *Examples of Topics for a Program of Continuing Education in the Area of Food and Agriculture using Stages in the Food–Agriculture Cycle as "Syllabus" Headings*

Stage in the food–agriculture cycle	Developed country	Developing country
Primary production	The impact of mechanization on animal farming	Alternative animal production — fish and poultry farming
Processing	Nutritional values of packaged foods	Traditional food preservation methods for maximum nutrition
Storage, supply and distribution	Policy in regard to national surplus	Conservation of resources through effective storage
Consumption	Maintenance of balanced diet to avoid obesity	Diversification of food preferences

TABLE 5. *Examples of Topics for a Secondary School Program about Food and Agriculture introduced through Conventional Subjects*

Subject	Developed country	Developing country
Agriculture	Effects of pollution	Soil fertility
Biology	The nature of food	Basic food requirements
Domestic science	Additives in food	Traditional cooking
Economics	International trade in food commodities	Cash flow at the local market
Geography	Effects of drought on food production	Conservation of soil and water
Health and physical education	Importance of balanced diet	Alternative sources of protein
Industrial arts	Maintenance of farm machines	Making basic farm tools
Language-arts	Writing a report on food preferences in the community	Giving a talk on food hygiene
Mathematics	Analysis of trade statistics	Maintaining a family budget
Physical science	Chemical analysis of food	Energy values of food

problem solving. There should be lots of opportunities for field visits, visits to community centres, and to food production and food processing facilities. Wherever possible, work experience should be provided in relevant areas of employment. Small group methods are especially important because of the need to develop appropriate attitudes.

In the non-formal and informal sectors where the targets are mainly adults, the teaching methods should be very carefully worked out. While some reliance must be placed on simply supplying information through talks, special publications, and by means of the mass media, the most effective programs will involve direct interventions which encourage practical participatory learning.

Some of the techniques especially suitable for adult groups include the following:

(i) *Small group work*: Apart from the classical discussion groups adults especially appreciate problem solving groups and need to be shown how to apply techniques such as brainstorming and force-field analysis. Mirroring techniques are especially useful when there is some internal group conflict — such as when there are opposed views about whether or not to build a new well or to introduce irrigation into an area: such techniques allow each group to see itself as seen by others and this tends to help in solving community problems.

(ii) *Simulation*: Since simulation involves a risk free model of reality it can help identify areas of difficulty or conflict and facilitate both basic learning and the solving of problems. Role play, for example, is usually especially effective. In communities with good reading skills, in-basket (in-tray) simulations can also be very effective. For example, a scenario could be established in which a member of a local government council could review all correspondence and relevant papers in his or her in-tray in relation to a proposal to build a cannery in a specified area of a particular town and make a decision based on the evidence. In less literate communities an interpersonal simulation game could focus on the solution of this type of problem.

(iii) *Dramatic and semi-dramatic methods*: Many adults enjoy being involved in sociodrama where they read from prepared scripts or to take part in creative drama about issues relevant to them. Good dramatic scenarios might be: (i) a family disagreement about a proposed innovation in farming, (ii) a women's group discussing the pros and cons of breast feeding using a particular family episode as a focus, (iii) conflict in the community about a certain fast food chain and its methods of advertising . . . and so on.

(iv) *Practical work*: Most adults enjoy active practical involvement in a learning experience. "Practical" work can involve planning as well as a "hands-on" activity. Take, for example the idea of a certain community (say a village or a suburban area of a large city) wishing to establish a communal vegetable garden — practical work could be organized on a variety of aspects ranging from paper and pencil or verbal planning meetings through to the actual organization, development, maintenance and administration of the garden.

(v) *Experiential (on-job) learning*: This type of learning involves either (i) direct intervention in the day-to-day work of the individual or (ii) the provision of work experience for people (say school students) not yet in full-time employment. This method has wide applications. Work experience can be integrated into a program of formal education with students working for two or three weeks on farms, in food processing factories, in the food distribution industry, in research laboratories and so on. In advanced food-processing industries in developed countries, on-job training can be given to improve efficiency, and on farms on-the-spot training can be provided on new techniques. The method is especially suitable in developing countries where effective traditional methods of agriculture, food processing, food consumption and so on can be analysed and used as the basis of an effective program of mass education.

(vi) *Independent self-paced learning*: While no program should rely on self-paced learning as its main method of instruction, resources such as programmed booklets; programmed audio-tape recordings; programmed video-tapes; slide-tape programs and audio-tutorials all have a place. They can be used in programs of distance education or as a focus for discussion during a workshop. They are especially useful for providing step-by-step instruction on a technique — such as use of a particular piece of farm equipment; to show how to build a vermin proof granary; to give guidance in planning nutritious meals for the family; to advise on organizing and implementing a reducing diet, and so on.

The point to stress about methods is that mere reliance on, say, the mass media or on a "field officer" visiting local communities to give formal talks is largely ineffective. If real improvements are to occur in attitudes, knowledge and skill, a variety of techniques is required all designed to encourage active involvement in the processes of learning.

Who should teach and how they could be trained

The type of program advocated involves a major national commitment and would need to call on a considerable cross-section of expertise. Clearly it would be economically impossible for any country or province to employ thousands of full-time teachers so what is suggested is that a register of suitable teachers be established and that these teachers be employed for only a few hours per week within the program. The teachers could be recruited from many sectors of the community and the following list is only to give some idea of the possibilities.

   (i) School teachers
  (ii) College and university lecturers
 (iii) Health officers
 (iv) High school graduates
  (v) Social workers
 (vi) Family planners
 (vii) Teachers in basic education and literacy programs
(viii) Dieticians
 (ix) Cooking demonstrators
  (x) Farmers
 (xi) Food processing employees
 (xii) District nurses
(xiii) Citizens knowledgeable about effective traditional practices
(xiv) Sports and physical education instructors

Indeed any informed citizen meeting specified basic requirements in terms of knowledge, commitment and ability to communicate, and willing to undertake a short retraining program could be considered eligible. Lack of formal educational background should not be a barrier. Each person recruited would bring some knowledge of a specialized aspect of the food–agriculture cycle to the program. Very few if any, at least at first, could be expected to be familiar with all aspects. They would need to be trained and to work as members of regional and/or local teams, pooling and sharing their expertise. Their main task would be to work directly in the community as change agents or facilitators aiming to help people to help themselves.

Training of these people need not be massive. The most appropriate model might be through participatory workshops, each involving eight to ten hours of training (over a weekend or spread over two evenings). The workshops could perhaps be designed using a minicourse format [2] which involves an application of the principles of educational technology to achieve a set of clearly specified objectives aimed to develop both understanding and practical skill. Perhaps, to achieve registration, only two or three such workshops would be required for basic retraining and others could be attended as required at a later stage to expand knowledge and to extend skills. Incidentally, the minicourse model has been used to good effect in Thailand to retrain school teachers for part-time (evening) work in the non formal sector where they give courses for adults to prepare for re-entry into a nominated stage of formal education.[3] It is a relatively small step to extend this idea to a broader spectrum of trainees for working in the informal sector in this program of continuing education.

The minicourse type workshop is designed to bring together a group of adults with widely varying backgrounds but with a common interest and commitment and to involve them in a type of training which encourages them to share and build on one-another's knowledge and expertise. If team-building techniques are added to this approach then minicourses could be used to train many hundreds of teams, some of whom could train others, and so within a few months a whole national program for the total community could get under way.

There remains the question of who should design and present these minicourses. An answer is that this could involve four levels. Firstly a total "syllabus" for a continuing education program about the food–agriculture cycle would need to be designed centrally (see below on co-ordination and administration). Secondly, a small group of experts, themselves a team whose members would see the cycle from different view points and different background, would design the minicourses and write training manuals. Thirdly, a panel of minicourse leaders would need to be recruited, mainly from the teaching, health and agricultural professions, and given training (perhaps over one or two weeks) in (i) how to present minicourses and (ii) the philosophy content and methods of the continuing education program. These people would then become the trainers of the trainers and would mount the regional minicourses. Fourthly, after a few months, further trainers of the trainers could be chosen from the more able and willing participants in the minicourse workshops. These people could then train others at local level.

How such a program could be co-ordinated

The main centre of focus for a holistic continuing education program about all aspects of the food–agriculture cycle and their implications, is the development and co-ordination of the work of the hundreds, perhaps thousands, part-time teacher-facilitators needed to work with all sectors of the community. Such a program, while multi-disciplinary in content and multi-level in organization, nevertheless requires strong central co-ordination.

The most appropriate co-ordinating agency would be a government department and though strong contenders would be the Ministry of Agriculture and the Ministry of Health, the most appropriate would be the Ministry of Education, and preferably the Adult Education section of that ministry. There is no doubt, however, that there should be the closest interdepartmental co-operation. The Ministry of Education is the most likely agency to co-ordinate this work because of its expertise in curriculum design; its knowledge of teaching methodologies and its access to training facilities. The approach, however, must be flexible and not constrained by philosophies, regulations and procedures of application in the formal sector of education. As previously discussed, if this type of program is seen in the same framework as schooling "it would be sapped of its vitality".

Several additional points can be made about the co-ordination of this type of program.

As mentioned before, a key task is to design a national "syllabus" and to train the trainers. Once these "leaders" have been trained some sort of regional administrative system is required perhaps co-ordinated by provincial offices of the Ministry of Education. These provincial offices should recruit local "teachers" and arrange their programs of minicourse training.

The actual teaching could be co-ordinated by local and regional committees of the teachers themselves. They could identify local needs, prepare appropriate materials and strategies and work as presenters and facilitators sometimes individually, sometimes with one or two others and sometimes as an intervention team.

Centrally the "experts" in ministry head office could provide support to regional and local groups by facilitating production of training materials; by helping with administrative aspects; by utilizing back-up resources of the mass media; by conducting writing workshops; by increasing the reportoire of minicourses available to teachers; to act as consultants and so on.

The decentralization of this type of program is, of course, essential since each local group will have its own special needs in relation to the food–agriculture cycle. It is important, however, that while attempting to meet special needs such a particular problem of crop diversification or a special nutritional problem or a general problem of prejudice against innovation, local teachers place these needs into the content of the whole food–agriculture cycle. Purely reflexive responses to local problems are not sufficient if the community, be it in the suburbs of Sydney or the highlands of East Africa, is to become willing and able to see the whole picture and to accept more responsibility for its own continuing development.

Several administrative bonuses emerge from this type of approach. The first is that costs would not be high. Since the retraining of teachers is very short-term and since the teachers are involved only part-time, the salary component would be small. In fact it could be made even smaller by offering incentives other than cash, especially for government employees. These could include improved opportunities for promotion, time off in lieu, extended vacation periods and the like. Some recruitment could be from voluntary groups — young farmers; peace-corps workers; community clubs; welfare agencies and so on. Since the "teachers" in this type of program are not conventional school teachers recruitment policy can be totally flexible.

The second administrative bonus is that once a total continuing education network of this type is established for one purpose — in this case to deal with the problems of the food–agriculture cycle — it can be used for other purposes. It could form the basis for a total program of community education involving aspects such as family planning; literacy campaigns; health education; the inservice education of school teachers and so on. The food–agriculture cycle could be seen as pivotal to a much broader approach to a total program of community education.

The third bonus is that many of the decisions to be made in the implementation of this type of program come from below — from the grass roots — rather than from above down. The people themselves are the real teachers and self help and self reliance become the predominant philosophy. This attitude is greatly facilitated by the team approach to training and to team work involved in actual work within the community.

A fourth bonus is that the model suggested provides an organic link between formal, non-formal and informal sectors of education. By recruiting school teachers into continuing education and by ensuring that the content of adult education runs parallel to relevant curriculum changes in the schools, the thread of lifelong learning remains unbroken and visible to all. School teachers, especially, by working within two sectors, enrich one by their experiences in the other. Undoubtedly this has been one of the gains in the non-formal sector in Thailand[3] and is a strong factor in ensuring the success of this type of program.

How the program could be evaluated

Evaluation of the ultimate effectiveness of lifelong continuing education can only be made in relation to long-term gains in the overall quality of life. By viewing the food–agriculture cycle as an entry point for a total program of community education, however, specific targets can be identified and measures obtained of specific gains.

This highlights the importance of setting national, regional and local short-term and longer-term goals, in both administrative and substantive terms. These goals should, of course, be sufficiently flexible to accommodate changing needs but nevertheless need to be specified as precisely as possible in a way which enables their achievement (or lack of achievement) to be clearly manifest to all. While this is characteristic of all good administration and all good teaching, it is especially important in broad spectrum programs of continuing education where elements, if not controlled, could become diffuse and ineffective.

To return to a consideration of the specific food-agriculture program any evaluative study would need to operationalize the agreed statements of aims by expressing them in terms of measurable and observable targets or expected outcomes. The following discussion gives examples for each of the broad aims suggested earlier.

Aim 1:   *Understand how food is produced, processed, preserved, marketed, conserved and managed in terms of the economy.*

Example of: Fruit growers of region X will be able to form and
Expected   manage a fruit marketing co-operative.
outcome

Evidence of: Twenty viable fruit marketing co-operatives to be
Attainment   established in region X by the end of 1986.

Aim 2:   *Appreciate how and why diversity in production of food is important to both the producer and the society at large and take action to increase diversification.*

Example of: Cattle farmers to develop the skill in establishing viable
Expected   fish farms on their properties by the end of 1986.
outcome

Evidence of: Fifteen percent of farmers in Western Province to have
Attainment   established viable fish farms by June 1987.

Aim 3:   *Understand factors influencing the consumption of food.*

Example of: Citizens will be able to plan practicable meals which
Expected   ensure provision of a balanced diet.
outcome

Evidence of: By December 1986 one representative of each family
Attainment   in Central City will have (i) attended a three hour
                workshop on nutrition *or* (ii) received a pamphlet
                describing how to prepare suitable meals *or* (iii)
                attended meetings held in the local primary schools to
                discuss this issue.

Aim 4:   *To appreciate that research and development should be
           encouraged.*

Example of: The majority of citizens will have an opportunity to react
Expected   to documentary material about research presented via
outcome   the mass media.

Evidence of: By 1985 a documentary video program on food research
Attainment   will have been produced and viewed in all major centres.

Aim 5:   *Develop skill in identifying and solving community-wide and
           personal problems which may arise from time to time in
           implementing the food–agriculture cycle.*

Example of: Community leaders will have developed skill in guiding
Expected   others in finding solutions to their problems.
outcome

Evidence of: At least two prominent citizens from each village
Attainment   community in Coastal Region, knowledgeable in local
                traditional farming practice, will have participated in
                problem-solving workshops held in the Provincial
                capital.

Aim 6:   *Understand each individual citizen's personal roles and respons-
           ibilities in the production, processing, supply, distribution and
           consumption of food to ensure the welfare (including the
           wellness) of the individual, the family, the community, the
           nation, and indeed of the world.*

Example of: The majority of citizens (of a developed country) will
Expected   appreciate that their country has a responsibility to effect
outcome   a more equitable distribution of food stocks world-wide.

Evidence of: By 1987 this concept will have been (i) introduced into
Attainment   the primary school social science syllabus (ii) integrated
                into the agriculture, biology, geography and economics
                syllabuses in the high schools and (iii) been the subject of
                an intensive campaign in the mass media.

It is immediately obvious from these examples that just as specific aspects of syllabus, objectives, and activities should be organized at regional and local levels, so too should most of the evaluation studies. As each local program is unique, its evaluation is also unique. The central co-ordinating authority, however, should provide resources to assist with collecting the necessary data and should co-ordinate all local reports to obtain a national overview.

This type of approach is highly pragmatic but is also very flexible. The expected outcomes and evidence for their attainment should be constantly reviewed and new targets set at least once each year. From time to time, say biennially, a national conference of regional chairpersons could be held to exchange views on programs, targets and evaluation studies and also to help in the interpretation of any centrally determined policies.

There is another implication. The national budget for such a program should be distributed so that only a relatively small proportion (perhaps at most only 25% or 30%) should be held by the central co-ordinating authority with the rest distributed to regional and/or local committees. The central budget should be for mounting national conferences; for producing resources to be used nation-wide; for maintaining a consultancy service for the region; for issuing national reports and for maintaining a modest central executive. Since the great majority of day-to-day activities, including the evaluative studies, occur locally and since many of the decisions need to be made quickly and on the spot, then local autonomy in the budget is vitally important — no matter how modest that budget may be.

Conclusion

In a recent report (1982) of FAO, the Director General, Edouard Saouma, wrote as follows:

> "The prolonged economic recession has imposed stress and distress on hundreds of millions of people in agriculture in different parts of the world. It is now over three years that the world economy has been plagued with recession; unemployment; declining demand, invest-ment and income; and rising trade protectionism; accompanied by an alarming rise in the burden of external debt of the developing world, currently estimated at $700 billion. International assistance pro-grames, including those of multi-lateral aid agencies, have been curtailed. On the other hand, military expenditures have still steadily grown and are now estimated to be about 4.5% of the world GNP."[4]

And elsewhere in the same report:

> "Food security should aim at three specific goals: to guarantee adequate production: to stabilize the flow of supplies to the utmost:

70 G. R. MEYER

and to guarantee access to available foods to those who need them. Obviously, production and trade are two of the main aspects of world food security, and the present crisis affects both of them. . . . The farmers of the rich countries have been hit by the crisis. But those in the Third World, especially landless farm workers and the poorer farmers, have been even more hard-hit in their ability to produce and to consume, as well as to export."

In our divided and complex world there is one thing we all share in common — the need for food security. Education alone cannot provide this. It cannot control droughts and other national disasters; it cannot prevent economic crises and it cannot give nourishment to the starving. But it can increase knowledge and skill in coping with these problems; it can help reduce the negative influence of fear and superstition; it can help in overcoming bias and prejudice; and it can help to increase tolerance and understanding between peoples. The food–agriculture cycle is not just another of those topics to be taken up as a "current fashion" in education — it lies at the heart of our survival as a species. Only a holistic approach of the type outlined in this paper would enable this message to reach all people in all countries of the world. Only then, perhaps, the world will see that there is indeed only one world and only then will the arms race give way to a race to improve the quality of life on this planet.

References

1. Keller, W. and Fillmore, C. M. Prevalence of protein-energy malnutrition, *World Health Statistics Quarterly*, Vol. 36, 1983, pp. 129–167. The statistics shown are from table 5, p. 147 (readers are strongly advised to consult the original paper for a full interpretation of these figures).
2. Meyer, G. Rex. The development of minicourses (with a basis in educational technology) for the in-service education of teachers and trainers, *Programmed Learning and Educational Technology*, Vol. 16, No. 1, February 1979, pp. 23–37. *Also see* Asian Programme of Educational Innovation for Development. *The Minicourse Approach: what it is and how it works.* Bangkok: Unesco Regional Office for Education in Asia and the Pacific, 1982.
3. Ministry of Education Thailand. *Proceedings of Workshops for the Development of the Minicourse for the Functional Education Level 3–4 Teacher Training Project.* Bangkok: Ministry of Education Department of Nonformal Education, 1982.
4. Saouma, Edouard. Foreword, *in* FAO, *The State of Food and Agriculture 1982*

8

Teaching About Nutrition in Primary and Secondary Schools

SHEILA A. TURNER
University of London Institute of Education, UK

> "Nutrition education is concerned with teaching and learning about knowledge, attitudes and practices related to food and the way it is used by the human body for energy, growth and development" (Unesco, 1983).

> "The aim of nutrition education is that all people shall know sufficient about the composition of foods and human physiological needs to be able to make sound choices about the foods they eat" (Hollingsworth, 1983).

Few people would disagree with these statements, although some would consider that they imply a view of nutrition education which does not give sufficient emphasis to other equally important aspects including those concerned with the socio-economic dimensions of the subject. The translation of the aim of nutrition education outlined above into appropriate and effective educational policies and strategies has been the subject of considerable debate during the past 50 years. The central questions concerning nutrition education, namely how it should be taught, what should be taught and by whom, are still pertinent; to many of us the answers appear as elusive as they were a decade ago. Amongst nutrition educators there is agreement, however, about the importance of including nutrition education as an integral and essential component of the school curriculum for all children. If we are to achieve the World Health Organization goal of health for all by the year 2000, then all of us who are teachers, whether of science or of geography, need to be more aware of the importance of nutrition education and the ways in which it can be incorporated more fully and effectively into the curriculum.

71

In what follows we will look specifically at the place of nutrition education in the school curriculum and the way in which it is taught at present; and suggest ways in which current practice might be improved. Although the emphasis will be on nutrition education in the United Kingdom, many of the issues raised apply to other parts of the world.

Teaching about nutrition poses particular problems. The first problem is that the subject of food is frequently an emotive issue. This problem is understandable since the importance of food extends beyond its obvious biological functions, such as those concerned with the growth and repair of cells or metabolic energy requirements; it extends into the social structures of every community and is part of religious and folklore traditions throughout the world. Nutrition education, if it is to be successful, must take into account the complex interactions which govern eating habits, including enconomic factors; this is not easy. The constraints under which many teachers work include lack of time, up-to-date information, appropriate teaching materials and sometimes encouragement from colleagues or superiors. Such constraints frequently inhibit the development of the imaginative and innovative approaches which are needed if subjects like nutrition are to be taught effectively. In many instances really successful teaching depends upon local initiatives and co-operation between teachers and members of the local community rather than implementing ideas produced by "experts". Nutrition education thus needs to go beyond the acquisition of facts; it should encourage the development of skills such as the ability to ask questions, to interpret data and to apply what has been learnt in the classroom in everyday life, it should also give greater understanding of the reasons for particular food habits and the socio-economic factors underlying food distribution and availability.

It is impossible to isolate what takes place in the classroom from the wider community. Schools are part of local communities and events which occur within the community may influence the educational system. Additionally the development of links between the nonformal systems of education, such as health and welfare programmes, and the use of informal education systems such as the media, merits examination. One reason why nutrition education has often failed in the past could be that there has been insufficient recognition given to the importance of liaison between the different sectors of education as well as between nutritionists and educators. Some consideration will therefore be given to the importance of projects involving the community and extracurricular activities, such as local visits.

In determining the place of nutrition education within the school curriculum it is important first to decide our reasons for teaching about food and nutrition. We need to define our aims and objectives! When educational projects or individual lessons "fail" there may be many reasons, including unrealistic or unreasonable expectations or unsuitable teaching material. Objectives which include changes in attitudes and behaviour are more difficult to achieve than those concerned with the "simple" acquisition of facts or basic skills. The achievement of an objective "to help the pupils make considered choices or decisions related to their health behaviour by increasing knowledge and clarifying the beliefs and values they hold" (Williams, 1981), requires skilled teaching in many areas of the curriculum.

In planning nutrition education programmes we need to be constantly aware of the knowledge and understanding which pupils bring with them to the classroom. The image of the pupil as an empty vessel into which "knowledge" is poured is a somewhat discredited analogy. Education in its widest sense encompasses not only those activities which take place in the classroom but all activities in which an individual engages. The effect of education within schools has to be seen in relation to the total experience of the individual child; the time actually spent in the classroom is but a small fraction of this total experience. Our knowledge of how pupils actually learn, particularly their understanding of ideas concerning food and nutrition, is an area about which we have limited information (Crockett, 1984; McLoughlin and Davies, 1984).

The place of nutrition education within the school curriculum

It is very unusual to find nutrition education as a separate subject in schools in any part of the world (Calloway *et al.*, 1979); indeed it is widely accepted that food and nutrition should be incorporated within the teaching of other subject areas. In the United Kingdom the amount of nutrition education which takes place varies considerably. There is naturally variation between that which occurs in primary schools and work in secondary schools. At primary level nutrition education very often forms part of thematic studies which include literature, mathematics, history and geography as well as science. In secondary schools nutrition education, when it is taught, normally appears as part of science courses, particularly biological science, or home economics. Some schools have health education courses in which nutrition education is one component: in some cases health education is a timetabled subject, in others it forms part of broadly based science courses.

It is apparent from the information we have about health education that there are still a number of "grey areas" in relation to the place of nutrition education in the school curriculum. Nutrition education does feature as part of the curriculum, often incidentally within a range of subjects. The amount, the content and teaching approach used, vary considerably. A first priority should be to ensure that schools develop policies about how such subjects should be incorporated into the curriculum and the emphasis which they should be given. The appointment of a senior teacher to coordinate health education in a school is often an important factor in the development of successful health education policies. The development of a school policy helps to prevent overlap between what is taught in different subject areas and allows a structured progression of work to take place from year to year. Such a policy may help in the development of interdisciplinary courses in which teachers with different specialisms participate. It should also encourage co-operation between staff and the exchange of ideas so essential for professional and curriculum development. Such a policy should also ensure that all pupils are involved in nutrition education throughout their school career. In England and Wales this implies that further consideration needs to be given to recent ideas and suggestions (DES, 1980), concerning a core of subjects which would be studied by all pupils up to 16. The proposals include the provision for all pupils to study science up to the age of 16 years and the recognition that "schools need to secure for all pupils opportunities for learning particularly likely to contribute to personal and social development" (DES, 1980). Health education is seen as one of the contexts in which such personal development could be furthered. More time spent on science, particularly for pupils of 14 to 16 years, could mean more time devoted to areas such as nutrition education. However such changes have implications for other subjects within the curriculum where nutrition education takes place, for example home economics. The number of pupils, particularly boys, studying home economics beyond the age of 13 is already small; a greater proportion of time devoted to science might reduce that number still further. Thus the place and importance of home economics within the school curriculum also needs to be assessed; it could be included for example as a part of a "life skills" course incorporating health and nutrition education, or, possibly, as part of more broadly based science courses for older pupils.

It is also important to consider ways in which nutrition education could be incorporated into the curriculum by modifying existing subject areas. Such restructuring may be limited to one or more subjects or have wider curriculum implications including the development of interdisciplinary courses. One approach, developed by the London Borough of Brent (Smith, 1984), has been to re-examine the place of subjects like home economics within the sschool curriculum. For pupils of 11–13 years "nutrition" has been substituted for home economics; this change has freed teachers and pupils from the constraints of traditional home economics courses and enabled new and more effective teaching programmes to be developed. Pupils between 14–16 years follow courses in personal and social education; these courses have a health component which includes nutrition education. Such courses are one way of ensuring that nutrition education is part of the curriculum for all pupils from 11–16 years.

Teaching approaches

In teaching about aspects of nutrition the teaching approach used will inevitably depend upon the type and location of the school. The requirements of primary and secondary school pupils are different and the development of appropriate courses for each level is important. Often constraints such as those imposed by lack of suitable teaching materials or by examination syllabuses militate against the development of imaginative and innovative teaching approaches. What is remarkable is the way in which so many teachers overcome these constraints. A recent survey (Turner and Ingle, 1984) highlighted the variety and range of teaching approaches utilized in teaching nutrition in many countries, particularly in primary schools. Drama, poetry, music and art were included in the subject areas in which teaching about food and nutrition featured in addition to mathematics, geography, history, science and technology, physical education and home science. Examples of some of these approaches are described in the Nutrition Education Series published by Unesco (Unesco, 1983). The value of a practical approach to nutrition education which involves first-hand experience is recognized by the majority of nutrition educators (Hamilton, 1983). This approach includes using the local environment as a basis for activities which will encourage children to be curious about their surroundings, to observe, explain, experiment and communicate their ideas and findings (Baez, 1980).

It is not my intention to provide a "content" list for courses in nutrition education, this will depend upon a variety of factors including the background and age of the pupils. Although examples will be given of topics which could be included in a teaching syllabus the emphasis will be on the type of systematic enquiries which will not only provide greater knowledge about nutrition but will also encourage children to think logically and critically, and enable them to develop social and life skills.

In many primary schools topics relating to nutrition are frequently incorporated within a theme which forms part of an integrated programme of work and which includes aspects of health education. A study of a staple food, for example rice, cassava, or bread; a visit to a local farm, market or the school kitchen could all form the basis of such work. Suggestions for possible starting points for the study of rice are shown in Fig. 1 which also indicates how links between subjects could be made. A study of rice could, for example, start with the examination of a single grain: the observation of its size, shape and colour encourage questions such as:

How big is the grain?

How many grains are needed for one meal?

Work in science and mathematics can be extended by germinating rice grains and measuring the growth of seedlings. A study of different types of rice and how they are used and cooked can lead to questions about how

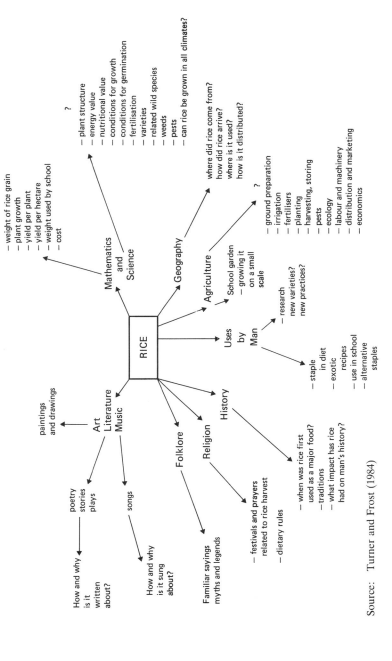

FIG 1.   Diagram to illustrate how work on rice could be developed in different subject areas.

Source: Turner and Frost (1984)

much is eaten by an individual (or a family) in a day, a month, a year — something which necessitates measurement and estimation. Work on the nutritional value of rice, the effect of cooking and different methods of cooking, the use of whole grain or "polished" rice could also be undertaken.

The starting point for such a study on rice need not necessarily be a mathematical or scientific one, indeed other subject areas such as geography may provide much more relevant and appropriate ways in which the social and economic aspects of food use, production and distribution can be introduced. Religious ceremonies and the way in which food is related to these, enable children to learn more about the complex interactions governing attitudes to food.

A range of practical activities is possible in addition to those linked to the preparation and cooking of food. Drama, games with a competitive element — for example a modified snakes and ladders (van der Vynckt, 1984) — or use of cartoon characters or puppets (Young, 1983) can all be utilized.

Visits to the local market or farms can help children's understanding of the importance of local crops in the life of the community. Links can also be made to extracurricular activities, such as school meals (Turner and Frost, 1984). The educational importance of extracurricular activities needs greater recognition. All too frequently they are seen as being isolated from that which takes place in the classroom. School meals, for example, can provide a basis not just for sound nutrition and social development but for a variety of learning experiences (Devadas, 1983). Activities related to school gardens can also provide a rich source of classroom material. Children need to have the experience of growing plants and looking after animals (Young, 1983). For some children such work in school may be their only experience of observing living things, discovering how the food they eat is produced, which plants are edible and which parts of the plant are eaten. For others, it may be an opportunity to learn more about selective breeding or experimenting with plants which could be grown as alternatives to those customarily planted in the area. Such gardens can be used to supply food for school meals and to introduce new and varied vegetables into the diet.

The greater integration of subject areas in primary schools permits an approach to teaching which is far broader and more flexible than that imposed by the traditionally subject orientated secondary school curriculum, which may be further restricted by externally imposed examination syllabuses. Teachers in primary schools are normally "generalists" rather than specialists and therefore often find it less difficult to make connexions between different subject areas than their colleagues in secondary schools. The opportunities for incidental nutrition education within topics such as that outlined for rice are more numerous. Much of the best health education occurs spontaneously in response to questions which pupils ask and this is more likely to occur in the less formal atmosphere of the primary school. It can be argued that many of the teaching approaches used so effectively in primary schools could be adopted more frequently in secondary schools. Additionally the ideas inherent in such interdisciplinary courses as "Man: a course of study" (Bruner, 1968), could be developed to produce very effective nutrition education projects for secondary schools. The aims of such courses include the development of understanding of such areas as social organizations and the use of language, encouraging children to ask questions, developing respect and confidence in pupils' own abilities. If nutrition education is to help pupils to gain greater understanding of the reasons for particular eating patterns and attitudes to food, then teaching approaches, including interdisciplinary courses, need to evolve and develop continuously. Traditionally such development has occurred more rapidly in the primary sector of education. Furthermore, within nutrition education we need to have a global perspective of innovative teaching practices at all levels.

In the United Kingdom there are currently a number of developments which could influence approaches to nutrition education in secondary schools during the next decade. One of these developments is the school-based curriculum development work being undertaken in some places. This work may involve groups outside the school and include the design of new interdisciplinary courses involving topics such as food and marketing. The way in which nutrition features in the school timetable in secondary schools in the London Borough of Brent has already been mentioned. This is, however, only one aspect of a much more ambitious programme which involves discussion between all those concerned with nutrition education in the community, including doctors, teachers, parents, pupils, school meals' supervisors and community dieticians. All schools in the borough, including primary and secondary schools, have been encouraged to develop their own teaching programme to meet the needs of their pupils. The teaching approach is based on the Aquarian scheme (Finch, 1978), which aims to give pupils first-hand experience of a range of different foods, allows them to select food, devise and test their own recipes; it also involves consideration of food habits. Pupils in Brent also assess their own work and discuss this assessment with their teachers. Curriculum development of this type requires commitment and hard work on the part of teachers plus in-service training. Teachers involved in nutrition education in Brent meet on a regular basis in groups which also include doctors and dieticians, they visit each other's schools and primary teachers have taught in secondary schools. One of the aims of the Brent Food and Health Group which initiated the nutrition education programme has been to encourage dialogue between different groups in the community, including parents and teachers. Thus parents have been invited into schools to learn about new teaching approaches and to discuss these with teachers. The views of pupils, parents and teachers on a range of health education related topics, including food and health, are being investigated by means of questionnaires. Such initiatives have been supported by recommendations of specialist committees concerning nutrition policy and dietary guidelines which have helped to create greater public awareness and interest in nutrition. The report of the National Advisory Committee on Nutrition Education (NACNE 1983), has enabled those involved in education to examine teaching approaches in the light of national recommendations regarding the intake of nutrients such as fats.

The provision of new teaching materials which encourage fresh thinking about teaching approaches related to health education could help teachers to re-examine and modify current practice. The Nuffield home economics materials (Nuffield-Chelsea Curriculum Trust, 1982) with their emphasis on food science and nutrition and health education 13–18 (Schools Council/ Health Education Council, 1981), are two examples. Many of the ideas and approaches advocated in the Nuffield Home economics books could be utilized within science courses. Both courses are designed to develop a wide range of skills including those related to decision-making and problem-solving. One of the aims of "health education 13–18" is to encourage non-didactic teaching approaches, for example small group discussions; it advocates that the methods used in personal and social education should encourage pupils to identify with real situations and experiences and give them opportunities to clarify attitudes and values. Topics covered include the nutritional needs of the body, nutrition and health, eating patterns and the pressures which influence peoples' choice of food.

Another factor which could influence nutrition education is the current debate on which subjects should be included in the curriculum for all pupils up to 16 years. Science is seen as an essential component (DES, 1981). The Secondary Science Curriculum Review (SSCR, 1984) recognizes that health education is an essential component of the education of all 11–16 year olds and should as far as possible "permeate science as a context for teaching". Health education is seen as part of science, biology, home economics and courses in personal and social education. The emphasis given to health education is encouraging.

Looking ahead to the year 2000 it is obvious that both the media and the increasing use of computer technology will have an important role to play in teaching. Communication technology is developing rapidly. Radio and television have been used in many regions of the world to assist in nutrition education projects. The role that computers could play in nutrition education has still to be realized; it is already apparent that good computer programs could be utilized in many ways at all levels of education. Simulation exercises can be used, for example, to enable menus to be planned, to calculate the cost of meals and their nutritional value as well as to demonstrate metabolic pathways in a more dynamic and understandable way than is normally possible (Turner and Ingle, 1984). Successful nutrition education is unlikely to become dependent upon the use of such new technology; caring, well-informed and imaginative teachers using more traditional teaching approaches will undoubtedly continue to be of more importance.

Ideas from the non-formal sectors of education could also be used by schools to develop new approaches to nutrition education. An example of this type of approach is the "child-to-child" project (Aaron and Hawes, 1979), which has developed a range of activities which can be used for health education. Co-operation is encouraged between different groups including community leaders, health workers, teachers, parents and children all of whom are involved in implementing activities designed to improve health. The section relating to food encourages children to observe and to ask questions; they may be asked to find out what a younger brother or sister eats at home during one day, how much they eat and how frequently they eat. This information is then related to practical studies, including work on the relative energy values of different foods. Other activities suggested involve children planning and cooking healthy meals at school and eating these together. The costs of such an exercise could be covered by children bringing one helping of a staple food, or a small contribution for a protein dish or vegetables. Vegetables and fruit could also be supplied by a school garden.

Nutrition education in many parts of the world is more forward looking and innovative than it is in many regions of the United Kingdom. It is rare for children in Britain to be undernourished and therefore nutrition education does not receive the priority or attention that it merits elsewhere. The problems of malnutrition in a society where the majority have access to sufficient and varied foods and yet can eat unwisely are only slowly being recognized. As educators we need to be aware of the risks attached to poor dietary habits and seek to ameliorate these through effective, appropriate and relevant teaching approaches.

Implications for teachers

Some of the suggestions made in previous sections have implications for teacher training and the provision of resource materials, as well as syllabus design. The place of nutrition education within interdisciplinary health education courses has also been examined; at the primary level this does not necessarily have major implications for the curriculum, as nutrition education is already incorporated into themes which cover many subject areas. The development of interdisciplinary courses in secondary schools is often more difficult — but it is possible!

As teachers, all of us need support and encouragement if we are to develop new teaching approaches, especially if these include unfamiliar concepts and subject content. Primary school teachers are normally "generalists", rarely has their training included any nutrition (Calloway *et al.* 1979); there are exceptions such as innovative schemes like the Namutamba Project (Kiyimba, 1984). Teachers may lack confidence in their ability to teach about aspects of food and nutrition — or to answer questions which pupils may ask! In-service training which will provide teachers with information and an opportunity to discuss common problems with other teachers is very important. The type of meetings described earlier where teachers meet with doctors, dieticians and community health workers can facilitate discussion about the content of nutrition courses and ensure that the information given by different groups is consistent. Workshops to produce low-cost teaching materials are also valuable. Such in-service work requires liaison between different organizations and government departments; support at local government level, from education officers and inspectors, and from teacher training institutions and universities, is important if in-service work is to be effective.

The most important resource in nutrition education is undoubtedly the individual teacher whose enthusiasm and imaginative approach can overcome problems posed by financial constraints and lack of equipment. Most nutrition education requires little specialized equipment; most of that which is required, particularly for primary schools, can be easily made using locally available low-cost materials (Dalgety, 1983).

Lack of appropriate resource materials is frequently cited by teachers as hindering curriculum development. Within nutrition education there is certainly a lack of suitable background material for teachers; one of the problems of a "young" science like nutrition is that our ideas are continuously being modified in the light of new research. For teachers to keep abreast of such developments is very difficult. Unesco has recently initiated a world-wide search for useful teaching ideas and teaching materials in nutrition education (van der Vynckt, 1984). The information collected will be available for teachers. Initiatives of this type which facilitate wider dissemination and exchange of ideas should help to alleviate problems concerning lack of resource materials.

Summary

The place of nutrition education in the school curriculum and some approaches to nutrition education have been examined. I have suggested that schools need to have a school policy about the way in which nutrition education should be incorporated into the corriculum across all subject areas. Although the emphasis has been on nutrition education within the United Kingom many of the ideas and approaches described are similar to work which is being undertaken in many parts of the world. The problems relating to nutrition vary in different parts of the world but the teaching approaches adopted in schools, particularly at primary level, have much in common. Undoubtedly the best teaching occurs where teachers have the necessary support and encouragement to develop courses which they feel confident to teach and which meet the needs of their pupils. Such courses should enable children to evaluate their eating habits and give them the confidence and knowledge to make "sound choices about the foods they eat" (Hollingsworth, 1983).

References

Aaron, A. and Hawes, H. W. R. (1979) *Child-to-Child*. London: Macmillan Press, Ltd.

Baez, A. V. (1980) Curiosity, creativity, competence and compassion — guidelines for science education in the year 2000. In: McFadden, C. P. (ed.), *World Trends in Science Education*. Halifax, Nova Scotia, 1980.

Brunner, J. (1968) *Toward a Theory of Instruction*. New York: W. W. Norton and Co. Inc.

Calloway, D. H., Gordon, H. F., Grodner, M. and Pye, O. (1979) *Position of Nutrition Education within Educational Systems*. Paris: Unesco.

Dalgety, F. (1983) Equipment for primary school science. In: Harlen W. (ed.), *New Trends in Primary School Science Education*, Vol. 1, pp. 133–148. Paris: Unesco.

Department of Education and Science (1980) *A View of the Curriculum*. HMI Series: Matters for Discussion, 11. London: HMSO.

Devadas, R. P. (1983) *The School Lunch Programme*. India: Ministry of Education.

Finch, I. (1978) The aquarian system. *Nutrition and Food Science*.

Hamilton, M. (1983) A suggested outline for the introduction of nutrition education at the primary school level in Jamaica. In: *Primary School Curriculum Planning and Selected Case Studies*. Nutrition Education Series, No. 4. Paris: Unesco.

Hollingsworth, D. (1983) Nutrition education. Paper given at VIth World Congress of Food Science and Technology in Dublin, September 1983.

Kiyimba, D. (1985) The place of nutrition in teacher's curriculum as a tool for rural development. In: Turner, S. A. and Ingle, R. B. (eds), *New Developments in Nutrition Education*. Paris: Unesco.

National Advisory Council on Health Education (1983) *A discussion paper on proposals for nutritional guidelines for health education in Britain*. London: Health Education Council.

Nuffield Chelsea Curriculum Trust (1982) *Nuffield Home Economics*. London: Hutchinson and Co.

Schools Council/Health Education Council Project (1981) *Health Education 13–16*. London: Forbes Publications.

Secondary Science Curriculum Review (1984) *Health and science education; proposals for action and consultation*. London: SSCR.

Smith, L. (1984) Nutrition education in the London borough of Brent. Paper given at a meeting of Nutrition Education Group, University of London Institute of Education.

Turner, S. A. and Frost, J. (1986) The contribution of science education to school feeding programmes. *School Feeding Programmes as a Potential Source of Learning* Paris/New Delhi, Unesco/UNICEF.

Turner, S. A. and Ingle, R. B. (1985) (Eds.) *New Developments in Nutrition Education* Nutrition Education Series, Issue 11. Paris: Unesco.

Van der Vynckt, S. (1984) Unesco and nutrition education. In: *Unesco Courier — Food for a Hungry World*. Paris: Unesco.

Unesco (1983) *Primary School Curriculum Planning and Selected Case Studies*. Nutrition Education Series, No. 4. Paris: Unesco.

Williams, T. (1981) Health education in secondary schools. In Cowley, J., David J. and Williams, T. (eds.), *Health Education in Schools*. London: Harper Row.

Young, B. L. (1983) The selection of processes, contexts and concepts and their relationship to methods of teaching. In: Harlen, W. (ed.), *New Trends in Primary School Science Education*, Vol. 1, pp. 7–16. Paris: Unesco.

9

Nutrition and Science Education

ISAIAS RAW
Brazil

The WHO defines health as a state of complete physical, mental and social well-being, and not merely the absence of disease or infirmity. There is no equivalent and accepted definition of the goals of science education, but it should include more than the simple acquisition of information and the learning of a few technical words. The learner should be able to find information, to review it critically by examining the evidence on which the information is based, to draw objective conclusions, and above all to acquire a skill to solve problems, both professional and those in daily life. If possible, he or she should become capable of producing, on the basis of available knowledge, new hypotheses and submitting them to the scrutiny of further evidence and experimentation.

Nutrition—a natural topic for science education

To achieve the main objective of science education—the acquisition of a scientific attitude—students must be exposed to problems needing to be solved. In the process of trying to solve a problem, they should learn to search for information and to check its reliability. This is achieved if the students can perform some real open-ended experiments that will allow them to make observations, collect data and interpret them. That, in turn, should lead to a conclusion which can be validated by further experiments. In this process, the problems selected are more a means than a goal.

Yet science education cannot be just an intellectual exercise and there is always a body of knowledge that one expects to be acquired at each level. This body of knowledge is another empirical choice, frequently imposed on the education system. In the primary school, even at higher levels of education, it is always easier if we start with problems and issues which are relevant to the learner. In this way, the student is not just motivated, but it also facilitates the transfer from school learning (which is generally temporarily stored for retrieval in examinations) to be internalized as a scientifically rational attitude which will be used in facing daily problems. In my experience with students from primary school to university, in Brazil and the United States, self-centred courses are those which motivate students best—and nutrition is the more frequently chosen topic whenever students have a choice.[1]

Nutrition is an ideal theme around which a proper science course can be developed. I have been involved in one such as a way to attract non-college bound students to take a science course. Called "What People Eat", it starts with a real open-ended experiment, the analysis of the student's own diet. Each student collects an exact duplicate of a one-day diet and brings it to the school laboratory. All the food and drinks are blended and dried. The dry powder is then the topic for analysis in a semester course.

Students who have never taken a real science course are provided with a "methods guide".[2] They are orientated to perform a few basic determinations: ash, carbon, hydrogen, nitrogen (or protein) content, as also fat and calorific content. They can use the guide to continue with other determinations. While using the laboratory on their own food, they are prepared to learn the basis of the methods being used and the significance of the data obtained, and are thus ready to take a formal science course, properly organized around food analysis and nutrition.[3] Not only was this approach used with non-college bound students, but also with highly motivated pre-medical students with significant success.[4]

Nutrition as a centre of interest can lead to a much wider integration, relating basic science problems with its applications, and through them with the social and cultural problems of society at large. Topics like the limits of food production on earth, food fads and cultural food habits always bring in a wide range of issues of social relevance.

In using "What People Eat" we encouraged students to observe rats maintained on a number of different diets which reproduce the extreme diets of some social group. One such diet that always led to intense discussion was a diet of corn and beans, used by North American Indians, when compared with a sole maize diet. Animals maintained on the maize diet were apparently normal, but they grew to half the size of those on corn-beans diet. If the maize diet were supplemented with beans, rats had a sudden burst of growth, but never reached those on the combined diet, remaining small, as do most deprived populations.

Nutrition in primary school science

In Brazil we produced a number of small units that guided primary school students to perform simple experiments related to nutrition and health. To understand the nature of food, those experiments must include both plant and animal nutrition. At the lower level, booklets contain illustrations of experiments, each with a single caption, frequently a question to be answered by performing the experiment. There is one on seeds that allow students (most of our population is now inner city) to observe the cycle of a plant, and some of its needs. Another uses house-flies as an experimental animal; students can raise them in bottles, and are asked to find out if they would survive just on sweets or soft drinks. They find out that to raise flies one needs milk (or another source of protein). Another presents students with a problem: they have a white powder from the kitchen and, without tasting it, they must find out what this powder is— and they examine a number of its properties.

Units for upper levels examine the requirements for plants to grow, plant respiration and photosynthesis, the production, transport and storage of starch. The caloric value of foods is compared using a simple calorimeter that can be built from aluminium foil. A more detailed experiment on animal nutrition is carried out with fruit-flies (*Drosophila*) using a diet of syrup, milk (casein), salts and vitamins, and it is possible to demonstrate the need for micronutrients.

A similar series was developed for health, starting with the observation of mouldy bread. Using oranges, students rediscover Koch postulates for the identification of the microbial cause of a disease (the rotting of the orange). With a small microscope or a glass bead microscope, they discover free-living microbes and investigate the theory of spontaneous origin of life.

The major emphasis of FUNBEC's approach for curriculum information was the introduction of open-ended experiments that students can perform with simple low cost equipment. This equipment is made available to schools, however this availability does not secure its use. To reach motivated students and thus to transfer the pressure on schools to perform experiments, led to providing self-motivated students with the same low cost equipment independently of the school: it thus always finds its way back into the schools. Two million such kits were used in a major out-of-school programme in Brazil.[6]

Nutrition in secondary school education

Major innovations in secondary school science were initiated in the United States by the National Science Foundation in the sixties and were followed by the Nuffield projects in the United Kingdom. These had a world-wide impact, through translations and adaptations, and acted as models. Unfortunately, they paid little attention to nutrition with the result that, apart from "What People Eat" and a Nuffield Advanced Chemistry book on *Food Science*[7] little was done about it. Perhaps the best resource for secondary school science teachers is Unesco's *Biology of Human Populations*, published in 1975.[8]

Transfer of information

Although I have taken science education to be a process leading to the acquisition of scientific skills for problem solving, it is impossible to learn all that is necessary through rediscovery or critical review of evidence. Science education must be balanced with some information transfer or teaching. But can such teaching change nutritional habits? This is apparently believed by some nutrition educators; they propose the integration into early school science of information through activities like counting teeth and even nursery rhymes.[9] It is possible, though not scientifically proven, that early school persuasion can affect children and change their eating behaviour. I doubt that schools can effectively in a few hours dramatically change deeply ingrained family food habits. However, I can probably shake traditional foundations of belief relating to health by showing through a small microscope microbes in dirty water, or worms and their eggs in the children's own stools. I can try to show the requirements for proteins and micronutrients in flies, but I am not sure that this information is transferred by the students to themselves.

The dilemma of two cultures

Whenever we discuss the education of young children, the attitude is that they are an empty void to be filled by the system. Schools frequently ignore completely that they provide a small fraction of their information, even of their education, the rest being provided by the family and in increasing proportions by society, especially through mass communication media. School teaching is kept separate to a large extent, without being absorbed into daily activities and behaviour.

The attitude of those professionally involved in nutrition, but basically outsiders, is to treat the young and even adults of the less educated classes and of less developed countries as grown children with a similar empty void, ready to accept as true the world of men wearing suits and ties, frequently with total disregard for popular culture. Popular culture was able to communicate even before the existence of the written word and to create and validate complementary diets (maize and beans, rice and beans, wheat and chickpeas or milk) with undoubted skill. In usual conditions, it seems an almost lost battle to defy the traditional culture, which dictates daily behaviour.

The two culture system is not limited to less educated populations. In the heart of Geneva, as in the middle of Africa, one can obtain healing plants (though properly packaged in Geneva) side by side with the wonders of modern medicine.

A large fraction of the population in the developing countries is in a process of change, moving to the city and being integrated in a money-centred culture, where for the first time a variety of foodstuffs can be purchased. This rapid transformation contributes to a break in the traditional food habits, and makes room not for rational nutritional education (which is, if it is at all, made available to children), but to publicity. The patent acceptance of coke drinks world over attests to this achievement.

The efficacy of publicity is even more obvious in the developed world. The counter-culture that bans processed foods, that replaced refined sugar with honey and ingests large amounts of vitamin C they believe to be natural cannot fight the coke establishment, accepting refined sugar, caffeine and phosphoric acid. More recently publicity has achieved to sell coke without sugar, and without caffeine, and maybe some day without even the coke flavour.

Nutrition education or food?

Probably the most potent measure has not been either a rational or empirical attempt to change nutrition habits, but through actual supply of a meal in schools that, besides essential calories and nutrients, provides an opportunity to try another diet, and eventually to accept it.

With the availability of minicomputers, one could even imagine students analysing what they are selecting in the cafeteria and thereby moving towards a healthier selection. This could be an efficient tool for nutrition education, not against under-nourishment, but against over-eating which contributes to the development of chronic diseases in later years.

This scenario, however, is foreign to two-thirds of the world child population, half of which is faced with death before the age of 5. Malnutrition is the cause of this. Can nutrition education contribute in any way?

Nutrition education in medical schools

If there is an area where nutrition education, in its broadest sense, is important, it is in the medical school curriculum. Both the fundamental scientific aspects and the socio-economic implications should be carefully woven into the curriculum. Although there has been some discussion, [5,10,11] practically nothing has yet been done.

References

1. Raw, I., Bromley, A., Pariser, E. R. and Vournakis, J. What People Eat—a chemistry programme based on nutrition, *J. Col. Science Teaching*: 177–178 (1975).
2. Raw, I. *What People Eat*, Laboratory guide, W. Kaufmann, Inc., Los Altos, CA, 1974.
3. Raw, I., Bromley, A., Pariser, E. R. and Vournakis, J. *What People Eat*, W. Kaufmann Inc., Los Altos, CA, 1974.
4. Raw, I. The integration of nutrition education in basic biomedical sciences, *Amer. J. Med. Educ.* **52**: 654–657 (1977).

5. Raw, I. and Rockwell, P. Health and science education—a natural partnership, *Principal* **57**: 85–90 (1978).
6. Raw, I. Science toys for science education, *Impact* **32**: 467–472.
7. *Nuffield Advance Science-Food Science*, Penguin Books, London 1971.
8. *Teacher's Study Guide on the Biology of Human Populations—Africa*, UNESCO, Paris, 1975.
9. Squire, E., Learning about food within the primary school curriculum, in *Preventive Nutrition and Society*, M. R. Turner (edit), Academic Press, London, 1981 pp 197.
10. Frankle, R. T. Nutrition education in the medical school curriculum: a proposal for action: a curriculum design. *Amer. J. Clin. Nutrition* **29**: 105–109 (1976).
11. Vitale, J. J. Nutrition education in the preclinical period of medical education, *Amer. J. Clin. Nutrition* **30**: 801–802 (1977).

10

Food Preservation and Storage

S. K. MAJUMDER
Central Food Technology Research Institute, Mysore, India

The trend of migration from rural to urban areas has posed problems of food supply in quality and quantity. One influence is the changing pattern of living style and aspirations. The trend towards processing food has led to meat, fish and poultry being over-cooked, fruit and vegetables being over-processed and raw grains being refined into milled products. These lead to loss of nutrients and increased waste, as well as wasteful energy consumption. Processing to produce so-called pure and refined products has been responsible for lack of nutritional balance. Disturbances in the homeostatic limits and imbalances in metabolism have been the results. These have led to the increased incidence of chronic metabolic diseases and neurological disorders.

To meet this situation, current education in food science should be broadened to include more nutrition and hygiene, together with some microbiology, entomology and biochemistry and reference to microtoxins, xenobiotics and toxicology.

The traditional processes in food manufacture involve milling, germination, fermentation, cooking, dehydration and drying, granulation and extrusion. Most of these are directed towards improving storage characteristics. The extent of the loss of nutrients depends on the type of processes. Refining in modern mills, debranning and polishing decrease many essential constituents. The fermentation process in traditional practices, however, tends to increase important nutritive constituents, improve digestibility and promote biosynthesis of essential food items such as vitamins, and thereby the nutritive value is increased. Germination can improve the acceptability of the products, but even more important is the biosynthesis of vitamins and the increase in nutritive qualities. In spite of their merits such products manufactured traditionally on the home-scale do not reach national marketing channels. With urbanization, it is becoming imperative to upgrade the technologies so that traditional foods can be made available without affecting the nutritional qualities.

91

In developing countries in the tropics and sub-tropics, the main intake of calories is through cereals. Unfortunately, the ecosystems provide optimum conditions for the growth of insects, moulds, rodents and the production of toxins. Storage systems in the post-harvest period should therefore include freedom from infestation and treatment to prevent cross-infestation. Prophylactic and curative measures are required. Pre-harvest prophylaxis by spraying, field drying and processing, rodent control in the field, insect proofing and rodent proofing of structures could all augment food and nutrition supplies to a significantly larger extent than any other effort. Other techniques in warehouses, food-processing factories, as well as within homes could make further contributions. And all these require educational courses to draw attention to food security.

The old knowledge in textbooks is not adequate to cope with future needs. The educational policy should be more in terms of comparative biology rather than taxonomy and physiology. The comparative biology must include morphology and biochemical topics dealing with conservation. Curious phenomena have been observed in the physical limits of insects, moulds, mites, rodents and organisms responsible for biodegradation. Comparative biology could teach, for example, that the intergranular space is a limiting factor for the growth of the specific pest in the storage of pulses and legumes.

Unfortunately, the internal brain drain towards urban settlements has prevented the development of a self-employed technocrat-based industry using local rural resources. Training in post-harvest conservation should be a main aim of an education and training system which might reverse the brain drain. This will require new curricula as follows:

In the high school system:

(a) pre-harvest spraying and prophylaxis, equipment and application;
(b) threshing and solar dyring;
(c) straw baling techniques;
(d) pest control: rodents, birds, insects, moulds;
(e) post-harvest processing, cleaning, grading;
(f) packaging and containers for storage;
(g) disinfestation and fumigation techniques;
(h) storage in rural homes, sanitation;
(i) fruit and vegetable preservation;
(j) seed treatment, protection and processing;
(k) feed processing;
(l) agro-mechanics (pumps, sprayers, tractors, threshers, winnowers, pest control equipment);
(m) bee-keeping;
(n) animal/poultry/fish farming;

(o) sanitation, biogas, farm waste, energy utilization in the village home;

(p) solar energy.

In the pre-university system (post-harvest technology courses):

(a) disinfestation service systems;

(b) biosciences (including entomology, plant pathology, microbiology, animal nutrition);

(c) mechanics and mathematics;

(d) machine drawing and design;

(e) biometry and statistics;

(f) workshop;

(g) chemistry;

(h) physics;

(i) sugarcane processing;

(j) oil seed processing;

(l) dal milling;

(m) activated clay, carbon and ash production — principles and processes;

(n) bacterial insecticide production;

(o) basic book-keeping and costing;

(p) seed production technology;

(q) cold and cool storage: principles, design and operation

(r) warehousing;

(s) storage structures, handling systems and constructions (ballooning, CAP storage, silo, godown);

(t) material handling tools and machines;

(u) report writing and project preparation (small scale);

(v) banking and insurance;

(w) draughtsmanship;

(x) pesticide, fertilizer, growth regulator — formulations;

(y) plant protection technology;

(z) rodent control, mosquito control and fly control — integrated methods;

(za) abattoir management — sanitation and by-product usage.

In university courses on food science and technology:

(a) rural anthropology/sociology;

(b) rural economics;

(c) agribusiness;

(d) plant protection science and technology;

(e) animal husbandry, production in ecosystem and animal products;

(f) landscaping, contouring, cartography;

(g) graphics, printing, layout of publications for extension literature and commercial art, photography, xerography;
(h) information sources in food science and technology;
(i) unit operations and food engineering;
(j) safety, toxicology and behavioural assay;
(k) biotechnology, biophysics and computer science;
(l) floriculture, bonsai, plant propagation and greenhouse technology;
(m) tissue culture and cell culture;
(n) biochemistry and molecular biology;
(o) statistics, biometry and mathematics of food processes;
(p) organic chemistry of pesticide and semiochemicals;
(q) pest management, protectants, storage and food security systems;
(r) cereal science and post-harvest technology;
(s) oil seed technology;
(t) fruits and vegetables technology and plantation crop processing;
(u) dairying and dairy waste conservation;
(v) institutional kitchen design, equipment and management;
(w) traditional foods, manufacture and quality control;
(x) enology and fermentation industry;
(y) fumigation science and controlled atmosphere technology;
(z) radiation preservation and biophysics;
(za) quarantine, export controls, surveillance methods;
(zb) planning of food industry complexes;
(zc) ecology, environment and xenobiotic cycles.

References

1. Majumder, S. K. Protecting food from deterioration. *Proc. 3rd International Congress of Food Sci. & Technol.*, SOS/70, Washington, DC 1970, pp. 519–531.
2. Deosthale, Y. G. The nutritive value of foods and the significance of some household processes. *Food & Nutrition Bull.* Supplement 9, UNU, 1984.
3. Majumder, S. K. Inter-relationship between pre- and post-harvest production systems. *Proc. UNU Workshop on the Management of R & D Institutions in the Area of Food Science & Technology,* 1979, pp. 17–26.
4. Majumder, S. K. Nutritional implications of recently developed techniques of storage and pest control. *Food & Nutrition Bull.* Supplement 9, 1984.

11

New Directions for the Teaching of Food and Agriculture

CHEONG-HOONG DIONG
Department of Continuing Education, Singapore

The teaching of school biology still places considerable emphasis on the content, more specifically on the structure of the knowledge within the discipline. Seldom do teachers go beyond the boundaries of the subject to discuss the issues and social relevance or values and implications of what they teach to society. Teachers are either ill-informed or are constrained by the curriculum time to do so. Hence most of them adopt the more traditional teaching approaches that encourage rote memory. The "teach-to-pass the examination" and "complete-the-syllabus" practices predominate in the classroom.

School biology education to be socially relevant and personally meaningful to the students must be beyond this status quo. Bybee (1979) wrote.

> "In the next decade policies for science education programs should include appropriate cognitive, affective, psychomotor and social objectives to: (1) fulfill basic human needs and facilitate personal development; (2) maintain and improve the physical and human environment; (3) conserve and efficiently use natural resources; (4) develop greater community at the local, regional, national and global levels."

The biology curriculum in schools should not just focus on giving knowledge. It should also perform a useful educational function for school leavers. Teachers should recognize that although they may not have the answers to all the biology-related social issues, they have the moral obligation to prepare school children to be able to cope with these and to be better problem-solvers. This can come about if students are given a

95

FAE-D*

wider perspective on societal issues that are related to the biological knowledge they learn in the classrooms. A future-now orientation is desirable since school children in today's schools will have to cope with a future very different from today in the twenty-first century.

How can biology teaching be redirected towards greater recognition of personal and social issues? One suggestion would be for teachers to modernize their teaching strategies. Many of the basic biological concepts at all school levels can be taught using a relevant context. To do this, biology teachers should identify those topics in the syllabus content that can have important implications for society and the individuals as members of the society. Thus, within the syllabus which normally organize the content under certain headings (living things, cell biology, nutrition, reproduction and growth, responses and control, diversity, genetics, evolution, ecology), topics such as food production and nutrition, population and energy can be further identified as those which contribute directly to the biology–society interphase. The relevance of the subject will emerge when we begin to examine the interdependence between biology and technology and sociology and its applications and social values, (Tamir, 1980).

The topic food

The topic food has a spiral sequence in the science curriculum. At the lower primary level, students learn the names of foodstuffs and such concepts as "plants make food" and "living things need food to grow". The concept of food as energy is introduced with simple food chains in the upper primary level. The consumptive aspects of food is stressed at the primary level, and also at the secondary level. Food is taught as part of life processes when studying nutrition and it is further treated as providing important organic molecules for physiological functions at the upper secondary level.

Food as presently taught in the schools emphasizes pure scientific knowledge. This does not necessarily give students a conceptual understanding of what food is and the relevance of the subject to their lives. One may argue that since food, as an item, is all too familiar to school children, the conceptual understanding of the subject would be facilitated. On the contrary, the student's familiarity with the topic presents a greater challenge to teachers. School children come to class with their own ideas, conceptions or beliefs — right or wrong — about food. Some of these ideas are held strongly and teachers may find it difficult to alter student's conceptions.

Figure 1 attempts to analyse the key concepts in the food topic. The map identifies the interrelated subconcepts — food components, nutritive value, functions of food components, human needs, health, malnutrition, food processing, agriculture — and shows the relationships and dependencies between one idea and another. It can be seen from the map that the two subconcepts that are central to the understanding of the food topic are the knowledge on food components and food production or agriculture. Food production and the relationship between food and agriculture are not presently taught in the classrooms, although the existing syllabus content could be extended to include food-related concepts. For this subject to be socially relevant and meaningful to school children, teachers can further

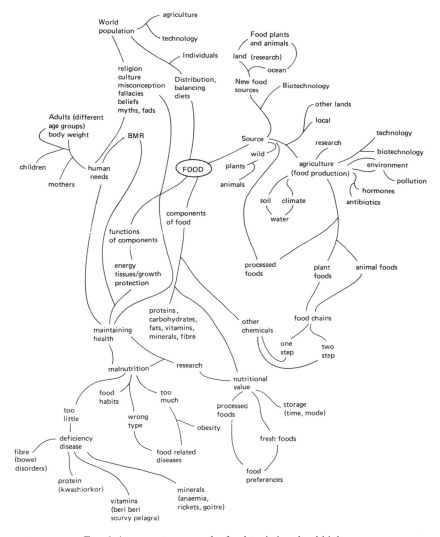

FIG. 1 A concept map on the food topic in school biology.

develop around the basic concepts to introduce the other relevant food-related concepts.

New directions for teaching the topic of food

Seeking out new directions for teaching the food topic can start with a search for an understanding of the social problems of food and nutrition and our role in society.

In an urban society like Singapore, there is a wide variety of food which is readily available all year round. There is no fear of food shortage. The food industry imports food from all over the world. The society has come to accept processed, preserved, and convenience foods, with little concern about adulteration by pesticides through agricultural practices or chemical additives during food processing. School children can name common food products, but are generally unaware about where the food comes from, or what the food plants look like. The nutritional problems are those of overconsumption, and poor food habits. Obesity among school children has been a growing concern. About 2% of children are obese when they enter Primary 1. By the time they reach Primary 6, 20% of the school children are obese, 10% definitely so by the Harvard Standard weight–height table. The shift in disease pattern in the last two decades, from communicable diseases (e.g. tuberculosis, malaria) to food-related diseases (cardiovascular diseases, diabetes) has led to a concern for better food and nutrition education.

The school curriculum should take cognizance of the food and nutrition problems in the society to ensure that the teaching of the food topic in the science curricula can be rendered personally meaningful and socially relevant to students. Since food habits are difficult to change in later years, primary schooling should help students to cultivate wise food habits and desired attitudes to food and to develop a conceptual understanding of what food is to them and their society. The children's perspective about food can be broadened by extending their experience about food around them to food that comes from other lands and the ways they are kept fresh from source to consumer. The food production concepts and the linkages between biology and agriculture are more appropriate at the secondary levels. Tables 1 and 2 give examples of how other food-related concepts can be built around existing topics in the biology curriculum. This confirms that many of the basic concepts in school biology can be taught with a social context.

Teaching strategies

There are a variety of teaching methods, some of which are more teacher-centred than others. The teaching approach is often affected

TABLE 1. *Teaching the food topic in primary schools with a social perspective*

Existing topics	New topics or amplification around existing topics
Common foodstuffs	Include local food examples also to introduce these ideas: (1) Food: from source to you — where they come from. (2) Why some foods are not available certain times of year. (3) Food plants and animals — characteristics and general understanding of conditions necessary for their growth.
Balanced diet	Concept of food and health, and their correlation. Introduce social perspective, e.g. my food + your food = our food. Forming wise food habits; evaluating your own diet; developing healthy lifestyle — the food way. Problems of balancing diets in some countries.
Food chain	Introduce man into food chain and dicuss how man and other factors (climate, soil, pests) can affect his food chains. Examples of man's food chains from poor countries of developing world and western countries.
Food preservation	Ideas on why food preservation is necessary, what we are preserving in foodstuffs, with simple examples of processing or preservation methods. Link this idea with food production and consumption.

TABLE 2. *Some redirections in teaching the food topic in secondary biology*

Existing topics	New topics or amplification around existing topics
Food relationships Food chains Balance in nature	Man's relationship with the earth to the food they eat. Discuss the one-step food chain (plant-to-man) in poor countries of the developing world, and the two-step food chain (plant-animal-man) in affluent countries in the west. Implications of food-grain shortage in, say, India and the US to introduce concepts like starvation. Introduce the world food chain — production, marketing, preparation and consumption. Explain how pesticides and other chemicals enter the food chains and the possible effects of these on health. Introduce concept of biological magnification, i.e. the concentration of hormones, antibiotics, chemicals in man's food chains. Disruption of natural food chains and balance in environment resulting from man's undesirable activities — eating of exotic wild plants and animals that are high up in the natural food chain.

TABLE 2. *(Continued)*

Existing topics	New topics or amplification around existing topics
Storage of food reserves by plants and animals	Amplify on how plants store their food to how and why man stores plant foods as reserves and consumption in other places. Examples of plant storage products (e.g. potato, onions, maize grain, pea seed, orange) and how these are stored for transportation from source to consumer.
	Extend this topic on storage of food reserves to include undesirable storage of excess fat to discuss obesity.
Genetics	Use of genetics of plant breeding. Crop improvement. Hybrid varieties that have more pest-resistance and shorter flowering time. Double cropping to increase food yields.
Population studies	Introduce the concept that food is the single most important factor that limits population growth. Discuss population growth and world food as a resource.
Micro-organisms (e.g. bacteria, fungi), health and disease	Microbes that improve soil fertility and are useful to food production aspects in agriculture. Food spoilage and control. Reducing bacterial growth in foods. Food processing and preservation — canning, pasteurization, ionizing radiation, low temperature, dehydration, drying, salting and freezing.
	Preservation of foods by fermentation using harmless micro-organisms.
	Food poisoning.
Soil	Soil management practices to sustain plant yield. Fertilizers and agricultural technology to improve soil (e.g. irrigation methods). Hydrologic cycle.
Animal nutrition	Extend the topic on digestion and assimilation to include the effects of food additives and the potentially harmful residues (pesticides, antibiotics, hormones, fertilizers) in fresh and processed foods on the human body.
	Animal food production.
Holophytic nutrition in plants Nitrogen cycle Photosynthesis	Man's part in the nitrogen cycle. Show how the knowledge of the nitrogen cycle can help a farmer or gardener produce better crop yields. Illustrate the interdependence between biology and agriculture.
	Introduce the concept of food production — plants as primary producers. Discuss some agricultural practices that affect food production, including growing vegetables in soilless medium (hydroponics) and manipulation of wavelength and light intensity.
	Importance of food production in relation to population needs.
	New sources of plant food including algae. Advances in food technology to develop vegetable proteins for world population: Role of biotechnology.

by such factors as: types of instructional objectives, subject-matter, availability of resources, class size and type of pupils and instructional time. Some of the methods that are suitable for teaching this topic are discussed below.

Experimental approach

The experimental model encourages students to ask questions, use science process skills to learn concepts and to understand problems. This approach also brings students into direct encounter with objects. The following examples illustrate the experimental approach to teach the concept of food preservation.

— provide students with commercially prepared bread (with additives) and organically prepared bread (without additives). They could taste them to discuss preference and palatability. Ask students to observe what happens to the two kinds of bread over the next few days. Discuss also the idea of shelf-life. The activity can be repeated with other fresh food (e.g. tomato, fish or meat, vegetables, fruits) or with processed foods.

— provide students with two glasses of sterile milk. Place one in the refrigerator and the other on a bench. Observe and compare changes during the week.

— provide students with vegetable seeds (e.g. *Ipomea aquatica)* to investigate the effects of fertilizer treatment or soil conditions on plant growth. The science garden is ideal for this kind of experimental work.

Role play

This can be a very effective strategy to help students understand the issues and the problems about the subject. For instance, in the topic on food production or processing, students could assume the different roles — agricultural officer, manager of a local food processing plant, consumer protection group representative, farmer, public health officer — to study the issues associated with the use of chemicals in the production and processing of foodstuffs. Teachers will have to give adequate guidance and refer students to the resource materials or even encourage them to interview such officers before they role-play. Role-play can help students to see the value of biological knowledge to issues related to the food concept, and also the need for recognizing different forms of judgement about an issue (Rao and Pritchard, 1984).

Project work

Teachers can organize students into groups to undertake projects. With some guidance from the teachers, students involved in project work are capable of learning beyond what is in the textbooks. Project work often gives teachers additional opportunities to link knowledge to other subject areas. Exemplars of project work in the food topic are:

— collect food labels to study nutrients, common preservations or additives. Make a chart showing classes of food additives.
— on a large world map, identify the major food-producing countries. Cut out pictures of plant foods and animal foods from magazines to construct the theme of "food people eat". Construct a typical meal for people in some countries.
— make a chart showing metabolic requirements of children, adolescents, adults, expectant mothers and the aged.
— list the fresh foods (meat, dairy products, vegetables, fruits) which students in the class frequently eat. For each of them, find where they are grown, how far they must be transported, and how long they must be stored.

Clarification of values

This allows students to determine their values and attitudes through structured activities. To arrive at a set of values as a guide to good habits, for instance, they have to go though a valuing process to clarify what they think or believe about food items, their food preferences and how these relate to health. The learning activities should be structured to include (i) making choices about the food items they would select to eat for, say, breakfast, (ii) prizing, where they are called on to explain their choice, (iii) acting, where they relate their choices to the subject matter of the school course and perhaps make alternative choices. Value clarification strategies should always be followed by discussion and additional instruction on the subject.

Using questions to guide enquiry

Teachers can devise a variety of questioning techniques to stimulate students interest in the subject. There are questions that call for higher cognitive processes, yet others can be used to approach the affective domain. Michaelis *et al*. (1976) illustrate how questions can be used to guide enquiry:

(a) *Cognitive*

Knowledge: What food nutrients do all of us need? In what foods may they be found?

Comprehensions: Can you explain in your own words why we need vitamins and minerals? What problems may arise if the soil in which food plants are raised is not fertilized?

Application: How can we use what we have learned to improve our eating habits? How can we check to be sure we have a balanced diet?

Analysis: What is meant by the statement that this cereal contains one-half of the minimum daily requirements? Who can analyse this menu to find out if essential nutrients are included?

Synthesis: Who can organise what we have learned about vital nutrients into a set rule for good eating habits? What soil conditions are necessary to produce vegetables that contain vitamins and minerals?

Evaluation: Are the claims in this advertisement consistent with what we have learned about vitamins? Which of the three dinner menus on the chalkboard is best in terms of our criteria for balanced meals?

(b) *Affective*

Receiving: How did you feel as you read about beriberi? Did you notice anything surprising in the film on vitamins and growth?

Responding: Do you eat vegetables because you have to or because you want to? In what ways do you feel it was helpful to make rules for good eating habits?

Valuing: Why are vital nutrients important to us as individuals and as a country? Why should all of us be concerned about soil conditions?

Organizations: Who can describe the plight of individuals suffering from malnutrition? How would you feel if you were in a country where it was difficult to have a balanced diet?

Characterization: How do you feel about changing your eating habits as new information about food becomes available? What place should health values have in one's view of the good life?

Problem solving

The problem-solving strategy is used extensively in food and nutrition education programmes. This approach is useful for students to learn cognitive and affective information. The problem-solving strategy leads students to recognize, and identify the problems, to gather or interpret data, and to formulate solutions, alternative action plans which can be evaluated by other experiential, experimental or project activities.

The importance of food and nutrition education for a society cannot be underestimated. Many countries have national policies and health programmes to ensure high health standards for a healthy population. Whilst formal education on this subject with a societal context is important for school children, the non-formal system, including adult and community education, needs also to be considered. School teachers, teacher educators, extension workers, community leaders and health education officers, among others, can individually and together do much to educate our school children — the emerging world citizens — and contribute to building a robust and healthy society.

References

Bybee, R. (1979). The new transformation of science education. *Science Education* **61**(1): 85–92.

Michaelis, J. U., R. H. Grossman and L. F. Scott (1976) *New Design for the Elementary School Curriculum.* McGraw Hill Book Company, New York, USA.

Rao, A. N. and A. J. Pritchard (1984) *Agriculture and Biology Teaching*, UNESCO, Paris.

Tamir, P., J. H. Adler and A. Poljakof — Maybehr (1980) Biological education towards the year 2000. Pages 229–238 in Imahori, K., R. A. Kille and Y. Koshila (eds) *Proceedings of the Eighth Biennial Conference of the AABE,* Asian Association for Biology Education.

B. Case Studies

12

Food and Agriculture in the Science Education Programme in Nigeria

EUNICE A. C. OKEKE

Faculty of Education, University of Nigeria, Nsukka, Nigeria

Science education aims through observation, experimentation and systematic enquiry to expose pupils to the nature of science, as well as to promote awareness of the biological and physical environment. It should equip the recipients with knowledge and skills for effective grappling with the many problems in life. One of these problems is the provision of an adequate food supply for everyone. Any nation which cannot feed her citizens can easily lose her sovereignty through dependence on other nations for her food supply. In fact, food supply has political implications capable of influencing not only international relations but also the stability of a nation.

Nigeria has been a sovereign nation since 1960. She has an estimated population of over 90 million. She is blessed with a wide land mass stretching over varied climatic regions. This geographical factor is an asset in the production of a variety of foods for her people. The foods that grow well in one region can be produced in large quantity for distribution to those other regions where these crops do not thrive.

In the region of the tropical forests, the climate can sustain trees and such vegetation which thrives where humidity, temperature and rainfall are high. Cultivated plants include palm trees, the oil bean tree, iroko, rubber and food crops such as cassava and yam. In the savanna scrubland, characterized by tall grasses and shrubs, ground-nuts and other grains such as corn and millet are grown and animal husbandry is prominent. There are also the highlands and the Obudu table land with temperate climatic conditions, where the temperature may occasionally fall to freezing point. With such variations of climatic conditions in one country, the potential for growing enough food for home consumption is high.

The following questions arise and an attempt will be made to answer them.

1. What foods are produced and eaten by Nigerians and what are their methods of production?
2. Are the foods produced in sufficient quantity?
3. What measures are being taken to ensure an adequate supply of food and agricultural products through formal and informal science education?
4. What are barriers hindering maximum effectiveness of the educational programme in the area of food and agriculture?
5. Can anything still be done to ensure that, through education in science, food and agricultural production will be maximised to meet human needs?

Food and agricultural practices

In Nigeria a variety of food items are eaten, which can be classified as follows:

Carbohydrates – yam, cocoyam, cassava, rice, maize, guineacorn, plantain, millet, potatoes.
Protein – fish, beans, snails, milk, beef, mutton, chicken, eggs.
Fats and oil – palm oil, coconut oil, melon.
Vitamins – vegetables, fruits and some foods mentioned above.

These food items are prepared in a variety of ways. For example, an average family in the southern part of Nigeria can have a meal of yam cooked with a large quantity of vegetables, adding a little fish or crayfish and palm oil. Another very common food in Nigeria is foofoo made out of yam, cocoyam, cassava or rice flour and eaten with soup which is prepared in different ways, but incorporating meat or fish, oil, vegetables and a little water. In fact, all kinds of food can be prepared from the flour of any of the carbohydrate foods. Different types of food can be identified with different states and with different ethnic groups.

Food production in Nigeria has been predominantly, until recent times, a highly individualized affair. One man with his wife (or wives) and children cultivate their own family portion of land, planting those food crops they think the family will need in order to survive. Any extra after harvest is sold for cash in order to pay for the other needs of the family. With the coming and spread of Western education, most children now attend schools and are thus away in the mornings when their parents are busy on their farms. Consequently attending school came to be seen as an alternative to farming. The latter being laborious, most children after completing primary or secondary education do not want to return to the farms. The result is that today agriculture in land cultivation, in animal husbandry and in fishing is carried out by illiterates and men and women whose age range is 40–60 years. For cultivation, especially in the southern rain forest region, the only farm implements are the hoe and the knife. The amount of work that a man can do in a day using these is naturally small and hence the annual income of a farmer is usually very low. The introduction of new implements, new methods of farming and new varieties of crop are mostly unknown to these illiterate farmers. Where they do know, their illiteracy acts as a barrier to trying out new ideas. The result is very poor yield.

In short, the amount of food produced by these illiterate and aged farmers, who control the food and agricultural production in Nigeria for the many young people who have emigrated to the towns, is grossly insufficient. A report of the Federal Office of Statistics in Lagos shows that the agricultural contribution to the Gross Domestic Product (GDP) fell from 64% in 1960/61 to 23% in 1976/77 and is at an even lower level today. At the present time, Nigeria spends much of her scarce foreign currency on importing food to feed a people who live in a country blessed with a wide variety of climatic conditions capable of supporting nearly all kinds of food production.

The long-term solution

The long-term solution to the problems of food and agriculture lies in a relevant science education programme. Education provides the basis for the introduction of vital innovations and new techniques necessary for enhanced agricultural productivity whether crop or animal husbandry, animal health and veterinary medicine, forestry, fisheries, food technology, irrigation, plant quarantine, processing of agricultural products, home or farm management (Yaycock, 1983).

Formal education in Nigeria includes 6 years of primary education, followed by 5 years of secondary education. Post-secondary education in polytechnics or in teacher training is for 2–3 years and university education 4–5 years.

The primary school curriculum includes some elementary science to acquaint pupils with their environment, including such topics as air, water, work, your body, simple machines, etc. The use of the guided discovery method of teaching is advocated to enable pupils to acquire scientific skills and attitudes. There is little or nothing on food and agriculture in the science taught. There is, however, another subject, agriculture and home economics, which is expected to introduce children to these topics. They learn about farm implements, hoes and knives, and simple farm practices, and they keep a school farm where this is possible. A problem is that in primary schools one teacher will teach all subjects, and the majority of teachers lack the competence and the interest required to teach so widely. The teacher can "kill or save" a subject like science or agriculture.

There appears to be no national policy on agricultural education at the primary school level, nor is there at the secondary level. Because of the type of science and agriculture taught at the primary school, children leave with the impression that agriculture is drudgery and science magical. Yaycock (1983) pointed out the "risk of creating in the minds of young pupils antagonism to agriculture as a result of premature exposure to the often dull, badly organised and heavy manual work in school farms/gardens".

This raises two issues. Can science and agriculture be taught as an integrated whole, geared towards solving human needs? Can the teachers with their limited educational background cope with science and agriculture in a way that will benefit the pupils and make them aware of the importance of food? Could the agriculture education planners, curriculum experts and the government begin to develop a policy in this direction?

In the lower classes of secondary schools, science is taught with an integrated approach using the Nigerian Integrated Science Project (NISP), launched in 1971 by the Science Teachers' Association of Nigeria (STAN). It aims at introducing pupils to the fundamental unity of science. By using themes rather than physics, chemistry or biology topics, a pupil can acquire a holistic view of science problems. Examples of themes found in NISP are "You as a Living Thing", "Saving Energy", "Controlling the Environment". However the content of NISP reveals that there is no direct effort to introduce pupils to food and agriculture.

In the upper secondary school, students study separate subjects: biology, chemistry, physics, health science, agriculture. The three science subjects which include aspects of food and agriculture are biology, agricultural science and health science. In biology, students study classes of food and carry out food tests. Although the curriculum lists aspects of agriculture, including farm practices in crop science, soil science and animal husbandry, in practice the syllabus is so extensive that many students sit for the certificate examinations without exposure to it. Furthermore, most of the biology graduate teachers did no agriculture in their university career and their competence to teach any aspect of farm operations is questionable.

However, the agricultural science offered at the upper secondary level aims at equipping students with the theory and practice of agriculture. The curriculum covers such areas as general principles of agriculture, crop farming, animal husbandry, soil science, food storage and preservation, etc., a curriculum acceptable to experts in agricultural science if it is properly executed. The failure of the curriculum to achieve its objectives has been traced to the shortage of qualified teachers, lack of facilities for practical work and inflexible timetables making such work possible.

In post-secondary institutions and in the universities, science is packaged into separate disciplines. There is no focus on food production in any of the science curricula, except in agriculture and this means that only a very small proportion of those who study science have any awareness of food and agriculture, which are of such importance to Nigeria.

Barriers in food and agriculture production

The Nigerian government is fully aware of the importance of food and agriculture and it has demonstrated its desire to make Nigeria self-reliant in food production. Despite the good intentions, the quantity and quality of food produced is inadequate and Nigeria still depends on imported food such as rice.

One of the barriers is the poor image of agriculture. This can be traced to the time when Western education was introduced: bright children competed to get white collar jobs, while the failures had no option but to return to the farms. Ignorance of new techniques forms another barrier, and even when there is adequate dissemination of information, the conservatism of farmers may lead them to resist change. Resistance to change is a common feature in most people because of fear of the unknown, but it has also been documented that the less educated one is, the more one is resistant to change.

Another barrier is the land tenure system. In Nigeria, land is owned in portions by families. As families multiply, the family land is shared out so that one family may own minute parcels of land in several locations. Mechanized agriculture flourishes better where land is extensive. Since one cannot employ a tractor for a portion of land not much larger than the tractor, the farming resorts to hoeing. The strong adherence to family lands and their gradual subdivision affects food and agriculture negatively throughout Nigeria.

Another barrier is the present science curriculum, which is not sufficiently directed towards the environment, and towards food and agriculture in particular. Even the agriculture taught at the senior secondary school is largely theoretical and most of the science teaching is "non-functional". The effect of concentrating on theoretical issues, combined with the lack of professionally qualified science teachers and the low level motivation of the students, discourage a move towards more functional curricula. Furthermore at the university level, the employers of agricultural graduates have criticized these graduates as often inadequately prepared for functioning as agricultural experts as they were deficient in practical skills. A new curriculum that would incorporate practical agriculture is advocated. Large *functional* farms attached to the universities would create opportunities for the acquisition of such practical knowledge. The present lack of these facilities because of poor funding has been recognized as contributing to the low state of agricultural education. It is also unfortunate that other science graduates are not exposed to some environmental issues such as food and agriculture.

Conclusion

Science education could form the bedrock for attaining the national goals in terms of self-reliance. The federal government realized this when it adopted the 60%/40% ratio for science/arts admissions to the universities. Though a greater number of science graduates are turned out yearly, their impact on a society in pursuit of self-reliance is remarkably small and the curriculum must therefore be at fault.

The goals will only be achieved when the curriculum at all levels from primary school to university emphasize those issues, such as food and agriculture, on which self-reliance will depend. The curriculum offered to everyone should include:

1. Food as a basic need of mankind.
2. Nigerian foods and the foods of other countries.
3. Classification of foods and their nutrients.
4. Food production through agriculture.
5. Potentials for food production in Nigeria.
6. Agricultural products for consumption and export.
7. Crop production processes.
8. Animal husbandry.
9. Soil maintenance and enrichment.
10. Food storage, preservation and marketing.
11. Careers in food and agriculture.

The government can launch short-term measures and support informal education, but only formal science education can form the basis for a long-term solution to the nation's food needs. A science curriculum which provides learning experiences in food and agriculture, as well as other content, is needed. Then food and agriculture will flourish and one human need will have been met.

Reference

Yaycock, J. Y. (1983) Agriculture, education and national development: the state of agricultural education in Nigeria. A paper presented at the 6th Annual Conference of the Nigerian Association for Agricultural Education, Zaria.

13

Educational Production Units

C. D. YANDILA
University of Zambia

In 1975 President Kenneth Kaunda announced that with immediate effect all educational institutions in Zambia would be production units. Following this announcement guidelines on how to organize production units were prepared by the Ministry of Education and circulated to all educational institutions in the country. Each was directed to establish a production unit committee, consisting of teachers, pupils and members of parent–teachers' associations. The committees were empowered to decide on the type of production to be engaged in and to determine their production targets.

The concept of production units is similar to the concept of young farmers' clubs, which were common in Zambian schools during the era 1953–63. Membership of the young farmers' clubs was voluntary: the idea was to have a small school vegetable garden maintained by pupils, supervised by their teachers. But because participation was voluntary, both on the part of teachers and pupils, young farmers' clubs did not become widespread in Zambia. Another reason for their decline was that pupils considered working in a school garden a punishment: they resented having to do manual work.

The production units introduced in 1975 had a wider perspective. All institutions of learning, at all levels, were directed to establish units. This meant that participation was compulsory for both teachers and pupils. The units covered all areas of manual work: agriculture, fishing, woodwork and metalwork. The major objectives are:

1. to provide an opportunity for pupils to apply scientific knowledge, methods and skills to real life situations in farming and other fields,
2. to cultivate in pupils the right attitude to manual work,
3. to motivate young people to play an active role in their own development and that of their communities,
4. to provide opportunities for theory and practice to interact,

5. to put knowledge acquired in classroom, laboratory or workshop to the test,
6. to produce food for consumption.

These objectives reflect the sentiments in Zambia's national development plans of 1966, 1971 and 1979. In each of these it was a stated government policy to encourage agriculture and food production among the peoples of Zambia. It was recognised that Zambia had good fertile agricultural land and, if people used it effectively, Zambia could soon be self-sufficient in food production. It was intended that Zambia's economy should no longer be based on minerals, but instead on agriculture.

The introduction of production units received overwhelming support from the public, teachers and pupils. From the very first season, 1975/76, the output was commendable: 7000 bags of maize and 100,000 kg of vegetables. One district produced 306 bags of cotton, 30,000 kg of sunflower seed, 1880 kg of tobacco and 141,374 chickens!

The organization of a production unit

At each educational institution a committee is established—pupils, teachers and parents. They keep the financial records. Initially capital funds are raised from various sources: short term bank loans, school funds, parent-teacher's association funds, as well as personal contributions from business houses and individuals. In some cases the unit is allocated land within the school grounds for its activities, but in most cases land is obtained outside either from local councils or chiefs. Because of these differences in obtaining land, there is no standard size of land allocated to the units. Institutions in rural areas tend to have access to larger pieces of land than those in urban areas. Most production units are involved in plant and animal production. Some are also involved in non-agricultural activities such as sewing or bakery.

A few institutions have large well-organized production units which employ paid workers in various projects. Such institutions become reliable suppliers of farm produce to the consumers. The produce may include chickens, cattle, eggs, maize, sunflower, soya beans, cotton, rabbits and groundnuts. The units in the Eastern Province give good examples of how well production units are organized. Let us consider them in detail.

Production units in the Eastern Province

These are well organised, supplying food to consumers in the region. The money raised from such sales is used to expand the units. Table 1 summarizes the production from all primary schools in the province for the 1983/84 season.

TABLE 1. *Produce from all Primary Schools in Eastern Province of Zambia for the 1983/1984 Season*

Commodity	Production	Value
Maize	8220 bags × 90 kg	K208,895.50
Sunflower	478 bags × 80 kg	K11,069.00
Cotton	11,923 kg	K9,349.16
Beans	65 bags	K3,517.50
Ground nuts	31 bags	K2,360.04
Vegetables	10 kg	K18.00

Total earnings K235,209.20

The total earnings were K235,209.20. There are, of course, fewer secondary schools in the province, but they earned K161,412.77 and the produce included:

green maize ducks   cattle
dry maize   chicken   pigs
sunflower   doves   rabbits
vegetables   eggs   sheep
fruits   goats

Conclusion

From an observer's standpoint, production units are a successful educational venture in Zambia, based on the fact that (a) extra food is produced which would not otherwise be available, (b) profits are made from the sale of the produce, (c) pupils participate actively in the units, thereby acquiring appropriate skills for running small-scale farms. However the units face many problems. For example, those engaged in poultry have difficulties in obtaining stock-feeds. Transport to bring stock-feeds or to carry produce to markets is a serious problem. Tools and implements are not readily available. Sufficient water for crops and animals has not always been easy. Some units have found it difficult to obtain land to expand their activities.

In addition, most units face the problem of lack of commitment by teachers, pupils and parents. Much of the work is done by a few committed people. Lack of knowledge of management of people, materials and money is a common problem. Another problem is that pupils may spend too much time on the production unit at the expense of their academic work if not properly organised, and this may affect performance in school leaving examinations.

However, the concept of the production units is a commendable one and where teachers and pupils are committed the objects have been achieved.

Food has been produced, which might have been in short supply; funds have been raised; pupils have applied their science book-knowledge to agriculture. Furthermore, some pupils have become very interested in farming and have gone into it afterwards.

The future of production units in Zambia depends on a number of factors. First there is a need to modify the present science curricula at the primary and secondary levels so that more practical work and projects are taught than at present. This requires that graduation examinations be more orientated towards the processes and skills of science. Perhaps there should be a separation between certification and selection examinations with certification examinations based on the practical work which should be emphasized in production units, and selection examinations based on theoretical knowledge. Secondly, there is a need for each production unit committee periodically and systematically to evaluate its activities. This should include finding out whether the stated objectives are being met, whether the pupils are applying scientific principles in agriculture, whether they are becoming interested in agriculture and acquiring management, production and marketing skills, whether food is being produced and profits realized. Also the committees need to determine whether more land, tools and equipment should be obtained to meet the expansion demands of the unit, and whether machinery needs to be replaced. It will also be necessary to decide which ventures are profitable, and which are preferred by the consumers and at which stage of the year.

If every educational institution were to run a well-organized unit, more food could be produced to feed the entire population avoiding Zambia's dependence on imported food like rice, corn and wheat; it would lower food prices; raise standards of living; as well as having educational advantages of great value.

14

Mites and Mirids: A resource management and applied studies approach to science education

A. J. PRITCHARD
Department of Education, Southampton University, UK

Much school science teaching is academic, seeing science as valuable for only its own pursuit, posing questions internal to its own logic as the only interesting and useful ones. This often alienates pupils who are more interested in the uses of science and the impact of its discoveries on society. To overcome this we should attempt to develop a more applied approach in science teaching with new starting points related to immediate local problems. We can assume that this approach will also benefit those children who find the pursuit of pure science intrinsically interesting: it will broaden their view of science.

There are, I feel, two aims we should be pursuing in science education at the moment: (a) through the education of future scientists, making our scientific communities more responsive to human and social need, (b) making the ideas and processes of science more widely available so that more people will feel confident enough to draw effectively upon them and the skills of scientific communities in helping resolve everyday problems. For such aims to be realised, we need to develop an appropriate curriculum framework, and to develop a wider range of classroom strategies than are commonly used today.

Any curriculum framework aiming at a science education with well-defined and diverse social functions for contemporary societies, will involve coordination between the separate sciences. It will need to see the sciences, and the roles they play in relation to contemporary needs such as health, maintenance and development of resources, technology, etc. In attempting to develop a framework, it is useful to explore the concept of resources. The conflicting demands on resources by human populations, which are expanding and in which individual consumption is increasing, are becoming more apparent in the changing patterns of resource exploitation. The human impact on the biosphere is growing very rapidly and social and economic problems in many parts of the world are such that there may be local over-exploitation of resources in order for communities simply to survive.

A resource is something that can be taken from the environment and used in some way; quite simply it is something which meets a human need. The status of a resource changes from one culture to another, and with time, and with the build up of science and technology within a culture. Until something is identified as a resource it is simply a neutral component of an ubiquitous background, a resource is culturally perceived. If a society has not developed a technology capable of using, say, uranium, this substance, even if known to it, cannot be recognised as a resource, since there is no use for which it is required or to which it can be put. The interesting feature of using the idea of resources in elaborating some of the structure of science programmes is that it immediately places science firmly into a "human needs" context.

A science education programme incorporating exploration of resources will inevitably bring together examples of agricultural techniques and practice together with the ideas and procedures of the pure sciences—particularly the biological sciences. It will also inevitably require a consideration of the "cultural" context. In terms of methods of teaching, both the scientific inquiry mode and the social decision-making mode would be incorporated. For example selective weedkiller as a topic can be dealt with in an inquiry mode, using experiments designed to investigate plant hormones, and further experiments on the effectiveness of particular herbicides (knowledge studies); issues of social concern can be discussed such as the broader ecological significance of the wide-spread use of such substances (issue studies). It is the careful mixture of different teaching strategies, and the way in which "problems" are arrived at which will help pupils to seek scientific knowledge in order to solve practical problems.

It may be helpful to see this mixture in terms of an applied studies approach in which the selection of content and teaching/learning strategies is seen to be not only dependent upon the internal logic of science but also related to the immediate needs and interests of the pupils and the future relevance to them as adults. Science teachers could be expected not only to teach about the process of, say, photosynthesis and soil structure but also to engage pupils in planning (and carrying out, in some instances) effective cropping practice in local situations.

Any attempt to help pupils to engage successfully with resource issues and to consider effective agricultural practices would involve the pupils coming to an understanding of the principles that the existence of animals and plants is dependent upon their position within populations and communities; the interaction within such populations and communities; the interaction between the abiotic and biotic components of an environment; and also that a species' continued survival over time is dependent upon its ability to adapt to the circumstances in which it lives. Such principles spply to human population also.

In order to sustain the interest and enthusiasm of pupils in such a way as to develop the sorts of skills and understanding discussed earlier the use of a variety of teaching strategies and the careful sequencing of them is called for. Among strategies currently in use in science programmes that may be relevant are:

1. Laboratory practical work,
2. Field work (a) biological; (b) social science,
3. Formal lectures and talks,
4. Audio-visual presentation,
5. Simulation and role play,
6. Computer simulation,
7. Seminar discussion,
8. Experiential activities (e.g. work experience, visits, conservation work),
9. Projects.

There are many ways in which resource management and applied studies approaches may be incorporated into science education programmes, but the essential feature must be to place the science subject matter in an appropriate context. I give here an example of a possible applied studies approach. The context in this case is Britain, but such an approach used with more appropriate examples could be used elsewhere in the world.

Red spider mites and integrated pest management

The small red mite (*Panonychus ulmi*) emerged as a serious pest in apple orchards in Britain with the use of DDT as an insecticide. Apple farming is an important economic activity in parts of Britain and the economic welfare of many families in such areas is dependent upon successful apple crops. Other families are dependent also upon effective apple farming to provide them with an important item of their diet at prices which they can afford. The economics of fruit farming is clearly of importance to a community, both for producers and for consumers. This might be an interesting starting point for some groups of pupils, particularly in areas where fruit farming is a significant economic activity. A programme of work centred on the problems of pest control, aiming to teach some ecology within an issues studies framework, may be developed as a short project.

Stage 1. The pupils explore the elements that contribute to the cost of apples, up to the point when the crop is ready to leave the farm for distribution to the shops. This could be guided class discussion, together with small group work, to establish ideas about possible component costs (for example various forms of labour, petrol for machinery, packaging materials, storage, fertilisers, pesticides, etc.). Those pupils from families engaged in fruit farming may be able to make special contributions from their family experience.

Stage 2. The work is developed into a planned farm visit, during which small groups of pupils take on different tasks (for example interviewing, collecting data on costing), leading to the presentation, in appropriate forms, of their findings (edited tape-recordings, bar charts on overhead projector trans-parency, photographs, etc.) and identification of the relative costs of chemical pesticides in apple production.

Stage 3. At this stage, a more formal presentation, possibly including a film, by the teacher of the general problem of pests in agriculture, with some examples of changes in pests associated with particular changes in agricultural practice. This could be developed into a short study by the pupils of changes in recent years in pests and pest control, in this case in apple farming. Reference back to the information gathered from the farm visit, together with looking at, for instance, the farming notes in back copies of the local newspaper, would reveal that the red spider mite is a relatively recent pest and a costly one. Thus, a problem is identified—why should this mite be a pest now, when it was not formerly a pest?

Stage 4. A second farm visit: (a) to collect samples of the fauna of the apple trees. The pupils working in small groups collect fauna by picking leaves from selected trees and tapping whole branches of the same tree over a tray. (The collecting techniques need not be treated fully as sampling techniques.) (b) to look at the effects which red spider mites have on the trees and discuss with the farmer how this affects his crop.

Stage 5. Laboratory observation of the field samples involving:

(a) a study, with the aid of notes, film-strips and photographs of the life-cycle and feeding behaviour of red spider mites;
(b) separation into groups of the fauna collected, using a simple key written for this exercise;
(c) estimation of numbers of each group and construction of a simple pyramid of numbers;
(d) a study (from information provided) of the feeding relationships of red spider mites; the identification of simple predator/prey relation-ships.

Stage 6. An exploration of the problem—why have red spider mites fairly recently become pests of economic importance in apple farming? This could be through a study using available data in the form of problem-solving exercises. This approach lends itself to individual, small group and whole class activities. The pupils are provided with a short introduction, describing the experiments carried out and data presented in a suitable form, together with questions which involve a careful consideration of the data. The form of presentation of the data, other forms of evidence and the structuring of the questions need to be related to the age and ability of the pupils.

In this case the use of DDT as an insecticide had reduced the number of mirids. These mirids (*Blepharidopterus angelatus*) had previously kept the mites in check with the result that the mites now became a much more serious pest of the apple trees (Muir, 1966). Data can be presented to the pupils in the form found in a research paper or in a simpler form using transparent sheets for easy comparison of population changes on an overhead projector. Questions would need to be asked to guide pupils through the data, involving a consideration of the changes in the population of the mites and the mirids. Pupils would also have to draw upon their earlier work on the life-cycle, breeding habits and feeding relationships of the insects.

Stage 7. A general consideration of integrated pest management programmes as part of orchard management, with some examples of practices in orchards other than apple orchards, perhaps in other parts of the world which produce crops sold in the locality of the school.

15

Food Technology Education in Papua New Guinea

M. R. BAQAR

Papua New Guinea University of Technology, Lae, Papua New Guinea

The needs of education and training in food technologies differ significantly between countries. In developing countries, special curricula have to be devised to train people to work in relatively primitive food industries, whereas in developed countries courses are designed to meet the needs of a highly sophisticated and mechanized food industry.

Papua New Guinea in the Pacific Ocean is slightly less than 450 000 square kilometers and supports a population of 3 million. Until the 1970s the country's economy depended almost entirely on exports of primary agricultural produce; now mining has become the largest economic activity, providing 55% of export earnings. Food production is predominantly based on subsistence agricultural systems in either a humid tropical or a highland tropical environment. Village subsistence production is mainly the cultivation of traditional staples — sweet potatoes, taro, yam, banana, cassava and sago. Sweet potato provides the major food energy requirement of the population. Traditional staples are generally supplemented by coconuts, pig meat, fish and a wide range of indigenous fruits, vegetables and nuts. Major food exports are cocoa beans, coffee, copra, copra oil, palm oil, tea and fish.

Despite the fact that there is sufficient raw material of agricultural and marine origin available, there is as yet little food processed. The government has now recognized the importance and need for the systematic development of food processing industries as is evident by the food and nutrition policy[1] which aims first to reduce food imports by encouraging the establishment of a fully integrated food industry, supported by a rapid increase in both subsistence and domestic production during the next decade. Secondly, the government aims to improve nutritional standards by increasing average food consumption through an increased food production plan.

Food technology education

The Papua New Guinea University of Technology is relatively new and its aim is to provide education for a relatively small number of students in various fields of technology. The aims of the food and nutrition policy cannot be achieved unless there is a sufficient number of Papua New Guineans trained in all aspects of food technology to promote the aims and to assess and supervise progress. Food technology is a new field of study in Papua New Guinea[2], but 38 graduates have been produced in the period 1978–1984.

In Papua New Guinea, education is not compulsory and students attend community schools for primary education from the age of 7 (grades 1 to 6) and secondary education is provided by 100 provincial schools (grades 7 to 10) and four national high schools (grades 11 and 12). The food technology course at the university is 5 years in length for grade 10 graduates and 4 years for those who have completed grade 12. The degree course is designed to produce professional food technologists who will pursue careers in industry, teaching and government research organizations.

Students study physics, chemistry, biology, mathematics in the first year of the four year course. Food technology studies start in the second year. Industrial training occupies 16 weeks of the third year. The final year is mainly devoted to the technology of processing foods. In addition, each student initiates work on an individual research project which occupies him for four hours per week in consultation with his supervisor. Some of the research projects of students are outlined below:

— ascorbic acid content of fruit and vegetables grown in PNG;
— nutritive value of fresh, sun-dried and dehydrated green leafy vegetables;
— chemical control of tomatoes ripening;
— potential of tomato sauce production in PNG;
— production of tropical fruit juices;
— wine production from locally grown fruits;
— jam production from lemon fruit;
— stability of palm oil;
— incorporating non-wheat flour into bread and biscuit making;
— design and operation of a solar drier;
— bacteriological examination of frozen and cooked foods.

Food technology training requires not only laboratory facilities, but also a pilot plant where the basic principles of operation of food equipment can be taught. The university is fortunate to have a well-equipped pilot plant, a joint operation with the department of primary industry. However, there are at present no certificate or diploma courses for individuals wishing to be technicians in the food industry. There is an urgent need for such technicians, in industry, research and teaching organizations.

The content of the curriculum for the B.Sc. degree in food technology is not based on what is needed in developed countries, but is consciously designed to fulfill the needs of Papua New Guinea. It is considered more appropriate to stress the methods of reducing food losses and to develop processing methods relevant to the local scene rather than studying in depth more sophisticated methods.

References

1. Lepani, C. A. (1977) *Food and Nutrition Policy for Papua New Guinea.* Available from National Planning Office, Port Moresby.
2. Baqar, M. R. and Stewart, D. S. (1979) Training of food technologists in Papua New Guinea. *Food Technology in Australia* **31**, No. 10, 434–437.

16

Village Orientated Topics in Papua New Guinea

FRIEDHELM GOELENBOTH
Wau Ecology Institute, Papua New Guinea

If education is to contribute more fully to the overall development of the country, educational planning must concern itself with well-defined final goals, for example the type of society and the type of development which the country is trying to achieve. It is only within this context that one can plan an adequate education system which will ensure that the knowledge, skills and attitudes which the system attempts to develop in its students will make the maximum contribution to society.

Because Papua New Guinea is predominantly an agricultural country (more than 85% of the population of 3 million live in villages where subsistence farming and small scale fishing is the main source of nutrition), the government schools have been provided with specific aims in their syllabuses for the teaching of agriculture. These are as follows.

Grade 1.   Learn the names of domestic plants and animals. Look for differences in plants and animals. Listen to legends about gardens and animals.

Grade 2.   Be aware of social activities in making gardens. Identify garden plants and the parts of plants used for food. Study the uses and behaviour of village animals.

Grade 3.   Understand how land is used in the community; what is involved in gardening; how traditional village activities and the daily routines of gardening are interwoven. Be aware of plant and animal growth.

Grade 4.   Find out what the local community understands by the term "land ownership". See how existing methods of gardening could be improved. Look at the growth of animals and examine some of the habits of migratory animals.

Grade 5.   Be aware of how they get rights of land, to hunt and to fish. Know that a person cannot have rights without also having

FAE-E*

obligations. Continue with the school garden, using improved ways of farming. Share in the traditional skills and knowledge of the older village people.

Grade 6. Understand something of the rules about land no longer controlled by village people. Continue with group garden projects. Better care for domestic animals. Understand how the villager can get agricultural advice and help.

Grade 7. Understand problems of improved subsistence farming; cultivation and maintenance, harvesting and replanting. Make students aware of nutrition problems.

Grade 8. Continuation of improved subsistence farming. Understand plant problems, pests and diseases and the planting and care of trees.

Grade 9. To understand interrelationship of soil, plants and animals. To provide a basic understanding of the theory and practice associated with the development, and management of the more important agricultural activities in the students' district and in the country.

Grade 10. To foster an appreciation of, and to create an interest in, agriculture as an essential part of development in PNG.

The above system — as also an alternative syllabus used in the vernacular school system of the Lutheran Church — aims to provide students with knowledge which will enable them to assist in direct material improvement of village life after their graduation. Unfortunately, most students are not able to go to a high school after grade 6, nor can such students find employment — and very often students and parents realize that the educational knowledge received is "just too little to give any real help to the village community" (Kemelfield, 1976). It is important to realize that the schools have very often created "job seekers" and not "job makers" (Bude, 1973) and this leads to increasing unemployment, a drift to towns, uncontrolled urbanization, crime and change from traditional ways of life and values.

Development of environment-orientated education

Following the techniques developed by Paulo Friere in South America (Friere, 1972), an analysis of life in different regions of PNG identified key topics, for example, coffee, pig, sweet potato in the Central Highlands; banana, cattle, coconut and traffic in the Markham-Ramu region; seafood, copra, coconut and taro in the Coast-Island region. It was proposed that education would be enhanced if there was a concentration on the key topics in the appropriate region. For example, in the Highlands discussion and instruction should take place around the key topic, pig, and the teaching would include the following (Table 1).

TABLE 1

Theoretical instruction	Project instruction
1. Traditional pig husbandry	1. Measuring of land plots and preparing of gardens
2. Traditional tribal stories of the pig	2. Nutrition of pigs and planting of crops
3. The pig as a nutritive animal	3. Designing and drawing and building of a pig house
4. The pig exchange ceremonies	4. Preparing and buying of pig feed and cleaning of the pig house
5. Prohibition of Lutheran adherents to participation in pig exchange ceremonies	5. Composting of organic materials, use of manure and planting of new crops
6. Decision making in PNG	6. Care of pigs and breeding of pigs
7. Modern pig husbandry	7. Pig diseases
8. Animal husbandry in other countries	8. Butchering of the pig
9. Budget calculation and bookkeeping	9. Buying and selling of pigs

Other key topics should be taught in a similar way. By starting with topics from the daily lives of village people in a given area, there are immediate improvements in the value of the education provided. After 5 years of preliminary studies, the Wau Ecology Institute started in 1982 a Rural Development and Subsistence Agriculture education programme based on village-orientated topics. Such education programmes have shown that it is possible to improve conditions in the villages, making them more attractive to young people, thereby encouraging them to remain there. The programme has given them the skills to manage a better life there. By identifying topics in this way, and integrating them into formal and non-formal education, the educational system can greatly contribute to self-reliance and the economic well-being of Papua New Guinea.

References

Bude, U. (1973) Ruralisation-information-participation, In: *Entwicklung und Zusammenarbeit* No. 6. Bad Godesberg, Germany.

Freire, P. (1972) *Consciencization for Liberation.* CIGOP Publication, Washington, U.S.A.

Goeltenboth, F. (ed.) (1985) *Subsistence Agriculture Improvement Manual*, Handbook No. 10. Wau Ecology Institute, Wau, Papua New Guinea (in print).

Kemelfield, G. (1976) Planting the seed: a proposal for community-based education. In: Thomas, E. B. (ed.) (1976) *The Papua New Guinea Education.* Oxford University Press, Melbourne, Australia.

17

Teaching Agriculture and Food Nutrition in Fiji

GUNASAGARON PILLAI
University of the South Pacific, Fiji

The advent of European colonists in Fiji at the turn of the last century has had a profound impact on the life-style of the Fijians. The colonists' need for cheap labour resulted in the introduction of Indian labourers who today comprise just over 50% of the total population of the country. Recent demographic trends, rapid urbanization and current recession have engendered malnutrition in their wake. Nutritional deprivation which normally afflicts the poorer sections of the community, specially those inhabiting urban centres, stems largely from discontinuance of traditional nutritional habits and the concomitant reliance on food of low nutritive value. In response to the increasing incidence of malnutrition, the Fiji Cabinet set up the National Food and Nutrition Committee (NFNC) in 1976 whose object is:

> "Food of adequate nutritional standard must be made available to every member of the community in order to maintain physical and mental health and to enable people to realize their potential."

NFNC has launched a multi-pronged strategy to ameliorate food and nutritional standards of the people of Fiji. The school curriculum, not surprisingly, has become an important vehicle for fostering an awareness of the pivotal role of wholesome food in the life and well-being of the people. The curriculum unit of the Ministry of Education, working with NFNC, has produced a variety of courses to achieve its goals: basic science, modern studies, multicraft agriculture, agriculture science, biological science.

In primary education (6 years' schooling), food and nutrition topics comprise an integral part of the curriculum and in higher classes account for one pupil contact hour per week. Furthermore, the school garden programme requires each pupil to undertake an hour's gardening per week.

131

In secondary education (6 years' schooling) the basic science course in the first four forms incorporates elements of food and nutrition, particularly as a source of energy. Modern studies is compulsory in Forms III and IV and it consists of two parts: (a) selected topics aimed at the development of basic economic concepts, including commercial understanding and skills, (b) a project, which includes activities such as raising chicken for meat and growing common vegetables.

Two agriculture-oriented courses, multicraft agriculture and agricultural science, are options available to the academically less able. The former has been designed to develop skills in agricultural planning and management, including keeping proper records of farm management and financial transactions. Students are encouraged to carry out the project component of the course at their own homes in the hope that it will ensure self-employment at the end of their schooling. The course is offered by twenty centres in Fiji and is funded by an annual grant from the New Zealand government. The agricultural science course consists of two options, namely field and animal husbandry. The former is offered by eight schools and the latter is available in only one school.

Food and nutrition constitute an important component of the biology syllabuses of the NZ School Certificate and the NZ University Entrance examination. The former is taken at the end of form V and the latter in form VI.

18

The Need for Educational Change to Increase Food Production

B. L. PRADHAN

Indian Institute of Hill Economy, Darjeeling, India

There is an explosion of population; there is also an explosion of knowledge. Unfortunately these two phenomena are closely accompanied by the explosion of problems everywhere, the hardest hit being the developing nations. The world has failed to use its vast store of knowledge towards solving the problems of hunger, malnutrition and famine.

Science and technology are the essential means of progress. Hence the message of science and technology must be propagated, and its application to the production of food encouraged. However, the resolution of this dissemination problem is not sufficient. In India's agricultural sector, an environment for the acceptance and application of science and technology has to be created where it does not now exist.

In the last three and a half decades there has been tremendous progress, saving India successfully from the onslaught of hunger. It is indeed new agricultural technology which has placed India on the threshold of the Green Revolution. At the present time, India is well placed so far as availability of foodgrains is concerned. But the production of foodgrains seems to have reached a limit, and the gap between supply and demand must necessarily widen tremendously as the population escalates as it must do. Apart from this, the changes in diet towards fulfilling nutritional requirements is sure to put pressure on the demand for food such as meat, milk, eggs, butter, fish, vegetables and so on. Furthermore, the demand for raw materials like jute, cotton and sugar cane would add further pressures on available farm land. Added to this, the expansion of cities, towns and villages, the demand for better housing facilities, the extension and expansion of roads, highways, railroads, irrigation canals, schools and playing fields, is sure to cut drastically the extent of farm land.

Under the existing set-up, much of India's agriculture is organized under peasant proprietorship. In 1953–4 agricultural holdings of less than 1 acre

133

in size formed 31% of the total number of holdings; in 1961–2 this proportion had risen to 37% and in 1971–2 it was 44%. Within this framework India can never build up a stable environment for the introduction of new technology. Modern techniques of production call for sizeable holdings, but the system of peasant proprietorship has the inherent tendency of continuously subdividing and fragmenting the holdings. Despite the abolition of the zamindari system, the growth of uneconomic holdings has been on the increase.

It is this subdivision and fragmentation of holdings which has been mainly responsible for accentuating the problem of rural unemployment, overcrowding of cities and towns, growth of slums and, above all, making the increasing problem of poverty less and less amenable to solution. The greater the scale of production and the greater the extent of diversification on a farm, the greater is the economic growth. In terms of profitability and productivity a small farm cannot compare with a large farm. The multifarious activities that a large-scale farm is capable of undertaking with accumulating financial resources at its command widens the scope of employment opportunities and ever-rising returns. And, to crown it all, it is only the large farm which provides scope for mechanization and the use of scientific techniques. Furthermore, a small farm fails to free our people from the drudgery of hard manual labour. The aspirations of the increasing number of educated young people in our villages are to free themselves from this drudgery. India offers many examples of small farm owners leaving their "mini-farms" to the care of wives and children in order to go to the towns for better jobs: such farms are then inadequately maintained and managed.

Education in science and technology becomes meaningful only when the knowledge and skills gained can bear fruitful returns.

Disseminating a knowledge of science and technology to millions of small farmers may ultimately be a waste of energy because of the impossibility of its application.

The stumbling block to progress is our agrarian set-up with its inherent bias towards endless subdivision of holdings. It is not possible, under the conditions prevalent in India, to allow a limited number of people as proprietors to hold large areas of farm land. Hence the only way to keep the farm large in size is to adopt co-operative farming.

Co-operative farming is a prelude to effective use of science and technology in agriculture, but this is not easily affected where the right to landed property has been given great sanctity. Hence co-operativization will be very slowly achieved, and for many years it will serve as a model only. Nevertheless, the importance of co-operative farming as the alternative to secure the rapid growth and modernization of India's rural economy should be inculcated in our students who will bear the brunt of forming such production organizations.

Before young people take on the responsibilities of adulthood, they should have compulsory vocational training which should include the place of science and technology in agriculture and food production. An appropriate allocation might be mother tongue 20%, English 10%, another language 10%, vocational training 20%, mathematics 10%, general science 10%, social studies 20%. As an alternative to the social studies, a student should be allowed to opt for another vocational course specialising in skill development.

The vocational training related to farming processes might include the following:

I.   1. Silage making: construction of a silo pit, various types of grasses, their nutrient value, cultivation propagation, fodder farming as a check to soil erosion.
     2. Food preservation: meat curing, fish drying, chutney making, traditional and modern methods of foodgrain storage, vegetable drying, grading, etc.
     3. Poultry farming, pisciculture, apiculture.
     4. Pig and goat rearing. Mushroom cultivation.
     5. Animal diseases and treatment.

II. 1. Seed farming: cabbage, carrot, etc.
     2. Maize, paddy, cotton cultivation.
     3. Use of micro-nutrients.
     4. Soil chemistry.
     5. Bamboo cultivation, silviculture.
     6. Flood irrigation, sprinkler irrigation.
     7. Compost making.
     8. Floriculture.
     9. Marketing.

III. 1. Agricultural economics, emphasis on co-operative farming.
     2. Farm management.

Our educational system in general, and vocational education in particular, should be reoriented to make more intensive use of our endowment of resources. These natural resources are unlimited and economic activities based on such resources are bound to help India's economy. In this agriculture and agro-based industries should have pride of place, and this should be reflected in education.

19

A Syllabus for Agriculture Education for Elementary School Pupils in Jordan

A. BADRAN, E. BAYDOUN, M. SUBBARINI
Yarmouk University, Jordan

The Jordanian Ministry of Education (JME) is the sole institution in charge of general education and the system is completely centralized. The JME takes care of all aspects of the educational process, including private schools, which are expected to comply with the policies and guidelines of JME. The stages of education are elementary (age 6–12), intermediate (age 12–14) and secondary (age 15–18). Like the majority of Arab states, Jordan has a 6–3–3 educational ladder. The 12 years of general education are preceded by 2 years of kindergarten for children aged 4–6 years. The kindergarten stage is conducted by the private sector. Education is compulsory for the 9 years up to the age of 16.

Secondary education is diversified into vocational centres (two years), vocational schools, academic schools (arts and science streams) and comprehensive schools. In addition to the general education schools, the JME is in charge of a group of non-formal programmes, such as adult education, evening classes, summer courses and enrichment classes.

Agriculture education: an historical perspective

Agriculture was a school subject from the early days of education in Jordan (1920s), though it was a school subject provided only for male pupils. Girls were and still are given nursing, baby care and home economics. Agriculture as a subject would begin in the fourth elementary class (age 10). When the Elementary School Certificate Examination was introduced agriculture was included as a subject for male non-Moslem pupils (Moslem pupils were taught Islamic religion instead).

The content and methodology of teaching agriculture was different in rural areas from that in urbanized ones. More emphasis was given to

137

practical work in rural schools. The general guidelines highlighted that "the main goal of agriculture education is to instil in pupils agricultural attitudes, strengthen relations within villages and develop satisfaction with rural life". When the East Bank and the West Bank were unified in 1950, agriculture remained as a school subject in elementary schools until 1977/78 when new syllabuses were introduced in elementary schools and agriculture disappeared as a separate school subject.[2]

Status of agriculture education in elementary schools

With agriculture no longer a separate school subject in elementary schools, even related topics are not prominent in the science syllabuses, as seen in the following survey of the six science textbooks in elementary schools.

Class	Total pages	Related pages	Percentage	Topics related to agriculture
1st	91	1.25	1.4%	Farmers and farming. How farmers plant seeds and harvest fields
2nd	113	4	3.5%	Taking care of plants (cotton, onion, pine seedlings). Why water plants? Milking a cow.
3rd	164	9	5.5%	Projected agriculture. How plants grow and reproduce. Fertilizers. How soil is formed.
4th	184	25	13.6%	Conventional and modern ways of farming. Production and storage of wheat. Planting trees. Poultry and fish farming.
5th	146	0	0	—
6th	179	0	0	—

Reconsideration of the place of agriculture in the curriculum has raised the following issues:

1. The goals of compulsory education in Jordan stresses that children in elementary and intermediate schools should be helped to (a) develop appreciation of manual work and be aware of the importance of related vocations in Jordanian society, (b) develop attitudes which will encourage their spending leisure time in healthy and fruitful activities, (c) get acquainted with and understand their natural and man-made environment, (d) express their innate inclinations and abilities in order to follow an appropriate career, (e) develop appreciation of nature and respect for life, (f) adopt a scientific approach to problem-solving.

2. Agriculture is not mere farming; it is a means for the production of the food which is necessary for sustaining health and strength in the whole of society (Jordan, like other Arab states, is not self-sufficient in food).[3,4]

3. The percentage of elementary textbooks devoted to food-related topics is small as was found for agriculture.

Class	Total pages	Related pages	Percentage
1st	91	11.2	12.3%
2nd	113	6.1	5.4%
3rd	164	4.2	2.6%
4th	184	1	0.5%
5th	146	9.2	6.3%
6th	179	3	1.7%

4. The objectives of science education in their domains (cognitive, psycho-motor and affective) can be attained through real, concrete situations involving the interaction of Man and the environment; agriculture provides an ideal area from which pupils can acquire an understanding of scientific concepts and develop scientific skills and attitudes.

A proposed syllabus for agriculture education in elementary schools

Based on the above considerations and the views on science education in official texts, the following framework is suggested for agricultural education as a major part of the science syllabus in the Jordanian elementary school system.

Year 1: Agriculture

(a) What is it? An activity controlled by man for producing "agricultural products" for the well-being of society.

(b) Agriculture in Jordan: limitations (soil, water, pests, climatic factors); what is soil (formation, types, improvement); agricultural products.

Year 2: Conventional versus unconventional methods

(a) Conventional ways (seeding, irrigation, control, harvesting).

(b) Unconventional ways: irrigation (drip, showering); hydroponics, plastic greenhouses; types of pest; natural, manual, chemical and biological control; fertilizers and crop rotation; preserving genetic diversity.

Year 3: Agriculture as a source of food

(a) Sources of food: animal production, plant production, fisheries.
(b) Photosynthesis.

Year 4: Agriculture for recreation and leisure

(a) School gardens.
(b) Gardens at home.
(c) Indoor plants (how to rear them, how to care for them).

Year 5: Food

(a) Sources of food.
(b) Types of food needed for a balanced diet leading to health.
(c) Preservation of food.
(d) The journey of food through the body (digestion, absorption, transport, assimilation).
(e) Health awareness: storage, poisoning, mishandling of food; diets of special groups (babies, school children, expectant mothers, etc); results of imbalance of diet (malnutrition, obesity).

References

1. Jordan Ministry of Education (1980) *History of Education in Jordan 1921–1970.* Division of Educational Documentation, Jordan Ministry of Education, Amman.
2. Shami, M. A. and Fonda, H. M. (1979) *Educational Innovations in Jordan 1976–1979.* Jordan Ministry of Education, Amman.
3. Salman, A. (1982) Animal production and its role in agriculture development, Proceeding of the *Symposium on Development of Agriculture in Kuwait.* Kuwait Foundation for the Advancement of Science, Kuwait.
4. Al-Kassim, S. (1982) *Food Problems in Arab States — An Analytical View.* A Shuman Establishment, Amman, Jordan.

20

The Food and Agriculture Topic in the Science in Society Project

MALCOLM OAKES
Bordesley Centre, Birmingham, UK

The "Science in Society" course is designed as a 1 year, post-16 course for use in the sixth forms of British schools. Its purpose as stated in the teacher's guide is:

> "to give a better understanding of the place of science and technology in the world today and an awareness that it is only through the wise use of them that the future of mankind is assured".

The materials were developed for students able to display good literacy and numeracy skills. Nevertheless, the course has been used successfully with students of a broader range of ability. It is expected that many of the students pursuing the course will have met elements of the topics previously in their school curriculum. In particular, work in biology will have emphasized the concept of the balanced diet and the roles of food in the processes of life. These will have been taught with an emphasis on practical work. Complementary work may have been followed in home economics. Except in geography, however, it is unlikely that issues associated with the supply of food to both the developing and developed nations will have been raised. The food and agriculture topic in the course seeks to raise issues that may, therefore, be new to the students. To do this, problems have to be overcome. For example, most of the teachers concerned are science specialists who have to adopt a different style of teaching to that with which they are accustomed or for which they have been trained. Consequently two student readers are provided (one on food, one on agriculture) plus a detailed section of suggestions and outlines for teaching schemes in a teacher's guide.

The readers contain a range of papers that are designed to inform the students. Hence the need for reasonable reading skills. Indeed, it is the stated hope that the course will lead to an improvement in their abilities to comprehend written material and to assess its validity. Nevertheless, with less able students it is possible for teachers to extract the essential aspects of the topic. The papers in each reader, written by experts in their field, are:

Book D	Book E
Nutrition and diet	Ecology and food production
Alternative sources of protein	Energy in agriculture
Food in the future	Energy to live
Food processing, packaging and distribution	Agriculture and the environment
	Farming today
The world's food supply	Soil — our true wealth
Data	Data

All the papers inform and they attempt to place the issues in context. There are a number of different approaches which the teacher can use in the classroom and detailed suggestions are given in the teacher's guide, which is the real basis for the course. Particularly for the teacher whose background knowledge of the topic is limited, the guide indicates a range of approaches and suggests what might be profitable lines of study.

The guidance begins with a list of objectives on which the material is based.

Objectives

It is hoped that, as a result of studying this unit, the students will appreciate

(*a*) the nature of food and the importance of different nutrients;

(*b*) that agriculture is the basis of most food production and that the increased world population can be fed only by an increase in production obtained by improvements in agricultural technology;

(*c*) that such improvements are inevitably accompanied by detrimental effects on the environment;

(*d*) that energy is an essential requirement for high productivity in agriculture and that inreased food output will require an increase in the energy input;

(*e*) that food processing is an essential activity if food is to be consumed a long way from the place of production and to avoid waste of surplus stocks;

(*f*) that, while one of the western world's problems is over-consumption, a large proportion of the world's population is still undernourished and that there are many countries which are wealthy and yet still suffer from malnutrition through lack of education on the nature of food;

(*g*) the possibilities of alternative food sources;

(*h*) some of the problems of the developing world in obtaining adequate food supplies.

To facilitate the development of these objectives the topic is divided into eight sections. They are analysed briefly in the introduction to enable to the teacher to have an overview. The sections are:

The world's food supply
Nutrition and diet — what people eat
History of food production
Ecology and agriculture
Agriculture and the environment
Food processing, packaging and distribution
Alternative food sources
The world's food supply

For example, section 8 states:

Aim   To conclude and summarize the topic by returning to the problems of maintaining and increasing the world food supply in order to feed a growing population.
Activities   Reading paper D5 in the Reader *Food*. Analysis of food by country of origin. Comparison of different countries using data (D6). Discussion.
Resources   Paper *The world's food supply* (D5), *Data* (D6). Film *Food or famine*. Discussion questions in this guide.

The range of activities covered in each section include some reading; various discussions; the use of the data; tasting exercises; analysis of foods by country of origin; a study of food labels and forms of packaging; film viewing; the use of an audio-tape; a visit to a farm and a visit to a supermarket; a simulation exercise.

Schools may not have time to benefit from all the suggested activities, but the variety of suggestions means that teachers can develop their own approaches.

The films which were recommended were those found to be particularly helpful, though many others could be used. The following extract from the teacher's guide suggests how such a film might be used.

Film: Food or Famine

Food or Famine, a 16 mm sound film in colour, is obtainable on free loan from Shell Film Library, 25 The Burroughs, Hendon, London NW4 4AT (telephone 01-202 7803). It is very warmly recommended, and this would be an appropriate stage of the course to show it.

The following questions might usefully be posed to the class before the film is seen, and students can be encouraged to answer them afterwards, in writing or during discussion. (As mentioned in the General Introduction on p. 13 students usually get more out of a film if they have some task to think about during its showing: it prevents a passive attitude if there is something active to be done.)

1. *What parts of the Earth's surface are (a) suitable for food production now, (b) will always be unsuitable for food production?*
2. *What methods does man use to improve yields of crops?*
3. *Is there anything wrong with using chemical fertilizers instead of organic fertilizers such as manure?*
4. *Would it be better to devote our efforts to controlling the world's population rather than trying to grow ever more food to feed ever more people?*
5. *Do we want all the world's varied landscape to be turned into agricultural land?*
6. *Is the world food problem a scientific, an economic, a political, or a cultural problem?*

Tables of data are included in both the readers. The following extract is typical of the way in which it is suggested such data might be used.

Comparisons between different parts of the world

Data has been included in Readers D and E which is relevant to this part of the course. Table E7.1 for example, shows the use to which land is put in different regions of the world. Figures on international trade (E7.2) indicate the proportion of agricultural commodities exported from the country of origin. Two further tables show the percentage of working population engaged in agriculture (E7.4) and the average protein and energy supplies for different countries (D6.6). (Note that where FAO figures concerning energy are quoted they have been converted from kilocalories to kilojoules to maintain consistency throughout the course.)

The data can be made the basis for a number of informative exercises. Some possibilities are:

1. Look at the world agricultural regions map in an atlas. Is there any relationship between the land use in a region and the region's population density?
2. Plot on a graph the energy supply as a percentage of requirement (Table D6.6) against the percentage of the population engaged in agriculture (Table E7.4) for the following selection of countries: UK,

German Democratic Republic, Poland, Cuba, Brazil, Jamaica, Venezuela, China, Kenya, Indonesia, Malawi, and Nepal.

(a) Is there a noticeable general relationship between the percentage of people engaged in agriculture and the sufficiency of energy supply?
(b) Which countries do not fit the general relationship well? Can you suggest why they do not?
(c) Which of the developing countries has progressed furthest in its agricultural development, judging from your graph?

3. Use table D6.6 showing average *per capita* protein and energy supplies to decide for which countries the food supply improved between 1961 and 1970. How much improvement was there throughout the whole world over this period?
4. Look at the figures on international trade in Table E7.2 Why is much more coffee than wheat exported from the country of origin? Why is almost all the rubber production exported from the country of origin?

The simulation exercise for this topic is called the Hilltop Project and concerns the factors which influence the effective functioning of a farm and how the environment can influence this effectiveness. The first part introduces students to the economics of a farm. The second part considers why some farms in the Hilltop area are uneconomic. Evidence is produced, from which it is possible to deduce how the mineral content of the soil is affecting the farms.

The teacher can plan his own route through the material for the topic as a whole, but if guidance is needed the guide suggests two possible routes. It must be emphasized that neither of these routes is prescriptive: the course encourages teachers to develop their own routes and to use their own material. The one hope is that whatever is done discussion will be promoted, and the following is typical of the help given in the guide (this comes at the end of section 8).

Lesson	Route 1 (full treatment)	Route 2 (short treatment)
1	Discussion of world food supply. Tasting activity: food and non-food. Homework: read D1 (*Nutrition and diet*).	Short resumé of world food supply problems. Nutrition and diet discussion (assuming paper E1 already read). Homework: read E1 (*Ecology and food production.*)
2	Discussion of nutrition and diet. Initiate analysis of food consumption. Homework: research on history of food production.	Discussion of ecology and food production; food chains and webs; energy. Homework: read E4 (*Agriculture and the environment*).
3	Talks and discussion on history of food production.	Film *Food for thought*, followed by discussion Homework: read E5 (*Farming today*).
4	Follow up analysis of food consumption. Homework: read E1 (*Ecology and food production*) and/or E2 (*Energy in agriculture*).	Discussion on agriculture and the environment. Homework: read D4 (*Food processing, packaging, and distribution*).
5	Ecology; food chains and webs. Discussion: the importance of energy.	Discussion on food processing and packaging, initiated by samples brought in. Homework: read D5 (*The world's food supply*).
6	Film *Food for thought*, followed by discussion of film. Briefing on farm visit.	Film *Food or famine*, followed by discussion on world food supply.
7	Visit to a farm. Homework: read E4 (*Agriculture and the environment*).	
8	Discussion on *Agriculture and the environment* Homework: read D4 (*Food processing, packaging and distribution*).	
9	Discussion on food processing, initiated by samples. Cook and taste peas preserved by different methods.	
10	Food packaging, initiated by samples. Briefing on supermarket visit.	
11	Visit to supermarket. Homework: read D3 (*Food in the future*) and D2 (*Alternative sources of protein*).	

Lesson	Route 1 (full treatment)	Route 2 (short treatment)
12	Discussion of alternative food sources. Taste TVP samples. Homework: read D5 (*The world's food supply*).	
13	World food supply.	
14	Film *Food or famine*. Final discussion.	

Concluding discussion

The concluding discussion on this unit might revert back to some of the questions raised in the opening discussion. The teacher might care to break the class into small groups which could consider different aspects and then report their conclusions to the whole class: this technique does get all the students actively involved in the discussion.

1. *What do you think about the Dean of Bristol's message: 'Live simply that others may simply live'? Should there be a radical redistribution of food throughout the world? How could it be brought about?*

2. *What about the 'life-boat situation'? Is it better to save some and to repel boarding-parties which might sink the ship? Should we concentrate aid only on those countries with the greatest chance of survival?*

3. *What sort of aid is likely to be most effective? Food? Tractors? Chemical fertilizers and pesticides? Education and training in new agricultural techniques? Better storage?*

4. *Should we encourage the use of chemical fertilizers, pesticides, and herbicides? Do the advantages outweigh the disadvantages?*

5. *How is it possible for only 2.3% of the population in the UK to be involved in farming whereas in many parts of the world the figure is over 80%? Will this situation continue? Will the shortage of energy force us back to earlier methods of farming?*

6. *Ought we to change our eating habits? Should we change from animal protein to vegetable protein?*

7. *Which is more likely to help a developing country with a large proportion of its population working on farms: the setting up of a large agricultural organization with the latest agricultural equipment or the encouragement of the local farmers?*

8. *What decides whether a farmer plants a variety of crops or a monoculture of one type only? What are the advantages or disadvantages of each?*

9. *Is it better for a developing country to develop industry or to develop the quality of its farming? What are the advantages and disadvantages of each?*

10. *Are you optimistic or pessimistic about food supply in the future?*

Earlier in this chapter it was mentioned that most of the teachers of this course have been science teachers (though certainly not all). Their usual teaching has centred around practical work in a laboratory, where the benches may impose a structure on the organization of a class. Such teachers need to learn new techniques, for example how to promote a worthwhile discussion, how to organize a room for it, but experience has shown how a course of this nature helps teachers to become better communicators and certainly better informed on wider issues associated with his subject. It therefore influences all their teaching.

At the present time, there are strong pressures in the UK to introduce social, economic, environmental and technological aspects into the new syllabuses being developed for the General Certificate of Secondary Education. For the first time such aspects are being included in the mainstream science curriculum. The contribution from the "Science in Society" approach is that it suggests techniques for teaching as well as indicating some of the material which might be included in other science courses.

Reference

Science in Society: Teacher's Guide (1981) Association for Science Education, College Lane, Hatfield, UK.

21

Operation Cat Drop

CHRIS HALL
Malvern College, UK

Stability in the ecosystem

An important concept which should be incorporated into secondary school teaching is how all components of the ecosystem exist within a dynamic equilibrium, into which feedback mechanisms are built so that a change in one part of the system can be compensated by another part. This gives stability. If, however, the change is too severe for compensation, for example when poisons such as toxic heavy metals or pesticides are introduced into ecosystems, then breakdown of the ecosystem occurs. A classic case of such disturbance has been described under the code name Operation Cat Drop. It is a particularly valuable example to promote to discussion within the classroom.

Operation Cat Drop

This occurred in the Dayak areas of Borneo. The Dayaks are an agricultural society, who live in large communal huts called longhouses, each housing up to 500 people. In this region of Borneo malaria has been endemic until the World Health Organization (WHO) decided that this disease should be controlled by eradicating its mosquito vectors. The WHO sprayed every longhouse with DDT, the number of mosquitoes diminished, and the incidence of malaria dropped dramatically.

Unfortunately there were other responses to the introduction of DDT into the Dayak ecosystem. *Cockroaches* in the longhouses absorbed DDT, which then became concentrated in the *lizards* which ate them. The lizards in turn were eaten by domestic *cats*. The DDT became further concentrated at each stage, but this time the concentration was so high that it proved lethal to the cats. With the death of most of the Dayak cats, the *rat* population began to increase. There was a parallel increase in the number of rat parasites, such as *fleas* and *lice*. Some of the parasites were vectors for *sylvatic plague*. Operation Cat Drop was an attempt to parachute into the region a new population of domestic cats. This proved quite effective.

However, disturbance to the Dayak ecosystem was not so easily stopped. The thatched roofs of the longhouses were subject to damage by a caterpillar normally held in check by natural parasites and predators. The DDT killed caterpillars, predators and parasites alike. However, the caterpillars, as always in such cases, were the first population to recover. A caterpillar explosion resulted and when the rainy season started, the roofs of the Dayak longhouses were so ravaged by the caterpillars that they collapsed.

Ecologists consider that stability in an ecosystem is positively correlated with its diversity. A diverse ecosystem with many species is more stable than an ecosystem with few species, for example Arctic ecosystems which have poor diversity are generally unstable. Many tropical ones have a high diversity and are remarkably stable. Man-made ecosystems, especially agricultural ones, usually have a very low diversity and are readily disturbed.

Man is undoubtedly the single most significant member of the Earth's ecosystem. He has been responsible for many disruptions of the natural environment — clearing land for habitation and industry, and altering the balance of animal and plant life with the development of agriculture. These disruptions are often too great to be compensated for naturally. Pests arise as a result of such disturbances.

Topics in a biology or agriculture course

Awareness of such a cautionary tale as Operation Cat Drop is a useful basis for consideration of a whole range of issues which might be incorporated into biology or agriculture course.

What are the advantages and disadvantages when agricultural economics depends on monocultures? Every animal and plant species is a potential food source for another. It is only when these consumers and predators compete with man for the food that the term "pest" is applied. The species which we regard as pests were in existence long before agriculture. They only exist now in vast numbers as a result of monocultures to feed growing populations.

What methods of control should be adopted? In the UK, certain animal diseases have legally to be notified (anthrax, foot-and-mouth disease, rabies, swine vesicular disease) and with some diseases slaughter is compulsory for infected animals and those apparently healthy animals which have been on contact with them. This is a useful topic for discussion in the classroom, as is the issue of transporting animals and plants from one country to another. Should there be controls? Are they justified?

Cultural control methods should be considered (crop rotation, trap crops, adjusting the time of sowing and harvesting, encouraging rapid growth of crops, crop sanitation, breeding resistant varieties of crops).

Biological control is another topic of importance, as is radiation control and, of course, chemical control.

Man has created the problem of the pests. Continued interference with the Earth's ecosystem can only make the situation worse unless very great care is taken during development of an area to ensure that the natural balance of nature is affected as little as possible. Man has to realise that his present selfish attitude can only lead to ecological disaster. Respect for the environment is one of the things that any biological or agricultural course should inculcate into young people.

22

Food, Nutrition and Agriculture in the Malaysian Education System

ABDUL SALAM BABJI and ABDUL LATIFF MOHAMED
Kebangsaan University, Malaysia

The educational system in Malaysia needs to be geared towards a broader education encompassing food and agriculture. This will enable graduates from secondary schools, colleges and universities to appreciate the economic and technological problems of the country, and to come out with rational and practical decisions to overcome them. Furthermore, if the educational system is to produce work-ready graduates for the food and agriculture industries, a sound knowledge and understanding of food and agriculture can only be achieved by strengthening the existing curriculum at all levels.

In an agriculture-base country like Malaysia, ethnic customs and traditions have made the introduction and acceptance of food, nutrition and agriculture into the school curriculum difficult. Another formidable obstacle is the lack of sophistication in the utilization of science and technology, which it is necessary to acquire to achieve certain development goals. Lack of original thinking leads to a proneness to imitate, borrow, accept "wholesale" and indiscriminately practise the values and methods of other societies from different lands rather than to select or originate viable techniques relevant to the solution of local problems.

The inheritance of educational packages from overseas has totally excluded food, nutrition and agricultural subjects, which should have been a priority in an agricultural country like Malaysia. Furthermore, teachers are ignorant on these. The present curriculum and examination system has so captivated the teachers and the students that it has stifled efforts at diversifying the curriculum and providing something more valuable to the majority of the population (Osman Mohamed, 1973).

A good education system encompasses three main objectives. First, it imparts information and knowledge to the students. Secondly, it develops in them self-discipline, as well as positive thinking and attitudes. Thirdly, it provides them with the know-how to utilize and interpret methodologies and techniques. An appropriate curriculum in food and agriculture must be based on a sound knowledge of biological sciences and the introduction of biology must be such that it is suited to solving the current and future needs of Malaysia. Among the urgent needs in this country are increasing the agricultural output, control of pollution and improvement of the environment, and there is always the problem of the increasing human population.

Most of the changes have been brought about at the university level of education. In the 50s the biology curriculum emphasized morphology, taxonomy and anatomy. Development in the 60s was channelled towards experimental disciplines with an emphasis on laboratory experiments in the related fields of physiology, ecology, genetics and molecular biology. In the 70s it was genetic engineering. Today universities are channelled more towards national problems, such as increasing food production, reducing environmental pollution and maximizing utilization of natural resources and agricultural waste.

Changes and development of the curriculum also occurred at the primary and secondary school levels. Science was introduced even at the lower primary school. At the lower secondary level biology was taught according to guidelines laid down in 1969. This curriculum emphasized the need to investigate as well as acquiring knowledge, as also the need to integrate biology, physics and chemistry. Thus by the mid-70s students were exposed to practical laboratories where emphasis was given to the familiarization and utilization of equipment and apparatus: this teaching was comparable to many developed countries. At the pre-university matriculation level the curriculum was planned to meet the needs of different university entry requirements, Nordin (1982) stressed the need to review this in view of the fact that the bulk of students entering universities take up biology as their main subject.

The interesting question is where biology will lead in the years ahead. It is without doubt in our minds that the emphasis in education in Malaysia in the 90s must take into consideration the relationship of biology to agriculture, food and nutrition and the utilization of existing natural resources to meet the nation's requirements, which includes more and better food and an efficient system of environmental management.

Development in Malaysia

Agricultural development in Malaysia has been steady and progressive. Self-sufficiency in rice, poultry and eggs, a leading producer in palm oil, rubber, pepper and cocoa is something Malaysians can be proud of. Unlike many developing countries where food production can hardly keep pace with population growth, Malaysia has been quite successful in this respect.

However, food production must also provide an adequate diet for the whole nation. The nutritional status of diets expressed in terms of the average *per capita* showed Malasia to be in good standing when compared with other developing nations, but recent community nutrition studies by the Institute of Medical Research, Kuala Lumpur (1984) revealed that many infants and schoolchildren are undernourished. Thus a food policy should aim to improve nutrition and welfare of households in the lower income population. In the past Malaysia's food policy has emphasized food imports rather than domestic production because rubber oil palm traditionally grown in Malaysia provide the nation with greater income and foreign exchange earnings with which food and other consumer and industrial goods are imported. However, economic prosperity should not be used a sole yardstick for determining the level of development; the status of community or population nutrition should also be taken into account.

Clearly if Malaysia is to increase the levels of nutrition, productivity and the quality of life of the rural communities, it must increase the family food supply through increase of food production and land utilization. At the same time, nutrition education of schoolchildren, informal adult education to mothers, and vigilance of nutritionally related health problems should be intensified so as to ensure the proper utilization of nutrients.

Food, nutrition and agriculture in education

The inclusion of food, nutrition and agriculture has been neglected in the primary and secondary educational system until recently. Students are ignorant about food and nutrition: it is not surprising that many do not even know the names of local tropical fruits and vegetables grown in Malaysia. Besides students, teachers at these levels are not adequately trained and exposed to the subjects.

However, in the last ten years Malaysia took drastic steps to develop and train its own local scientists to meet the nation's requirement in agricultural development. This far-sightedness has resulted in a rapid development and establishment of agriculture, food science and technology, and nutrition programmes in local universities.

It is now felt that the present curriculum on nutrition and agricultural subjects in primary and secondary schools is inadequate when compared with the successful developments at college and university levels. Important in the country as a whole, it is particularly important in the rural areas where chronic undernourishment was found in 43% of pre-school children and anaemia was found in practically all sections of the community. A systematic approach to teaching food, nutrition and agriculture throughout schools should now be adopted and this will involve an extensive retraining of teachers.

References

Nordin, T. A. and Nor'Aini, D. (1982) *Pattern and Trends of Biology Education in Local Universities*. Research Priorities in Malaysian Biology Symposium on Biology. Universiti Kebangsaan Malaysia, Bangi.

Osman Mohamed (1973) *Education and Social Integration in Malaya,* Doctoral Dissertation, Department of History and Philosophy of Education. University of Nebraska, U.S.A.

23

Agricultural Aspects of Biology Education

WINSTON K. KING
University of West Indies, Barbados

The following table shows a suggested curriculum [after Rao and Pritchard (1984)]

Reference

Rao, A. N. and Pritchard, A. J. (1984) *Agriculture and Biology Teaching*, IUBS/CBE/ Unesco.

Area of concern	Concepts/Principles/Topics	Practical experiences for students	Teaching/Learning strategies	Developing values/Intellectual skills	Levels Lower	Higher
Agriculture						
(a) Factors affecting crop production	Biotic factors and interaction Concepts of limiting factors Concepts of tolerance Carrying capacity	Case studies Field work Designing remedial experiments Identification of visual symptoms of limiting factors	Project work Games Lecture Discussion	Awareness of conservation of soil and water resources Appreciating the need for proper management of soil and water resources Awareness of production limits of ecosystems	✓	✓
(b) Varietal improvement (c) Use of non-conventional food sources	Breeding Asexual reproduction Mutation Genetic conservation Introduction of new species	Field trip Performing asexual propagation methods Setting up school nurseries Actual breeding experiment in plants and animals	Lecture Discussion Audio-visual aids Case studies	Skills in analysis of pedigree Skills in breeding asexual propagation of plants Awareness of new role of heredity in development of organisms Awareness of negative and positive effects of breeding	✓ ✓	✓ ✓
(d) Pest and diseases control	Biotic relationship predator prey host specificity competition allelochemics Development of resistance to biocides (pesticides, weedicides	Field work Case study Experiments Familiarity with biocides (pesticides, weedicides, herbicides) and their uses Collection Preservation of specimens	Decision-making Games Lecture Discussion Audio-visual Use of biological specimens Use of resource persons including farmers	Awareness of important biotic relationship Develop attitude for conservation and maintenance and proper biotic relationship	✓	

Topic	Concepts	Learning activities/methods	Objectives	
	herbicides)		Skill for developing proper agricultural practices for pest and disease control and management (inter-cropping, multiple cropping, biological control)	✓ ✓
(e) Pollution (including bio-cides and agricultural waste management)	Food chain relationship Hydrologic cycle Material cycling	Case studies Monitoring studies using ecological indicators Field collection/preservation Identification of ecological indicators Collection and separation of biodegradable/non-biodegradable farm waste materials	Develop proper attitudes towards the use of pesticides, weedicides and fertilizers Appreciate value of farm waste as a source of energy and fertilizer Develop proper methods of agriculture waste disposal	✓
(f) Integrated farming systems for efficient resource utilization and management	Energy flow and material cycling Ecological efficiencies Homeostasis and steady state	Case studies Field work School projects on recycling Audio-visual, i.e. charts, slides Lecture Discussion Practical experiences in the farm Need resource assessment	Appreciate the value of diversified production system Appreciate the value of farm waste as alternative source of energy and fertilizer Develop proper management strategies for integrated farming	

24

Food Aspects of Biological Education

WINSTON K. KING

University of West Indies, Barbados

The list below shows how food and nutrition topics can be infused into biology education. [after the Handbook from the Caribbean Food and Nutrition Institute, Jamaica]

Biological Topics	Suggested Food Topics
	Food and Good Health
Food — types and functions	What is food?
Food and nourishment	Using food groups to guide nutrition
Food intake and age, sex, activity, special situations	Food groups for the Caribbean
Diet and occupation. Energy value	Meal planning with food groups
Balanced diet	Food — quantity and quality
Importance of local foods — cherries, guavas, grapefruits, peas, carrots, etc.	
Food from the sea. Fish farming.	
Common Caribbean foods — main nutrients	
	How to buy, store and prepare foods properly
Food storage and preservation methods and effectiveness	How to handle, store and prepare foods
Eradication of food pests —	
Preservation of food — drying, salting, etc.	
Food preparation and food quality	
Choosing the best foods for the purpose	

Biological Topics	Suggested Food Topics
	Nutrition during pregnancy and breast-feeding
What is anaemia?	Preventing anaemia in pregnancy
Foods which prevent anaemia	Nutrition problems during pregnancy
Preparing for birth. Fertilization and development. Birth and baby care	Identifying undernourished pregnant women
Choosing correct foods in pregnancy	Breast-feeding — value and suggestions
The value of breast milk	
	Young Child Feeding
Go, grow and glow foods	Feeding the young child:
Development of the young child	4–6 months; 6–12 months; 1 year and over
	Recipes for making young child's meals
	Malnutrition in Young Children
Diseases of malnutrition in young children	Signs of good nutrition
Function of food types	The growth chart
Causes of malnutrition	Protein — energy malnutrition
Anaemia — prevention and cure	Conditions which cause malnutrition
Combatting malnutrition	Anaemia in young children
	Diarrhoea
Diarrhoea — symptoms, prevention and cure. Causative agents	What is diarrhoea?
The importance of water in the body. Effects of diarrhoea — dehydration	Feeding in diarrhoea
Feeding in diarrhoea	Dehydration and diarrhoea
	Recovery from dehydration
	Prevention of diarrhoea
	Feeding Other Groups
Food types and functions	School children
Energy value of foods	Teenagers
Food and its relationship to age, sex and activities	Elderly people

Biological Topics	Suggested Food Topics
	Health Problems Related to Food and Nutrition
Diabetes — cause, symptoms, treatment	Diabetes
Diet and disease	High blood pressure
Feeding the Diabetic	
	Improving Health and Nutrition in the Community
Protecting the body against disease, e.g. polio, tetanus, measles, whooping cough	Immunization
Diseases — causes, prevention and cure	Family planning
The reproductive cycle. The Mentrual cycle. Methods of contraception	Correcting misconceptions
Fads and fantasies in food	Producing foods at home
Nutritional value of various foods	

Reference

Nutrition Handbook for Community Workers. CFNI, Jamaica, 1982

25

Topics on Food, Nutrition and Agriculture in Biology Teaching

DOLORES F. HERNANDEZ and VICTORIA B. BALTAZAR
Institute of Educational Development, University of the Philippines

Listed below are selected topics on food, nutrition and agriculture with corresponding subtopics or suggested activities and major questions on which to focus. A biology teacher in a rural area should be able to select those activities and topics which relate closely to the biology syllabus. The activities are intended for the age group 13–15, normally found in a biology class in the Philippines.

1. Microorganisms in plant nutrition

    1.1   Replenishment of minerals, vitamins and hormones required for plant growth through the activities of decomposers.

    1.2   How nitrogen-fixers in legumes and azolla release nitrogen for use by crops (i.e. rice).

        Activity: How to make compost (use one of several local references, e.g. Goodbye, Waste!)

        Question: What do microorganisms do to compost materials?
                How does composted material enrich the soil?

    1.3   Nitrogen content of plants and animals.

        Activity: Nitrogen in plant and animal protein

        Materials: reference materials such as *Guide to Nutrition; Food and Nutrition*; local plants and animals

        Procedure: Make a list of various plants and animals found in the farm or community and indicate the plant or animal part which has high protein content.

        Example: cassava — leafy top or shoot
                chicken — meat and eggs

Question: Which plant part has higher protein content, cassava tops or cassava root?

1.4   Points of entry in the biology syllabus for 1.1 to 1.3:

Soil conservation
Soil ecosystem
Cycles in the biosphere (nitrogen cycle)
Nutrients in food (protein)
Microorganisms and their activities
Substances needed for plant growth

2.   A farm as a modified ecosystem

2.1   Differences between the farm and natural ecosystems.

(a) closed or open system
(b) degree of management needed
(c) number of components

2.2   How agricultural ecosystems are developed from natural ecosystems.

2.21 Activity:

Prepare a table to show the difference between a farm and a natural ecosystem in the community:

Type of ecosystem	Natural	Farm
Closed/Open system Management Number of components		

2.22 Activity:

Examine and describe the growing of a single crop such as corn, peanut, or eggplant, as a system. Use the following diagram.

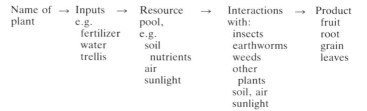

Name of →	Inputs →	Resource →	Interactions →	Product
plant	e.g.	pool,	with:	fruit
	fertilizer	e.g.	insects	root
	water	soil	earthworms	grain
	trellis	nutrients	weeds	leaves
		air	other	
		sunlight	plants	
			soil, air	
			sunlight	

Questions:

(a)   What will happen to the product if there is not enough control (inputs) over the farm ecosystem?

(b) Why does an agricultural ecosystem need more management than a natural ecosystem?

2.3   Food webs in the farm community

Activities:

2.31 Draw a food web present in the farm. Classify the organisms as producers, consumers, decomposers.

2.32 An investigation of a food web of a farm plant insect.

Materials: sample food web chart of common insects; collecting net; specimen bottles.

Procedure: Select one insect found in the local farm or garden. Perform a field investigation to identify dominant predators and parasites for nymph and adult. Collect insect predators from a quadrat. If there is an area where azolla grows, collect insect predators of rice leafhopper from one quadrat and compare the number of predator insects collected with that from the quadrat without azolla.

2.33 Population densities of farm/garden insects:

Materials: 30 × 30 cm board coated with sticky material

Procedure: Place the sticky board at a 45-degree angle at the base of a riceplant mound. Tap the base of the plant 5 times and count the number of insects that fall on the sticky board. Repeat this procedure on 3 randomly selected plants in one quadrat. Calculate population density based on number of plants in one quadrat, number of quadrats and area of field.

Questions: (a) What is the role of predator insects in a food web?
          (b) Which organism acts as a biological insecticide?
          (c) What is the effect of azolla on insect predators?
          (d) What happens to the food web in an abandoned farm?

2.4   Replacement of natural with artificial processes; e.g. artificial insemination, artificial hormones, fertilizers, artificial incubation, use of pesticides and herbicides, vaccines, control of temperature and daylength.

Activities:
2.41 Effect of varying amounts of fertilizers on plants, e.g. *pechay* (Chinese cabbage).

Procedure: Use varying amounts of compost, green manure, animal manure or chemical fertilizer in experimental plots. Compare rate of growth, size of leaves, and yield of experimental plants with untreated control plants over a period of 2 weeks.

2.42 Effect of growth hormones on rate of sprouting of vegetatively propagated plants.

Procedure: Soak the cut ends (below the nodes) of six stem and branch cuttings in rooting hormone before planting. Record rate of sprouting and compare with unsoaked cuttings.

2.43 List some of the things which are done in a farm community which change the balance of the natural ecosystem.

2.5   Effect of new farm technology on farm productivity

Activity: How to make a simple farm record and how to use it.

Procedure: Make a list of the number of crops in a planting season, total planting area, and total yield from a farm in the school or community. Record expenses and profits. Subtract total expenses from total profits to get the net profit. Report to class.
Use data obtained above as well as those obtained from interviews and questionnaires. List down which technology produces a higher yield: rainfed and transplanted or direct-seeded and irrigated. List down the advantages derived from tractors and mechanical threshing over carabao and manual threshing; use of compost and green manuring over expensive chemical fertilizers; use of biogas over electric energy. Determine the cost savings from the farm's financial record.

Questions: (a) What is the advantage of keeping a farm record?
(b) Which is the largest cash expenditure in a farmer's crop budget?

2.6   Points of entry for 2.1 to 2.5:

Ecosystems: Patterns within the environment
Components of an ecosystem
Interactions in an ecosystem; ecological interrelationships
Food web in a community
Population densities
Problems of man and his environment
Man challenges his environment

3. Structure and development of farm plants
3.1   Basic features of a farm plant

Activities:

3.11 Structure of a riceplant

Materials: young and mature riceplants; reference material on riceplant, e.g. *Science Principles in Rice Farming* by Vergara and Visperas

Procedure: Examine and sketch the parts of the plants. Label the following structures—leaf, blade, leaf veins, stem, sheath, seed, primary and other root structures, node, panicle, spikelet, spike. Examine a flowering panicle. Sketch and label the parts. Examine a seed. Sketch and label the following structures—awn, hull, endosperm, embryo.

Question: How is the number of spikelets related to the grain yield?

3.12 Stages in the development of a riceplant

Materials: rice plants approximately 4 weeks old, 8 weeks old, 12 weeks old (rice plants in vegetative, reproductive and ripening phases).

Procedure: Examine each of the 3 plants and record the observations in a chart.

Characteristics	4 wks old	8 wks old	12 wks old

No. of leaves
No. of tillers (new shoots)
No. of nodes
Average length of internode
(a) 1st internode (next
    to panicle)
(b) 4th or 5th internode
    (next to root)
Average height of plant
Average length of
  leaf blades
Leaf color			

Questions: What changes take place in (a) leaf size, (b) tiller numbers, (c) leaf numbers as the plant ages?
What things could affect the number of tillers that the plant develops?

3.2   Monocots and dicots

Activity: An introduction of community plants

Procedure: Select 5 plants from a nearby farm or garden and fill up a chart with the following headings—Plant number, Common name, Flower sketch, Height, Leaf shape, Growth pattern.

3.3   Life cycle of a plant

3.31 Activity: Stages of seed germination

Materials: 4 different seeds from the farm or garden; absorbent paper; large glass jar; marker.

Procedure: Line sides of glass jar with absorbent paper. Place each seed between glass wall and moist absorbent paper. Keep each seed apart. Record observations in a table and through illustration of one germinating seed.

Feature \ Seeds	A	B	C	D

No. of cotyledons
Cotyledons: fleshy or leafy?
Position of cotyledon after
  germination
Endosperm: present or
  absent?
First sign of germination
  noted (no. of days)
No. of leaves after 5 days
Length of epicotyl after
  5 days
Length of hypocotyl after
  5 days				

Question: Why must you keep seeds dry when storing them?

3.32 Activity: Life cycle of a farm plant

Procedure: Select one farm plant and sketch its life cycle. Identify its stages. Note the relation between length of life span and growth rate.

Question: What is an annual plant?

3.4   Points of entry for 3.1 to 3.3:

The seed plants: structure and development of flowering plants
Monocots and dicots

4. Limiting factors in the production of vegetables during the wet season (examples – tomatoes, corn, peanuts)

4.1   Activities:

4.11 Investigate rapid multiplication of insect pests, diseases, weeds.

4.12 Investigate effects of low light intensity, high night temperature, heavy rainfall, and flooding on tomatoes, cabbage, cucumber.

4.13 Investigate effects of wire trellis and plastic covers on quality of fruit yield in one experimental plot. Compare with control plot.

4.14 Investigate effect of water supply on yield, quality, and shelf life of fruit vegetables.

4.15 Investigate effect of degree of shading on the yield and quality of ginger.

Questions: What causes fruit-cracking of tomatoes? head-splitting of cabbage? rotting of cucumber?
What causes firmness, high sugar content, and good flavor in fruits and vegetables?

4.2   Points of entry:

Transport and osmoregulation in plants
Function of roots in plants
Ecological interrelationships
Factors that enhance spoilage

5. Farm animals as sources of food

The activities of 5.4, 5.8 and 5.9 can be done in collaboration with the teachers of the work experience classes/vocational classes.

5.1   Increasing livestock and poultry production through selective breeding, e.g. producing large eggs from small birds that eat less feed than larger birds; shortening the interval from oviposition to ovulation, thus increasing egg production.

5.2   Increasing animal sources of food by applying technology, e.g. sex removal in tilapia to produce male tilapias from females. (The male has more meat content.)

5.3   Reproductive period and life span of farm animals.

5.4   Increasing livestock and poultry production through improved feed and
           feeding practices. Use NSRC pamphlets on single cell protein to discuss
           how SCP is produced and utilized as poultry and hog feed.

           Questions: What can microorganisms produce from the farm wastes they
                      decompose?
                      How does SCP improve the diet of chickens?

5.5   Keeping farm animals free from parasitic worms

5.6   Energy substitutes for corn grain in poultry and swine rations, e.g. sorghum,
           sweet potato, coconut oil.

5.7   Improving digestibility of feed for ruminants, e.g. carabao, cattle, goat; how
           to make silage.

           Question: Why is silage easier to digest than rice straw?
                     What is the role of the bacteria?

5.8   Limitation to the use of rice bran as livestock feed

           Activity: Show how rice bran is often adulterated by some dealers with finely
                     ground rice hull which has very low feeding value. Discuss how nutrient
                     content in rice bran rapidly deteriorates in prolonged storage.

5.9   Increasing productivity and well-being of farm animals by reducing stressful
           conditions in the pen

           Activity:

5.91 Finding the pecking order of a flock by observing behavior of a flock of
     chicken at feeding time

           Questions: Which chickens are threatened most?
                      Which chicken feeds the most?

5.92 Test the effects of some factors such as beak trimming, toenail removal,
     decreasing group size, increasing space/hen, longer feeding trough,
     sanitation, on egg production.

           Question: Why would placing feeding troughs on the longer side of the pen
                     reduce aggressive behavior in chickens?

5.10   Instinctive behaviour in farm animals.

5.11   Activity: List down some instinctive behaviours of farm animals that allow
           them to live successfully in the farm.

           Question: Why do chickens bury their heads in their feathers during the
                     night?

5.12   Points of entry:

           Vertebrate and invertebrate animals: structural adaptations
           Patterns of inheritance: animal hybridization
           Ecological niche of animals

Animal life cycles
Microorganisms and their activities
Patterns of digestion in animals: ruminants and non-ruminants
Patterns of animal behaviour.

6.   Storage and preservation of harvest and food products

6.1   How to lengthen shelf life of seeds and other plant parts

6.11 Activity: How fruitflies locate their food

Procedure: Use an improvised apparatus to demonstrate how fruitflies locate their food.

Question: How will fruitflies be prevented from infesting fruits?

6.12 Activity: Preference test for rice weevils

Materials: grains of 3 rice varieties in small uncovered and marked plastic cages; 20 adult weevils, starved overnight; large screen cage.

Procedure: Place grains in plastic cages at random but forming a circle inside the screen cage. Release the weevils at the center of the circle. Count the number of weevils attracted to the test varieties 20 min., 40 min., 1 hour, and 2 hours after release. Repeat test 3 times to represent 4 trials. Cover plastic cages and count the weevils emerging on the 15th to 30th day from the first day of exposure to the insects. Record in a table.

Questions: Since larval and pupal development takes 30 days, what might have been the cause for early weevil emergence?
What is the increase in the original population?
Which rice variety is favoured by weevils?

6.2   Sanitation in the kitchen (or wherever food is stored and prepared)

Activity: List down sanitary practices in the kitchen.
List ways of handling food packed for school, the farm, or a picnic to avoid food poisoning. Visit the market, school cafeteria, stand, and list how raw and cooked food is improperly displayed, processed, handled, stored and sold.

Questions: How should salted foods be handled for storage?
Why should fried peanuts be sold in sealed plastic bags?
Why should cockroaches, flies, and rats be kept away from fruits and food?

6.3   Effect of microbial activity on food

Activity: List down kinds of food poisoning; discuss the methods of infection and corresponding prevention in farm products, dressed fowl, sausages, barbecued meat, canned sardine. Describe symptoms of food poisoning. Discuss why plant and animal products should be prepared under sanitary conditions.

Questions: Why is it not advisable to eat direct from the can?
Why is it advisable to wash off soil from fruits and vegetables before they are stored in the refrigerator?

6.4   Botulism—a common and dangerous type of food poisoning

           Activity: Use community resources (agencies and persons) to provide
           information on botulism, such as:

               (a) how the bacteria that produce the poison get into food;
               (b) where *Clostridrium botulinum* is found;
               (c) how these bacteria reproduce in improperly preserved food;
               (d) conditions suitable for botulinum poison production;
               (e) methods of prevention such as proper ways of preserving and canning
                   food in the home/community

6.5   Microbes as spoilage agents in farm produce and food products

           6.51 Activity: Perform simple experiments to investigate

               (a) influence of water in fruit, vegetable, meat and food on growth of
                   microbes (bacteria, yeasts, molds)
               (b) influence of water vapor in air on growth of bacteria and fungi on dry
                   food
               (c) temperature and growth of microbes on food; why food and farm
                   produce get spoiled in the refrigerator and cabinet
               (d) why most natural food get spoiled
               (e) effects of microbial activity on various farm products, e.g., tomato,
                   coconut meat, egg, fish, meat, cottage cheese, unpasteurized milk
                   (effects such as odor, color, texture)

           6.52 Activity: Preserving fresh eggs in oil

               Procedure: Heat vegetable oil slightly. Dip eggs in oil for 15 sec. Drain. Air-
                   dry for 20 min. Store. After 2 weeks, compare with control as to yolk
                   membrane, thickness of white, odor, stability of yolk.

               Questions: How did the oil preserve the egg?
                          What are the factors that favour growth of microorganisms in
                          food?
                          What is the effect of frequent power failure on foods in the
                          refrigerator/freezer?
                          How can the use of the refrigerator be made more effective in
                          food preservation?

6.6   How food preservation methods inhibit microbial activity

           Activities on food preservation 6.6–6.8 may be done in collaboration with
           the home economics teacher.

           6.61 Activity: How salt acts as a preservative

               Materials: Succulent plant, i.e. Caulerpa (green bulbous seaweed), tsp. salt

               Procedure: Place seaweed in two shallow containers. Sprinkle salt on one
                   seaweed. Observe what happens to the water in the seaweed. Compare
                   with unsalted seaweed.

           6.62 Activity: Test the effect of heat on egg white.

               Questions: How does salting minimize growth of bacteria in food?
                          How does heat preserve food?

6.7   Preservation of fruits and vegetables

6.71 Activity: Demonstrate a method for preserving fruits and vegetables in season, e.g. fermentation in brine-vinegar solution as in cucumber, papaya, carrot; in syrupy medium as in mango, breadfruit jam; drying as in banana chips; home canning and bottling as in tomato sauce; pasteurization as in coconut milk.

Evaluation will be through a food fair and such criteria as taste, flavor, texture, ease of preparation, technique, consumer demand, cost price.

Prepare a summary chart on fruit and vegetable preservation:

Fruit/ Vegetable	: Materials needed	: Preparation	: Actual procedure	: Packing

Question: Why are fermented fruits and vegetables often preferred over fresh ones?

6.8   Preservation of meat and animal products

Activity: Demonstrate a method of preserving meat and animal products, e.g. smoking – example, milkfish; salting—example, tilapia; drying—example, pork meat and bullfrog legs; fermenting—example, clam.

List down the procedure for each and share with classmates.

6.9   Additives for food processing and preservation

Activity: Additives in food labels
Procedure: Classify the additives indicated on the labels of various foodstuffs.
Consolidate in a chart:

Foodstuff	Additive	Function	Common usage	Class
E.g. "tocino"	saltpetre (potassium nitrate)	delays spoilage	curing	preservative

These classes may also be used:
leavening – ex., bread; thickener – ex., ice cream; emulsifier – ex., cake and frozen desserts; coloring – ex., *kare-kare*; flavoring – ex., beverages; nutrient supplement – ex., iodized salt and milk; bleaching – ex., white bread; clarifying – ex., gelatin and guava jelly.

Question: What is meant by "enriched rice"?

6.10   Points of entry for 6.1 to 6.9:

Patterns of animal behaviour
Structural adaptations of insects and rats
Life cycle of insects
How animals receive information

Asexual reproduction in plants
Nutrition and digestion
Economic importance of microorganisms
Economic importance of plants
Plasmolysis
Asexual reproduction in bacteria
Food preservation

7. Nutritional needs of adolescents

7.1   Nutrients in food

7.11 Activity: Indicator tests for nutrients in foodstuffs

Materials: Samples of various foodstuffs, including fresh fruits, raw egg white, fried peanuts; indicators – brown paper, iodine, Benedict's solution, dilute nitric acid; burner; test tubes and holder.

Procedure: Use the indicators to test for the presence of nutrients in the food samples. Nitric acid and Benedict's solution need a little heat to hasten reaction. Yellowish color is positive (+) for the acid and Benedict test; translucent spot is + for oil and black is + for starch.

Questions: Why is there a need to eat a variety of foodstuffs?
Is peanut a "junk" food? Explain.

7.2   Activities of the body and their nutrient needs

7.21 Activity: List and discuss metabolic processes, rapid growth and development that occur in boys and girls and the corresponding nutrients needed. Fill up table on *metabolic demands and nutrient needs of adolescents*:

Ex: Activities in body	Nutrients needed	Food source
Growth in length and weight of bone	Protein, calcium	Shellfish
Strengthening of bones	Calcium, vit. D	Anchovy (dilis)
Menstrual cycle	Iron	Phil. spinach (talinum)
Muscle development	Protein	Goby fry omelet

7.22 Activity: List external activities of boys and girls in one day and corresponding nutrients and food needed. Fill up chart. Example is shown below:

External activities	Nutrients needed	Food source
Work in farm	Starch, sugar	Cassava cake
Swimming, basketball	Starch, calcium, phosphorus	Shrimp ukoy
Reading, sewing	Vit. A; starch	Camote tops salad; rice

Question: What seems to be the nutrient needed to provide energy for external
activity?

7.23 Activity: List down common plants that can cure and prevent diseases common in the school/community such as skin disease and anemia

7.3   Points of entry:

Growth and development

8. Food and nutrition management

8.1   Nutrient conservation or deriving more nutrients from properly preserved and prepared food

Activity: Demonstrate ways of preparing food that retain nutrients. Prepare a list.

8.2   Food selection and budgeting or wise food selection for health and economy

Activities:

(a) Collect, preserve and display plant parts from the community that have nutritive and medicinal value.

(b) Use of kitchen, backyard, and spice garden to supply school and domestic needs. Example – pepper, ginger, onion.

(c) Use of neighborhood or barangay garden pool as a resource for fresh and cheap kitchen needs. Example – squash tops and flowers, guava.

(d) Use of recycled food. Ex. meat left-over omelet.

(e) Use of small fish instead of large, expensive ones. Ex. "talimusak" instead of pompano.

(f) Use of green leafy tops instead of pale vegetables like cabbage. Ex. *patola* tops, cassava tops, camote tops, stringbean tops.

(g) Use of fresh fruits in season and fruit juices instead of soft drinks and coffee.

(h) Use of brown rice instead of white, bran-less rice.

(i) Use of dried vegetable seeds instead of succulent vegetables like bottle gourd and radish that are sold for their weight but are low in nutrients.

A menu may be planned based on (a) to (i). A recipe may be prepared.

Question: Why are green leafy vegetables more nutritious than pale vegetables?

8.3   More nutrients for less cost

Activity: Show and tell how to make the most of some edible fruit, vegetable, weed, insect, mollusk, bird, and other animals in the community. Make a list of alternative, inexpensive protein sources. Then a menu using alternative sources of food. Look up recipes for alternate foods. Evaluation will be through a food fair. Prepare a similar list, recipe, and menu for alternative sources for other nutrients. Refer to examples:

Source	Recipe	Menu
Ex. Clam, frog's legs Cassava tops	Boil clam and cassava tops; cut fresh tomato over them and add fish sauce.	Fried frog's legs Clam with cassava tops and fish sauce

Examples of alternative sources for other nutrients:

Alternative source	Nutrient
Kutsarita tops and leaves	Vitamin A
Breadfruit	Vitamin B
Kulasiman (Purslane)	Vitamin C
Winged bean	Vitamin D
Phil. goby, *talimusak*	Calcium
Alamang (tiny shrimps)	Phosphorous
Pigweed (*kulitis*)	Ascorbic acid
Phil. spinach	Iron

Make a list of plants found in the community that can substitute for animal nutrients. Bring some to class for a show-and-tell.

Name of plant	Edible part	How propagated	Nutrient	How cooked

8.4   Alternative snacks for adolescents

Activity: Prepare a list of common junk foods and fad snacks that are sold in school and nearby stores and corresponding substitutes for more nutrients. From the list of better substitutes, plan a fun snack for the class.

Ex. Fad snack	Fun snack
Watermelon seeds Chips and Cola Fish ball	Yam ice cream Pressed sugar cane juice Porcupine ball (friend dilis) stuck into boiled quail eggs

8.5   Points of entry:
                    Nutrition and digestion
                    Nutrients in food
                    The human organism: reproductive system
                    Human ovarian cycle
                    Cell respiration and calories
                    Economic importance of plant and animal parts and products.

C. Discussion of Issues

26

Discussion of Issues

A. N. RAO

(a) Introduction

The chapters already included in this volume resulted from papers which were specially written for the conference on "Science and Technology Education and Future Human Needs" held in Bangalore in India. A particularly important part of the conference were the workshops into which participants from nearly eighty countries were divided. These brought together people with very diverse backgrounds and training. Their own experiences and immediate needs varied considerably, but they were united in their concern that food and agriculture was a topic of importance which needed a place within the curriculum.

Whereas the earlier papers express, on the whole, the experiences and opinions of individuals, reports on the discussions in the workshops present a consensus of opinion of the group as a whole, as well as identifying issues on which there were different opinions. These reports are therefore included here as an important contribution to further debate and a useful basis for follow-up meetings in different parts of the world which will inevitably take place in the years ahead.

Workshop	Chairman	Rapporteur
1. Food production	K. S. Krishna Sastry	M. Oakes
2. Food consumption	C. Hall	E. A. C. Okeke
3. Land use and food	Sheila Turner	Padma Asuri
4. Nutrition and health	Sheila Turner	Padma Asuri
5. Preservation and storage of food	E. Rugumayo	C. D. Yandila
6. Biotechnology	A. N. Rao	L. H. Grimme
7. Appropriate technology	K. S. Krishna Sastry	M. K. S. Rao
8. Food, agriculture and ethics	Cheong Siew Yoong	P. D. Pages
9. Educational aspects	A. J. Pritchard	C. H. Diong

(b) Food production

The first workshop was an opportunity for participants to explore not only the topic of food production, but also the philosophy underlying both the workshops and the conference as a whole. It was agreed that, in the first instance, vocational courses should not be considered, but the changes which might be appropriate in the basic syllabuses used in formal teaching. Many times throughout the discussion the question was raised what should be done about the existing science curriculum as a whole. It was agreed, however, that the main emphasis was that enrichment materials to include in the curriculum were being sought. The point was made that since education was expanding rapidly in the rural areas of many countries like India, there is a need to enrich the curriculum with materials relevant to daily life.

Running counter to this proposal, the fear was expressed that existing basic science courses wuld become diluted or diverted from their traditional objectives of exploring/discovering scientific principles. Reassurances were given that this was not the intention. Indeed, the intention was to create a curriculum that is more relevant to the needs of the children so that the numbers receiving a good scientific education are increased.

A point that was raised on more than one occasion was that rural children who experience the more advanced curriculum of the pure sciences are often those who leave the countryside and take with them their training. Enrichment must, therefore, be for **all** science courses so that **all** pupils will benefit. Maybe the ones who leave the countryside will return to it and enhance it in course of time.

The level of understanding need not be a problem. For instance, if a practical activity carried out by pupils results in an increased yield of crop, for example by addition of nitrogen to the soil, they will appreciate the significance of the result even though they do not understand the details of the principle. Understanding the details can follow at a later stage.

It is also worth bearing in mind that education does not begin or end in school. People who use technology in farming will have experienced to the full the relevance of much of that which we may wish to present to the children. Experienced farmers may appear to be old-fashioned and set in their way, but they also have a lot to lose if their crops fail. Nevertheless, with proper encouragement, they can appreciate the significance of the use of scientific methods to solve their problems. Examples were cited of such farmers using trial strips to ascertain which were the best crops or growing conditions for their farms.

The question of how to tackle the issues involved is an important one. For instance, should we confront children with the serious issues that face agriculture, and if so at which age/level? Or should we set out simply to create an awareness of the significance of agriculture, food production and its importance? The general feeling of the group was that the latter approach was the most appropriate as a starting point and with younger pupils. Issues could then be introduced to the older secondary pupils.

The participants divided into discussion groups to consider which aspects of food production, as an agricultural activity, were appropriate for inclusion in the school curriculum. Whereas some topics were new, there were others which already appear in existing syllabuses, but which might be given a new importance by emphasizing their relevance to food production. The discussion groups were asked to consider, first, whether the topics listed were valid subjects for inclusion in the school curriculum, and, secondly, at what level they were appropriate. It was agreed to restrict the levels to primary and secondary in the first instance. It was also agreed not to consider teaching methods at this stage, as this would be left to later workshops. The aspects of food production which were identified were as follows.

1. Farming is an enterprise

An important general point to be included in appropriate courses at all levels is that farming is an enterprise and profit is important. It can make an economic contribution and it is not simply a subsistence way of life.

2. The need

Another general point is that there is a need for increased food production and, depending upon the circumstances of the individual country, the priority may be (i) increased production, (ii) increased quality.

It was agreed that the topic of food production could be used as a starting point at many levels. For instance, the progression

$$\text{HOME} \rightarrow \text{COMMUNITY} \rightarrow \text{COUNTRY} \rightarrow \text{THE WORLD}$$

could be followed from the primary stage onwards. Primary pupils would begin with the familiar situation of the home, whilst upper secondary pupils could consider the issues associated with the country and the world.

3. The study of seeds of crop plants

This is a well-used topic, particularly in primary courses. Some countries have a largely rural population and schooling that does not extend far beyond the primary years. In such countries it would be valuable to introduce such pupils to the seeds of a range of locally available crop plants. The aim being to emphasize the differences between them; for instance during germination. Such an approach would begin the process of building up a body of knowledge and understanding appropriate to their future needs.

4. Factors required for growth and productivity

Topics (i)–(v) are likely to be included in many general science/biology courses. The points listed emphasize what was considered appropriate and relevant to the promotion of work related to food production.

(i)   Soil — top soil; good quality a prerequisite for increased yield.
      — soil erosion; prevention of.
      — soil microbes; their importance.
(ii) Plant nutrients — sixteen elements have been demonstrated to be essential for plant growth. If one or more of them is deficient, then yields are low. Such work should include organic and inorganic sources of nutrients and their availability to plants.
(iii) Water — essential compound for plant growth. Lack of water or deficiency of water results in a decrease of biomass production. Drought conditions lead to famine. Water requirements differ from crop to crop.
(iv) Temperature — crop distribution is related to temperature range.
(v)   Light — the efficient use of solar energy, e.g. the production of a crop leaf area that maximizes the utilization of the incident light.

All these points can be introduced in very general terms at the primary level. They can then be developed through lower secondary up to upper secondary where the detailed work will occur with necessary theoretical knowledge and laboratory demonstrations. They can be part of plant ecology and physiology. Crop plants of local importance should be selected and used as examples.

5. Variety

Hybrids and improved varieties are produced that enable the farmer to obtain: (i) increased yields and (ii) resistance to pests and diseases. These points can be illustrated using local vegetable and field crops. Reference to the Green Revolution and the significant costs of technology in these developments is important. To be introduced at upper secondary level, as part of plant genetics.

6. Pests and pest control

In an attempt to increase productivity the use of pesticides has become a practice. This leads to problems of residues and health hazards. The issues involved are many and the study of the concept of the ecosystem is important. To be introduced at secondary level.

7. *Yield*

Actual yields versus potential yields.

There are theoretical maximum yields, best practice yields and working yields of the average farmer. The differences between these are wide. Consequently, the point should be developed at secondary level so that the student begins to appreciate that significant progress is possible.

8. *Input/Output ratios*

These are important aspects when the farmer is striving to make a profit. They can be considered with reference to money and energy at secondary level.

9. *Animal production*

Whenever food animals are mentioned in syllabuses, particular emphasis should be given to the following:

Fisheries — Inland
                 Marine
                 Hatcheries
Cattle   — Milk breeds
                 Meat breeds
Poultry   — Broiler breeds
                 Egg breeds

A comparison of plant and animal food production and relative energy yields is also important. All these are topics at secondary levels.

Tertiary education

Although the discussion groups concentrated upon primary and secondary levels of schooling, comment had been made in the first workshop that tertiary education was an important factor. The point was made that if agricultural studies and biology exist side by side at the higher level it does not mean that the fundamental issues of agriculture will be covered in biology courses. Consequently, if biology has the higher status it is the future decision-makers who will miss the development of attitudes and the raising of awarness of agricultural issues. The suggestion was made that if university requirements influence what goes on elsewhere, then we should start with university courses.

Accordingly, topics covered at upper secondary and tertiary levels that are of significance with respect to food production were identified and are summarized in Fig. 1.

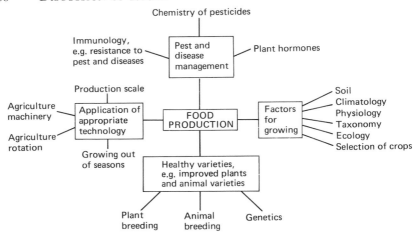

FIG. 1. Summary of topics covered at upper secondary and tertiary levels that are of significance with respect to food production.

(c) Food consumption

In this workshop the Chairman introduced the many aspects of food consumption, which is a large and complex topic. An outline illustrating the complexity is shown in Fig. 2 on page XX. To enable the discussion groups to structure their work, it was accepted that the aim of including this topic within education was to enable pupils as future parents to make wise decisions about what food they eat.

The objectives for the group were taken as the following: to identify factors which affect consumption of food in general, in other words why some countries or communities consume what they do; to identify factors which influence the individual's choice of food; to define clearly over-consumption and under-consumption and to identify the consequences of each; to highlight possible trends in future as they affect food consumption, for example the effect of biotechnology; to select appropriate content matter related to food consumption which is appropriate for different levels of education; to suggest approaches appropriate for the presentation of the subject matter at the various levels. The responses of the discussion groups to these issues were as follows.

1. General factors that affect food consumption in different countries

(i) Culture and tradition. People rear their children according to their own pattern of food consumption and this is passed on from generation to

generation with very strong associated beliefs and attitudes. Examples abound of food consumption based on cultural patterns and traditions. The Western communities are known to eat lots of sugar-based foods, while the Asian community favour highly spiced foods.

(ii) Geography/Climate. The geography and climatic conditions make natural demands on the human physiology. For instance, people who live in cold climates tend to drink hot beverages more often than those in warm climates, for understandable reasons.

(iii) Availability of food. People tend to consume what food they find available. You do not consume what is not available. Even if a Nigerian wanted to eat apples every day, he would not be able to because such foods are not available. In short, the ready availability of foods (fresh/preserved/processed) greatly influences the food consumed by any community.

(iv) Population. A large population reduces the amount of foods available for consumption. A highly populated country may resort to low-quality foods to ensure that every citizen is fed. A less populous country would have enough to choose from and may even import foods to increase the variety of food available for consumption.

(v) Religion. Religious traditions may forbid their followers from eating certain foods. Pork is not eaten by Hindus and Jews, for instance. This means that, even when pork is available, their religion does not permit its consumption.

2. Factors that influence individual's choice of food

The illustration below (Fig. 2) indicates those factors that were identified.

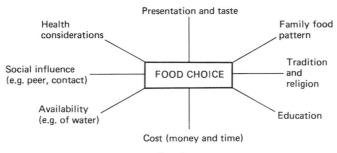

FIG. 2.

Each of these factors can be illustrated with examples. For example, some people eat certain foods because their peers eat them; while someone may prefer one food to another because through education he has recognized the nutritional value of that food.

3. Consequences of consumption

In looking at the consequences, the group considered over-consumption and under-consumption. The former relates to eating more than the body actually needs in carbohydrates, proteins, fats or vitamins, and can result in obesity, coronary heart disease, high blood pressure, strokes, etc., and tends to be prevalent in developed countries where there is much food. Under-consumption leads to anaemia, protein energy malnutrition, rickets blindness, intestinal disorders, etc., and these are prevalent in many developing countries.

4. The future

It is necessary to consider the use of biotechnology and genetic engineering to produce not just more foods, but food of varying taste and quality. Meat analogues are examples of such biotechnologically produced foods. Meat analogues are derived from textured vegetable proteins (t.v.p.) such as soya, groundnuts, pulses, etc. The amino acids lysine and methionine are added to raise them to the level of Class I protein. In looking to the future, children in upper secondary school need to be introduced to the influence of biotechnology on food production, which will ultimately affect food consumption. The advantages of meat analogues can be emphasized, namely longer storage life and less fuel needed for cooking. It is hoped that developing the right attitude to such foods will improve food consumption habits of children, the parents of tomorrow.

5. Food consumption in the science curriculum

The group recognized the importance of being aware of the consequences of inappropriate food consumption and agreed that the topic should certainly be an element in education at all levels — primary, secondary and tertiary.

At the primary level, it was suggested that the relationship between what we eat and how healthy we are should be stressed, together with a general treatment of the consequences of over-eating and under-eating. The use of a food diary was advocated as a way for pupils to become more aware of what they actually eat. This can lead to comparisons of what is eaten by different individuals, comparing perhaps what is eaten in other countries, noting cultural, geographical, climatic influences on choice. Simple analyses of what various meals contain and examination of some processed foods can be worthwhile exercises, as can a visit to the market place to see what foods are available.

The secondary school biology curricula of several countries cover many aspects of food. Often what was found missing was a necessary emphasis on the link between food consumed and the health of individuals. This extra dimension — awareness of conditions governing food choices including socio-economic factors, the effect of biotechnology, etc. — could be included without major syllabus revision. To do this, therefore, the following topics need to be included under the unit food/diet in the secondary school biology syllabus.

  (a) Food habits of individuals.
  (b) Factors affecting food consumption (in general and for individuals).
  (c) Consequences of consumption (over- and under-consumption).
  (d) Balanced diet (illustrated with common foods in the locality).
  (e) Effect of biotechnology with various examples of products.
  (f) Responsibilities of consumers (parents, pupils), policy makers/ authorities, manufacturers in ensuring correct food consumption.

Teaching strategies at the secondary level might include the following:

  (a) Formal teaching (didactic approach) using as many examples as possible to bring home to the children the relationship between food eaters and maintenance of good health.
  (b) Investigatory approaches such as in the building up of statistics on national consumption of certain foods; sugar and incidence of for example, diseases such as heart diseases/diabetes.
  (c) Talks by experts in nutrition and food processing and by medical doctors.
  (d) Use of supplementary reading materials relating to foods (in general), and health.
  (e) Problem-solving approach, creating hypothetical situations where for example individuals have got to demonstrate ability to choose rationally from given foods, and justify their choice. Case studies fall in this approach.
  (f) Use of posters, photographs that can influence attitudes of pupils to food consumption and health.
  (g) Simulation exercises.
  (h) Laboratory investigations, for example, the classification of foods according to calorific values.
  (i) Field trips to food processing industries and centres using bio-technology for food production.
  (j) Use of films and tape/slide presentations.

At the tertiary level, the topics can be treated in biological sciences or agricultural sciences. While it is important to direct the attention of the students to the relationship between food consumption and health, much emphasis would go to in-depth laboratory and problem-centred studies.

These include:

(a) Case studies of communities/family food consumption to establish patterns.
(b) Surveys of the incidence of common diseases in a community and establishing possible correlation between food consumption and health.
(c) Food analysis — fresh and processed foods.

Teaching strategy would be more of discovery approach rather than didactic. The discovery may be via experimental studies, or documented/reference materials. A talk by a biotechnologist followed by a factory visit could be most informative, highlighting the future trends in food production which ultimately will influence food consumption.

(d) Land use and food

In her introduction the chairman reminded the group about the interrelationship between the teacher and the pupil, the teacher and materials, and the pupil and the materials.

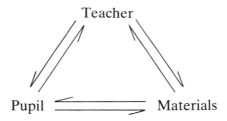

She emphasized that this relationship should be kept in view while planning resource materials for teaching. Learning in science calls for the transfer of ideas/concepts to the pupil. It also includes thinking about developing skills and attitudes such as curiosity, open-mindedness, sensitivity to living things. The aesthetic side of science should also not be forgotten.

In this workshop, speakers from the Land, Water and Mineral Resources group joined the Food and Agriculture group for discussion about ways in which the topics of soil, irrigation and land rehabilitation can be introduced to students.

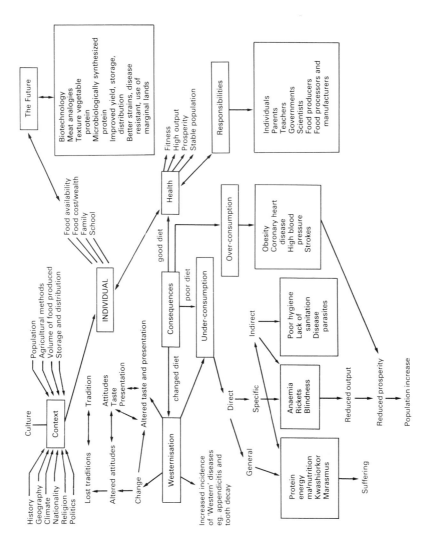

Fig. 3. Food consumption — outline analysis of the topic

Soil

This is an appropriate topic for primary schools. It can be taught through practical experiences using local types of soil. The importance of practical and observational activities was stressed. The work could form a foundation for ideas about conservation — for example, causes of erosion and desertification. At the secondary level appropriate aspects are (a) rock and soil; (b) different kinds of soil; (c) soil plant growth; and (d) conservation of soil resources. Whilst at the tertiary level appropriate aspects include (a) chemical, physical, microbiological properties; (b) taxonomy and mapping; (c) agricultural uses; (d) engineering uses; (e) biological implications; (f) conservation; and (g) soil ecosystem.

The value of soil as a linking topic for cross-curricular work was stressed. For instance, it could be used to integrate geography, biology and chemistry.

Irrigation

Water is an important input and is increasingly becoming a problematic resource as its availability is restricted. How to save and restrict its use and how to recycle for agricultural use are important topics. Students can be taught about "water" through involvement in local projects. Alternatively, case studies and simulations can be used to demonstrate how society and science interact. For instance, a case study on farmers of semi-arid areas opting for drip irrigation.

Land rehabilitation

Mining was used as an example to illustrate this topic. It was seen as a means of raising issues that relate to the role of science and technology in society.

(e) **Nutrition and health**

This workshop was a joint one with the Health group. Dr Srikantia of the University of Mysore gave a brief introduction to the topic of nutrition. The workshop was then divided into four groups which looked at approaches to teaching nutrition in the four areas of education.

I.   Primary schools.
II. Secondary schools.
III. Teacher education.
IV. Extension education.

Introduction

"We can give messages but how does one change attitudes and practices?" — Dr Srikantia.

The subject of nutrition and health involves complex ideas and there is considerable disagreement about what should be included in "nutrition education". There is agreement that it is important! Before we teach people about why certain foods should be eaten we must as individuals and teachers, understand what we eat and the constraints that operate in our choice of food — which include ethical, social, psychological and economic constraints. Individuals must also think in terms of food, not nutrients, when they produce, purchase or process foods.

In this introduction, Dr Srikantia suggested that "good nutrition is essential for good health" — in educational terms we need to define what is meant by "good health"! Is it just absence of disease?

As scientists we are aware that all nutrients come from "diets" which include water. We recognize that:

1. Foods differ in their nutrient content.
2. Many different combinations of food items can provide balanced diets.
3. Foods of animal origin — except milk — are not absolutely necessary for a healthy diet.
4. Satisfactory diets have two important dimensions, namely quantity and quality; if either is unsatisfactory, disease can result.
5. There are various grades of malnutrition with different health connotation — overeating can be as much of a health hazard as undereating.
6. The concept of basic food groups has its uses, but its applications in the formation of basic diets has its limitations.

There are also complex issues which teachers, teacher educators and older secondary school pupils and students need to consider. In an earlier workshop we looked at food production. Adequate food production in a country does not necessarily guarantee good nutrition for all — factors such as employment, status and purchasing power are also important. Food consumption is not the only factor which determines nutritional status. Non-food items including culture bound feeding practices during health and sickness; family size; lack of appropriate medical care, these are all important. Malnutrition is usually an expression of socio-economic interaction and solutions to the problems of malnutrition lie in correcting imbalances in these. At a basic level the solution of malnutrition is multifaceted. Education has a central role to play. Nutrition programmes and programmes involving, for example, control of infection also make a contribution.

It is difficult to demonstrate the effect of factors leading to malnutrition — it is after all impossible to demonstrate these experimentally in human beings!

Teaching at the primary school level

As stated in the introduction, nutrition is a complex and abstract concept involving ideas about diet and nutrients in the diet. Many adults find it difficult to understand these concepts and for young children it is impossible. Young children are not interested in nutrition. They are concerned with their own rumbling tummy and with the *things* they eat.

In teaching about nutrition we therefore have to start with things that children know about, and can handle and experiment with. Young children need *basic* simple, direct experience which will help them build up a "store" of concepts which will lead to understanding of the more complex issues later in life. They obtain these experiences at home, in their daily play and occupation. They can also be given experiences at school. Children can talk about these experiences and such discussion can lead to greater understanding. It is not necessary to relate only to what the children themselves eat. Their curiosity can be stimulated by the unusual, they can work with animals or plants in the very simple terms of "what happens if . . ." experiments. They are bound to get results which they learn to interpret.

A germinating bean brings its seed leaves (cotyledons) above the ground.

> "What happens if you pluck these off?"
> "What happens if you pluck only one off?"
> "What happens to the bean you leave alone?"

With help, children can both suggest and *do* experiments of this type and see what happens. In this case, the beans provide the answer to the questions asked. In talking about the results children (or the teacher) may well bring in the idea that cotyledons are a store of food. They will appreciate that this food is necessary for the young plant; and *we* eat the insides of the beans!

A further example could be cited here, although such activities could not normally be attempted on ethical grounds. In a classroom in Tanzania children fed their young chickens on different foods. Clear results emerged after a few days. The chicks were separated and marked for recognition, so they could be weighed daily and their growth recorded. Some chicks were fed on pure starch (cassava flour), others on maize bran and a third group on "wholesome" chicken feed. (The wholesomeness here was an act of faith.)

It soon became very clear that the "starchy chicks" did not grow well. The maize bran chicks grew fast in size and weight, but developed leg trouble. The "wholesome" chicks thrived — and so did the others when they were given proper chicken feed after a few days.

A rather complicated event became a comprehensible lesson for these children. Of course they could not understand the biochemical and metabolic processes involved, but they *did* establish a relation between the kinds of food and growth (or health) of these chickens. First-hand experience is of vital importance. It leads to children asking questions and this means they *want to know*. It also prepares the way for further learning based on understanding.

Secondary education (12–16 years)

Nutrition features as a significant element in biology and related science courses. The question is what and how should aspects be emphasized in order to create the awareness of human nutrition that we are seeking. Home economics courses are also addressing the same problem and within a school it would be helpful for work on nutrition to be co-ordinated.

In biology and similar courses nutrition is encountered mainly through work on food compounds (carbohydrates, vitamins, etc.) and the balance of such compounds in the diet. Examples include diet, food tests, work/ exercise, respiration, photosynthesis, digestion, food storage, growth, anabolism/catabolism. Thus there are many occasions for communicating information that could lead to heightened awareness of the issues.

Appropriate methods for introducing materials that could achieve this include the following.

Anecdotal evidence — When teacher embellishes his/her work with anecdotes, they make a significant impact because they are particular to that teacher. For instance, a teacher may comment upon evidence obtained from talking to the local doctor or dentist about the effects of nutritional deficiencies to be seen in the local community.

Investigations — Foods at home can be audited for energy or fibre content. Packaged foods can be studied for the information that can be obtained from the labels; for example, the ingredients and the relative amounts of each ingredient.

In addition, there are less commonly used methods such as *guided discussion, role play, data analysis* and *problem solving*. These methods are useful for they allow student to interact with the issues rather than being a passive recipient of information.

For all these approaches information can be conveyed through photographs, models, slides, tape/slide presentations and visits to markets and catering establishments.

What aspects of nutrition would you include in teacher education?

The group decided to define aspects in a wide sense (including awareness and attitudes) and tried to focus on teachers at the *primary education level*, who are limited in their own science education (it was even said that many non-science teachers are teaching science courses) and on teachers of the *secondary level*, who are scientifically trained. The objectives of a nutrition education curriculum at *primary level* cannot be implemented simply by taking nutrition education as an isolated teaching subject as such. It was felt that in all parts of a curriculum, where biology is to be taught, biological principles can be used for nutrition education. It was argued that the biology part of a curriculum should be used to inform about biological principles for teacher education, students and pupils. We thought about what pupils of the age 5–11 years should know in nutrition and what is expected as a "minimum knowledge" in nutrition (Badran *et al.*, see page 137) and what kind of attitudes should be achieved.

The objectives of nutrition education in primary schools were defined by Devadas (1985):

— To enable children and their parents to understand that proper nutrition is essential for good health and normal physical and mental development.
— To teach children about the selection, preparation, conservation and consumption of good quality foods.
— To help children develop desirable practices in relation to food, hygiene and environmental sanitation.

How can one realize the above and what experiences do primary school teachers need? Knowledge? Skills? Attitudes? Strategies? For the knowledge sector emphasis should be given to issues which are within the normal daily life experience of the children. These issues could be "healthy food" (balanced and uncontaminated diets) — food groups, local foods — food values — food chains — eating habits.

Among the subjects included in food and nutrition education Kiyimba (1985) has included:

— How to get food; growing food; food as a source for living.
— Basic methods of cookery (advantages and disadvantages of these methods). Methods of food preservation.
— The choice and cost of foods in different seasons with emphasis on local foods.

— The planning, preparation and serving of a day's balanced diet for the family.
— Special diets for infants, sick and old people, and on various occasions.
— Economy in the kitchen — care and use of leftovers.

Student teachers should be taught in the way we all would like them to teach, that is by integrating theory with practice based on local situations.

Nutrition education of teachers for *secondary education* is, in respect to the issues to be taught, not essentially different, but the qualitative and quantitative aspects of food (production, processing, consumption and nutrition) can be handled as "science and technology education". The school curriculum in which this can happen involves home economics, domestic science (both often restricted to girls' science education) or biology and chemistry.

The content of nutrition education should stress emphasis on the needs of the growing children themselves but also on those of the future homemakers. Moreover, particular concern should be paid to concepts of "healthy foods", in order to encourage a broad understanding of views on "balanced diets" in chemical terms (chemically balanced diets with its very limited approach towards health, contamination and food chains, etc.).

The transfer of scientific knowledge in food production and nutrition should not only stress how to feed children but also to implement good food habits. Science teaching should promote an understanding of science as a continually developing framework of ideas, and so nutrition education should not be dogmatic in saying what a "balanced diet" is. It should show the dynamics of the development of knowledge in nutrition to enable the children to judge for themselves and to educate for free choice and to realize the defined (limited) role science plays in terms of nutrition. With this it should be possible to rationalize nutritional matters and to distinguish judgements based on values, economy, morality, religion, etc.

The topic "right food habits" should be a subject of exploring. It might offer the opportunity to realize that the function of food habits not only relies on individual eating behaviours, but also be based on social impacts (McDonaldisation, Cocacolonialisation, etc.). Parry and Cursiter (1985) have demonstrated that exploring provides a valuable and interesting experience for teacher and students ("learning by doing").

Extension education

This group agreed that the target group for extension education should be rural adults, usually from marginal and small town families, and the family was the main goal.

The aims of such education were two-fold: to promote awareness of the importance of food and its nutritional value; to promote awareness of the various needs of different members of families. It was also hoped that it would encourage self-reliance. It was agreed that the main topics to include in such adult education programmes were:

— Role of safe water.
— Relation of food to health.
— Food values — traditional and the contribution to body's growth.
— Production of nutritionally desirable foods, crop planning.
— Postharvesting, hygiene, contamination, spoilage and promotion.
— Deficiency diseases and related problems. Malnutrition — causes, prevention.
— Meal planning.
— Diet, traditional diet, special diet.
— Food adulterants — additives.

It was also agreed that the methods would need to be designed after making a local appraisal of the situation and the course should be paced according to the audiences' needs. It was considered particularly important that women should be consulted in the planning. Appropriate activities could include simulated games, working together on field trips, undertaking joint projects, role-playing demonstrations, and arranging displays.

The strategies should include establishing links with local schools, involving the teachers as trainers, and also involving local organizations such as churches and temples as centres of learning. It was realized that there were bound to be problems associated with funding, the time factor, evaluation and involving women.

(f) Preservation and storage of food

Many Third World countries have in recent years experienced food shortages to varying degrees. One of the causes of food shortages in these countries is the loss of food through lack of proper and adequate facilities for preservation and storage after harvest. Estimates by the FAO of the amount of food lost ranges between 35 and 50% of all the food produced.

Schools and higher educational institutions have a role to play in sensitizing the children and students to the issues of food preservation and storage. Moreover, to have a greater impact, extension workers should include in their programmes those issues relevant to this important subject of preserving and storing food.

In this workshop we dealt with methods and techniques of food preservation and storage, and the various strategies considered appropriate for primary, secondary and tertiary levels of education, as well as the non-formal education sector.

The topics to be considered were:

1. Food losses and their causes.
2. Storage structures and systems.
3. Pest control methods — physical, chemical, biological and the underlying scientific principles.
4. Sources of pollution — pesticides (xenobiotics) cycle, residues and control.
5. Selective protectants, comparative biology, morphology, (structural), biochemistry (physiology) and immunology (pathology).

Primary school level

The general topics listed above should be dealt with according to the level of understanding of primary school children. Concepts and principles of food preservation and storage should be treated empirically by demonstration, observation and experiment. Teaching strategies might include the following:

— Because young children tend to learn new concepts and generalizations through activities of observation, experimentation, model building, handling objects, and by question-and-answer techniques, the entire unit should be activity based.
— The teacher may ask questions such as "Why do we refrigerate, can or bottle?" or, in rural areas, "Why do we dry, salt or store in barns?"
— Work should start by looking at food intake in the home. What did you eat today? Was it fresh? Did it come from a can, packet or a refrigerator?
— Children can visit markets or shops to examine the variety of produce and the range of preservation techniques. They might also be able to visit canning or bottling plants, etc.
— An awareness of the problems and methods of other countries should also be promoted and this could lead to activities such as drawing, model making or writing.
— Classroom activitites could also include simple techniques of *cooking, drying, salting, pickling*, etc. and the children could be encouraged to observe and record the changes in food so treated.
— Comparisons could be made between fresh and canned or dried food. How do they differ in appearance and taste? Such exercises could be carried out blindfold leading again to recording observations.
— Simple experiments illustrating the need for preservation techniques could be carried out.
— Fruit or bread could be left to go mouldy or meat left to attract flies —

how long is it before the food becomes inedible? Does cooked food or food processed in other ways last longer?

— Canned, dried and imported foods should be examined. How long ago was the fruit picked or the sheep killed? Why is it still fresh and not rotten? How was it preserved and transported?

— Here could also be introduced the fact that we like to eat things out of season.

— The effects of processing on the eating habits of the population could be studied — compare with other countries or previous generations. How have modern techniques shaped our lives, not only in terms of our diet, but also in terms of how often we need to go shopping, etc?

— Simple *models* could be made of storage huts, etc., from other countries — how well do they keep rats or mice out? This could be looked at by putting the models in cages of mice. Similar methods could compare sacks, boxes, cans, etc., as storage methods.

— The organization of shops and larders could be studied. Foods in cans placed next to soap for example do not pick up the smell or taste, whereas food in boxes do. This sort of exercise can lead to classifying activities.

— Some simple economic considerations could be examined with regard to fresh and packaged food and also out of season foods, etc., why are canned pears or out of season tomatoes more expensive than the in-season fresh variety?

— Cans and packages could be looked at for date stamping — how long will the food keep? Labels could be studied to look at the ingredients and preserving agents. Many preserved foods will contain sugar, salt, vinegar or some similar agents thereby linking back to methods of preservation.

— The basic advantages and disadvantages of various techniques of food preservation and storage can be discussed. Techniques that are cheaper and suitable for a particular community can also be encouraged.

The major aims of the activities at the primary level are as follows:

1. To satisfy the natural curiosity of young children.

2. To introduce young children to concepts and principles associated with food storage and preservation upon which future study and inquiry at the secondary level will be based.

3. To let the children carry out simple experiments and projects associated with food preservation and storage.

Secondary school level

The general topics introduced at primary level would be appropriate at the secondary level, but treated in a more sophisticated way. The major aims of activities at this level should include:

1. To provide pupils with skills in food preservation and storage commonly used in their regions and cultures.
2. To inform the pupils of different ways of food preservation and storage in different regions of the world.
3. To train pupils in appropriate modern food preparation and storage.
4. To acquaint pupils with new techniques of food preservation and storage as a preparation for advanced studies at tertiary level.

It was realized that we should start with traditional methods when introducing the subject. In India, for example, the traditional methods include the use of astrology: for astrological reasons, some farmers do not harvest during certain periods known as Sarvne because they are supposed to lead to problems and, in consequence, during the harvest periods themselves less care is taken since it is expected that the problems have been avoided!

It is, of course, essential to cover scientific principles in the teaching so that understanding could lead to a better use of scientific methods in the future. But it is not sufficient merely to state the bare essential of a topic and expect the pupils to appreciate their significance. Practical examples, either demonstrated by the teacher or better carried out by the pupils themselves, are essential to illustrate the significance of the scientific principles in the processes of preservation and storage.

It is unlikely that refrigeration, freezers, freeze-dried and irradiated foods will be available in many developing countries. Nevertheless, it was considered that information relating to such methods should be given as the pupils are being prepared for what lies in the future. If a process or device is introduced, its acceptance by the community may take place much more rapidly because of the previous reference to it. For instance, a very cheap refrigerator has recently been developed in Zambia and, if it proves to be successful, its popularity may spread very quickly.

The group also discussed new foods. For instance, the potato is being grown in India and it is the crop which is increasing most rapidly. If grown in warm parts of the country, storage by traditional UK methods will not be satisfactory as they are based on low temperatures. Maybe they will have to be stored as the sweet potato is stored in Zambia under a layer of organic matter, which insulates the heat and produces carbon dioxide to inhibit the growth of pests.

One way of improving the nutrition of an area is to improve the food supply of farm animals. In this context the concept of silage could be developed so that the minds of students are prepared for its acceptance at a later date. In the same context work can be carried out on fodder trees which are often cultivated for silage production.

Tertiary level

This level includes three categories: teacher training; pre-university; university. The common topics discussed in the primary and secondary levels could be discussed at this level but with more details given. More specific topics are listed below.

For teacher training:

(a) Pre-harvest biology and prophylaxis.
(b) Thrashing and solar drying.
(c) Pest control.
(d) Packaging and containers for storage.
(e) Disinfestation and fumigation techniques.
(f) Fruit and vegetable preservation processes.
(g) Seed treatment, protection and processing.

For pre-university (post-harvest technology courses):

(a) Biosciences (entomology, microbiology, nutrition, etc.).
(b) Principles and processes.
(c) Cold and cool storage: Principles, design and operation.

For university course in food science and technology:

(a) Safety, toxicology and behavioural assay.
(b) Organic chemistry of pesticide, and semi-chemicals.
(c) Pest management, protectants, storage and food security systems.
(d) Cereal science and postharvest technology.
(e) Fumigation science and controlled atmosphere technology.
(f) Radiation, preservation and biophysics.

At the tertiary level, a research project can be used in the teaching: the best way to get knowledge across in the area of food preservation and storage is by example. For example, an investigation of maize storage by small farmers, finding the relationship between moisture content and susceptibility to infection, relating this to harvesting techniques and storage methods. Such practical approaches do not add to the existing science syllabus, but enable science techniques to be learnt through relevant examples.

Non-formal level

It was identified that the following should be the clientele for non-formal educational programmes: those who have foods to preserve; those who do not have the opportunity for formal education, but need to know about post-harvest technology; those who need to update their knowledge; community leaders; extension workers, including health workers and teachers. The need of this group is knowledge on proper applications of technology and the skills to take advantage of them. It must also be realised that, of course, they also have the need for the necessary equipment and facilities and the economic capability to use them.

The educational approaches in educating this group need also to be non-formal. Efforts should be made to meet the actual groups and should not be confined to only a few teachers. Methods will involve TV and radio, informal discussions, seminars, exposures during field trips and so on.

(g) Biotechnology

After a brief introduction of the subject, the following topics were suggested for consideration for different levels of education.

At primary level, familiarization with bread, curds, yoghurt, cheese, sauces; and with man-made processed foods. At the secondary level, respiration and fermentation; yeasts; useful bacteria; hybridization; cytological implications. The suggestions for tertiary and post-graduate research were as follows:

Tertiary	Postgraduate research
1. Cytology, genetics, crop plants, animals.	1. Plant mass production–forestry, agriculture (tissue culture).
2. Principles of microbiology and plant tissue culture.	2. Protoplast fusion.
3. New methods in plant breeding.	3. Gene transfer and expression.
4. Economic implications of biotechnology (economic botany, biology).	4. Pest and disease control methods through gene manipulation.
5. Genetic resources.	
6. Starch — protein conversion. Yeasts, *Aspergillus*.	

Biotechnology was regarded as a major business opportunity which over the past 10 years has grown very rapidly. Although most biotechnology companies have targeted the pharmaceutical market (because the newly developed technologies are immediately applicable for products that can be used for maintenance of health or treatment of disease) the application of biotechnological processes in the agricultural field is fully developing at the research stage.

Concerns were expressed (a) on the socio-economic impact of these techniques, which needs strategic thinking in setting goals, and (b) on the risk of the privatization of biotechnology, which might restrict the free development of knowledge in this field creating dependence and restriction.

It was agreed that very little biotechnology has yet come into teaching and the workshop considered the possibilities at different levels.

Biotechnology at the primary level

It was agreed that, at this level, no "biotechnology" in its modern technique sense could be introduced, but the concepts already existing in "old biotechnologies" should be.

Plant propagation will lay the groundwork for a later understanding of the use and purpose of tissue cultures. Simple experiments mostly carried out in the home are exemplified by growing seeds (in glass tumblers with filter papers): what can grow (seeds, cuttings, "eyes" of potatoes, etc.); variability in growth of seeds; hydroponics, leading to various plant nutrients.

Common fermented foods could offer a good entrée into larger principles of biotechnology. Scientific thinking could be grown through doing and spectating. Simple examples are *making of bread* by leavening, the setting of *milk* to *yoghurt* or *curds,* and the slow fermentation of fruit juices to *wine* or *vinegar.* Simple changes in temperature, acidity, time, salt level, sugar level, and reassessing of observations offer wide scope for scientific understanding.

Seed and animal variation offers a means to background development for a later appreciation of artificial insemination, plant breeding and so on. Experiences which could be drawn on include farm familiarity with cows, sheep, and chicken in rural areas; keeping pets at home and at school; maintaining school gardens, indoors if necessary; visits to zoos and botanical gardens to see diversity.

The primary level is felt to be too early for a direct appreciation of the concepts of genetic engineering. Many of the "experiments" suggested above would develop attitudes and a knowledge base that would lead quite naturally to grappling with what genetic engineering can do, if not why.

Biotechnology at the secondary level

It was felt desirable to introduce the concept of biotechnology into the secondary schools. The aim of this introduction is to prepare students to understand biotechnology and its application in their adult life. More specifically, it is to develop the students' intellectual tools to appreciate the effects of modern biotechnology, at high levels, for example, gene transfer.

Biotechnology should not be viewed in a narrow sense at the secondary school level. The approach to its study should be to demonstrate that man can manipulate living processes through technology by showing various examples.

(a) Bread fermentation.
(b) Grafting.
(c) Hybridization.
(d) Animal breeding.
(e) Simple enzyme technology.

Other examples can be added, but they ought to be simple and demonstrable in the schools or experienced in their daily lives. It must, however, be accepted that teachers experience difficulty teaching biotechnology in schools, particularly when expectations are at a sophisticated level. These difficulties are that it is multidisciplinary (integrated science is best for introducing it); it demands a high level of understanding; the practical work requires high level skills and time is short and experiments can be expensive; above all, the teachers' background knowledge is often poor.

Biotechnology at the tertiary level

At the tertiary level full respect has to be given to biotechnology as "the integrated use of biochemistry, microbiology, cell biology and chemical engineering" in order to achieve the technological application of the capacities of microbes, cell cultures and tissue cultures. Biotechnology also involves knowledge and skills in genetic engineering, gene splicing techniques, rDNA cloning and immunological procedures.

This high technology needs a high capital growth industry which favours the further development in already developed countries. Private industries are getting involved in these upcoming techniques, making it possible that advances in biotechnology will not be freely accessible to the scientific community.

On the other hand, developing countries with their enormous genetic resources of plants and animals will foreseeably provide the raw material for this fast growing exploitation of gene potentials by Western industries without much financial gain.

Education and training in biotechnology could increase the availability of knowledge in techniques, and benefits might come out also for developing countries in the long term.

Target groups for education and training would include students who are going to be "professionals" (biologists, microbiologists, chemists, biochemists and agriculturists) as well as non-professionals (general science and biology students).

Topics identified to be included in a science teaching curriculum in biotechnology are:

(a) Principal techniques in microbiology including fermentation processes.
(b) Principal techniques in cell, tissue and organ culture.
(c) Principal techniques in cell fusion and gene insertion procedures.
(d) Principal biochemical techniques with proteins (enzyme technology).
(e) Principal techniques in gene splicing.
(f) Principal techniques of immunology.

This techniques-related approach should be embedded in a knowledge of organisms and life processes from the molecular and cellular levels through organs and organisms to populations and ecosystems.

A supporting knowledge of chemistry, physics and mathematics, including statistics and computer training is essential in most areas of biotechnology.

Likely developments in food and agriculture are related to reproduction biology (*in vitro* fertilization) and biological pest control. The educational process in the tertiary level should also be directed to increase the awareness among students of the need to maintain an open attitude towards economic management and research aspects, as well as to social implications of the technological developments.

Research and development thrust in biotechnology

The future curricula at primary, secondary and tertiary levels of education will provide young scientific research workers with adequate background to start research on relevant problems. It was identified that propagation of prospective plants, cloning for economic products, reactor design for culturing, production of biomass and primary metabolites, animal, cell and tissue culture development are most important fields of emerging "biotechnology". Priorities in these areas are as follows:

(i) *Propagation*: Tomato, cassava, maize, triticale, sugarcane and others.
(ii) *Cloning*: (a) Oil palm, cocoa, spices. (b) Cells of plants and microbes for secondary metabolites — flavour, enzymes, bioactive compounds.

(iii)   *Reactor design*: Continuous culture, downstream processes.

(iv)   *Primary metabolites and biomass production*: Plant cell, tissue and organ culture, animal cell and tissue culture developments.

(v)   *Supporting biotechnologies*: Anther culture, embryoid genesis, DNA engineering, monoclonal antibodies, protoplast/microcallus.

(vi)   *Research projects for development*:
   (a) Interaction of food constituents in cell biology, tissue and organ systems, cell behaviour and neuro-physiology.
   (b) Photo-autotrophic cell culture for production of primary products — food, feed, energy, bioactive industrial products, vitamins, enzymes, flavours, colours and others.
   (c) New requirements of downstream processes in biotechnology of submerged fermentations, live cell mass, viable biomass and biopesticides.
   (d) Biosynthesis and biotechnologies of meat analogues from oil seeds, cell cultures and tissue cultures.
   (e) Greenhouse technologies for plantation crops, spices, plant pesticides and plant drugs.

(b) Appropriate technology

Technology transfer in agriculture is a very complex and exciting process. It involves decision-making by millions of farm families spread over large areas. This is the basic difference between technology transfer in industry and in agriculture. In farming the farmer, as an individual, is a farm operator, seller, buyer, manager, all put together. A farmer's reaction to improved technologies is conditioned by several socio-psychological and economic factors. In the decision-making process the farmers pass through stages of knowing about the innovation, developing attitudes, trial adoption and a final decision to adopt, or to wait and see, or not to adopt. It takes a period of time for stabilization of the technology-transfer into a social system.

The appropriateness of a technology depends upon its compatibility with the existing situation. The relevance of the technology in terms of local applicability is a crucial factor, because there are great differences between farmers operating in different cultures.

To motivate the farmers to perceive correctly the advantages of the new technology calls for use of different methods of communication. The teaching methods needed to influence the farmers are different from the methods used in normal formal education. It is necessary to use a combination of mass media, group media and individual contact methods.

As part of the important process of transfer of technology, selected topics should be incorporated into the school curriculum. Above all, the emphasis should be that pupils at all schools develop an attitude of pride and a respect for the importance of agriculture and learn the simple skills related to the transfer of technology.

Pupils at primary level need to develop positive thinking about agriculture in the context of national importance. This can be assisted by giving examples of achievements of individual farmers and villages and by inviting leading farmers to speak to the pupils.

Pupils at the lower secondary level need to develop an attitude that agriculture is based upon use of scientific principles of biology, physics and chemistry. They need to understand that there is continuous research in agriculture to be transferred to farmers. This can be integrated with biology, chemistry and physics teaching while teaching about the sun as a source of energy, importance of plants in maintaining ecological balance, the principle of food or water movement in phloem and xylem, etc. Simple experiments to teach photosynthesis can be designed.

Students at higher secondary level need to understand different aspects of agricultural technology and the factors involved in different situations. Simple demonstrations in the school yard or visits to farms can open up new ways of thinking about integrating new technologies into existing conditions as means to influence farm families.

Science teachers need to be given training and orientation towards the different aspects of technology in agriculture. They may have to be trained to integrate aspects of technology into biology, chemistry and physics teaching.

Appropriate technology development

The degree of appropriateness of any technology is related to the situation in which it will be used, the users, the objectives and the policies surrounding the project. Therefore, a technology could be appropriate in different circumstances — it may be highly sophisticated or just simple traditional one.

Major considerations are:

1. The objectives for the use of the technology.
2. Socio-cultural acceptability.
3. Capability of the users' group in producing and maintaining the technology with local resources.

Specifically, for technology to be appropriate, the following criteria should be considered.

1. It should utilize the users' skills and knowledge.
2. It has the potential to increase production, reduce work/burden, save time, improve quality of products, etc.

3. It should utilize locally available materials or materials easily and cheaply obtainable within the country.
4. It should be based on techniques which are easily learned and transferable.
5. It should lend itself to production on a small scale, for example a few households or a group of individuals.
6. It should be within the economic capability of the users, in other words, affordable.

Users should be consulted in the planning and design of the technology.

Transfer of appropriate technology

The strategy which is much effective for this transfer is the so-called "Training and Visit", where the clientele or users are first trained on the technology considered appropriate, and an action plan is required of the trainees on how they will use the technology. Assistance, both technical and supplementary funding (if available) are extended to the trainees for project implementation. Once implemented, monitoring is accomplished by visits and *in situ* consultations until the technology has been fully adopted.

Training should not be the "spoon-feeding" type of teaching-learning activity. Underlying principles (scientific basis) should be explained and understood by the users of the technology being transferred.

Hand-in-hand with transferring knowledge and development of skills, direction on right attitudes and correct values should be taken up, e.g. productive use of time, attainment of excellence, persistence, co-operation, positive thinking, etc., would certainly add to the effectiveness of appropriate technology.

(i) Food, agriculture and ethics

In this workshop, two basic questions were posed: (1) What are the ethical issues? (2) How do we teach these issues? The issues which were identified are listed below, followed by suggestions on the teaching.

Food production and ethics

Two major ethical issues were raised concerning food production.

1. Crops to grow — for example, food vs tobacco or other cash crops. There should be priority on the part of the producers to meet the food requirements of the locality coupled with a concern for conserving soil and other resources.

2. Usage of pesticides and herbicides — modern agricultural technology involves inputs which when used indiscriminately imperil the lives of consumers. A better understanding, therefore, of these technologies has become imperative. Policies on monitoring the waiting periods between application and harvest, especially of food consumed fresh and raw, must be implemented.

Postharvest technology and ethics

The nutrition value, quality and quantitative availability of food products are largely dependent on the ethical standard and attitude of the producers and processors.

Postharvest technology involves grading, preservation, storage, transporting and other handling operations after production and harvesting. These should be guided by the principles of (1) food safety; (2) prevention of adulteration; (3) equitable distribution; (4) reasonable profitmaking; and (5) non-pollution of the environment.

To be included in the teaching of science and technology are: concepts of macro-level implications and global perspectives of food safety as influenced by postharvest technology; lessons on maintenance of nutritive quality and prevention of adulteration; information on local and/or national food and drug laws; ways and means of handling produce to effect equitable distribution not only in geographic terms but also of times; inexpensive technology using local raw materials with minimum energy requirements, techniques which reduce losses of harvests, etc.

Food consumption and nutrition

In schools the starting point for any discussion of food consumption should be what the children themselves eat. In many cases discussion of what individuals eat, or *choose to eat* — if they do have a choice — will lead to the question of "animal" consumption itself. Even very young children can appreciate reasons why they themselves or others, cannot eat meat or meat products. The majority of teachers will thus be faced by ethical questions concerning food consumption — for example, "Can a vegetarian eat eggs?" (The advent of large-scale egg production has meant the availability of non-fertilized eggs and increased consumption by vegetarians.) These questions will arise early in any study of food consumption and teachers therefore need to have thought through the issues prior to teaching the topic. As teachers we need to be aware of the background of our pupils — at an individual and local community level — aware of their needs — physical and mental — and the knowledge which they bring to the classroom. Frequently they are well informed of topical issues, for example, famine in Ethopia and will want to know why many children do not have sufficient to eat. Teaching in this area should not be prescriptive (i.e. no preaching!).

Global food distribution and the socio-economic, political aspects of this are in general not issues which children can appreciate or understand until upper secondary level. There are some issues which could be raised earlier including the "dumping" of food available for consumption and "cash crops". It is debatable whether most science teachers can, or should, introduce such debate into the classroom — "team" teaching with teachers of other disciplines may be appropriate here.

The role of advertising and the media was recognized in our discussions (see also Turner and Ingle (1985) *New Developments in Nutrition Education*, p. 212). We recognized the influence of advertising on what children eat (as well as other features in the marketing of products, such as sweets, which in themselves had little or no nutritional value).

The importance of food in religions throughout the world — and throughout history — was recognized.

Food supply and distribution and ethics

The subject of ethics in food supply and distribution can be presented at various levels of science education by examples of current problems affecting human population in the area of interest.

Some illustrations/examples of ethical questions in this particular area of food supply and distribution:

1. India's surplus of food could be exported. But it is stored. Can the government distribute surplus food through subsidy scheme?
2. School lunch programme: Some people think money spent could be better used in research and development.
3. European Economic Community — dumping of foods instead of distributing them where they are badly needed (price/market).
4. In the USA six million broiler chickens were destroyed because Dieldrin was detected by the Federal Department of Agriculture. If this was discovered in less developed countries what actions would be taken? Moral dilemma. There is no limit set on such chemicals.
5. Prohibited food colours in developed countries. Food products from developed countries are exported to less developed countries where the food colours are not even thought of by the Health and Food laws and regulations.

Biotechnology and ethics

1. Research workers employed in private sector are becoming very secretive and they are very profit-oriented or commercially-minded.

The flow of information is one-sided from the public to private sector and not the other way.

2. Patenting is common in industries and secrecy in operation is common among them. Unfortunately the same tendency is developing among other researchers.

3. Knowledge should not be withheld and it should be used for the benefit of all.

4. This topic is not very suitable for school teaching, but at tertiary or postgraduate level the implications should be made known.

5. Fear, fame and fortune are the possessions of scientists who are working in private sector and this type of unethical attitude is not to be encouraged.

Teaching and learning

Education has an important role in developing ethical values and social responsibility in both children and adults. When ethical issues are discussed it is essential that the pros and cons, positive and negative effects of decisions are presented. Moreover, ethical issues should be presented as complete as possible, limited only by the age and maturity of the learners. It is believed that the ethical issues dealt with by young children would be those that concern them or their community and which are within their understanding and experience. Ethical issues to be introduced to older children at secondary level could be those of regional or international significance and which may require understanding of people, environments and cultures in other countries.

Ethical issues should be discussed in the content of human concerns and activities. This being so, a holistic approach should be used when ethical issues are introduced in school education. The teacher should avoid developing prejudices but to develop in students the ability to evaluate different positions and values held by people with different social, economic and cultural backgrounds. In short, teachers should avoid authoritative teaching when ethical issues are discussed.

Skills to be developed

The skills required for considering ethical issues go beyond those normally developed in the teaching of science. The cognitive skills associated with scientific processes, observation, measurement, hypotheses formulation and theoretical modelling are inadequate when ethical questions are discussed. In view of the humanistic dimensions inherent in ethical issues, the skills to be developed would include:

1. Interpretation of data.
2. Value clarification.

3. Evaluation of "dilemma" positions.
4. Decision making.

Teaching–learning approach and methods

A multidisciplinary approach should be used when teaching ethical issues, bringing into the discussion ideas and concepts from various subject disciplines including those of the social sciences. The methods which are relevant include:

1. Library research/essay writing.
2. Field work.
3. Audio-visual methods
4. Role play or simulation.
5. Seminar, discussion and debates.
6. Experimental activities — work experience, visits, etc.
7. Projects/case studies.

The emphasis in teaching should focus on action learning, whether the learning is at a personal or collective level. At school, school projects focused on community service and the school environments can be used for students to examine different ethical issues related to food production, supply and distribution.

Teachers should be trained to include the teaching of ethical issues in science teaching in the schools. In teaching of ethical issues, teachers should leave students with a feeling of diversity of values and the ability to reach decisions that they can justify based on facts and reasoning. Within this context, it should be recognized that the teachers' opinions constitute one of a number of inputs and this being so, not necessarily the "correct" one. The validity and relevance of other opinions, including those of the students, should be recognized. Such an understanding can be developed if at the training level, student teachers are asked to speak and discuss an ethical issue of environmental concern including taking a stand based on factual understanding about the issue and decision making.

(j) Educational aspects

The workshops devoted to this topic set out to consider the following two issues:

1. Curriculum frameworks for primary and secondary science which would facilitate the development of science teaching programmes more responsive to human needs, and reflective of local situations.
2. Methods of development of a range of classroom strategies for primary and secondary science.

214 DISCUSSION OF ISSUES

Curriculum frameworks

Any curriculum framework aiming at a science education responsive to human needs in relation to agriculture, food and nutrition will need to:

(a) allow for co-ordination between the separate sciences and an integrated approach to science teaching;
(b) ensure that the biological principles relating to issues of food, nutrition and agriculture are taught within an ecological context;
(c) develop opportunities for understanding the role science and technology can play in helping to identify and resolve local problems of feeding, nutrition and agriculture.

The basic biological principles relevant to these areas of human needs that all science curricula should seek to incorporate involve the following:

(a) the existence of animals and plants (including human beings) is dependent upon:
    their position within populations and communities;
    their interaction within such populations and communities;
    the interaction between abiotic and biotic components of an environment.
(b) the existence of different levels of organisation and complexity in the biosphere which are interrelated (see above) these include individual organisms; populations and ecosystems.
(c) the principles of individuality and variability, development and evolution; communication and behaviour, cycling and recycling processes.

All these principles can be related to contemporary issues of feeding, nutrition and agriculture, as shown in the table below.

| Topics to be taught | Related principles | |
	Levels of complexity	Process
Diet	Individual	Variability
Food production Food distribution Food consumption	Population	Populations and community
Agricultural resources Management Development	Ecosystem	Interactions

Development of classroom strategies

Any curriculum strategy should seek to start from *local issues and needs* of food, agriculture and nutrition and to relate relevant science and technology to local *traditional practices*.

Such a strategy for developing classroom work (formal and non-formal) may usefully include the following.

(a) A descriptive framework for linking issues, science and technology and school science as a basis for developing learning activities starting from a relevant local issue (the topic).

(b) Concept mapping. An initial concept map/teacher's plan for teaching a topic on food production.

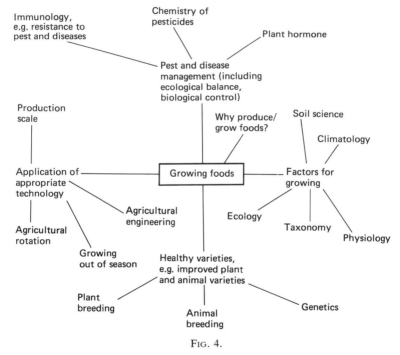

FIG. 4.

(c) Identification of a variety of pupil activities drawing on local resources:
   1. Case studies, using indigenous examples.
   2. Field trips and community studies, e.g. survey to study yields.
   3. Experiments including laboratory simulations, e.g. hydroponics, drip irrigation.
   4. School farm demonstrations, e.g. use of fertilizers, use of pest control measures, self-sustaining farms.
   5. Project work.

FAE–H

Topic (local issue)	Traditional practices	Related agriculture or food technology	Related school science	Curriculum framework
(i) How to manage pests? Problem of defining pest as a concept. Pest was defined as an organism which prevents maximizing agriculture production and naturally arise from man's infesting with natural environment.	In the past cultural method. Today mainly chemical control.	Today trends to use environmentally more suitable methods, e.g. selective chemicals, baits, integrated and biological control. *Methods of teaching* Experiments in and outside the lab. Case histories.	Balance between species. Adaptation and resistance. Mutation. Cyclic development of interrelated species.	Man's interference in nature. Balance in nature.
(ii) How do we store food?	Storage of maize by small farmers — grain drying.	Postharvest technology, e.g. preharvest prophylaxis	Concepts and principles. Respiration. Fungi. Water and life.	A biology course with an ecological dimension throughout.

References

Badran, A., Baydoun, E. and Subbarini, M. (1985) A frame syllabus for agriculture education for elementary school pupils in Jordan (Conference paper).

Devadas, R. P. (1985) Integration of nutrition and health education in the primary school of Tamil Nadu State, India. In *New Developments in Nutrition Education* (Ed. by S. A. Turner and R. B. Ingle), Nutrition Education Series, Issue 11, UNESCO.

Kiyimba, D. (1985) The place of nutrition in teacher's curriculum as a tool for rural development. In *New Developments in Nutrition Education* (Ed. by S. A. Turner and R. B. Ingle), Nutrition Education Series, Issue 11, UNESCO.

Parry, D. A. and Cursiter, M. C. (1985), Learning by doing — student participation in nutrition education surveys. In *New Developments in Nutrition Education* (Ed. by S. A. Turner and R. B. Ingle), Nutrition Education Series, Issue 11, UNESCO.

Postscript

Due to constraints in space and number of pages assigned to each volume, many of the articles submitted for Food and Agriculture section are not included in this volume. Hopefully, most of them will be published in other appropriate journals. As a consequence the names of some of the participants of the Food section are not individually mentioned in this volume. But their participation and contribution during discussion are greatly appreciated and their views are included in the foregoing pages. The Chairman and rapporteur (see page 181) prepared the summary of discussion of each workshop and after omitting some of the repetitions of extraneous points the discussion of issues was rewritten by the editor for this section.

This short postscript briefly explains the presentation of results obtained in different workshops and hopefully this would also clear the doubts that some of the participants of the Food section may have with regard to their individual contributions.

A. N. Rao

D. Other Papers

27

Continuing Education for Rural Women

PAULINA D. PAGES

Project Manager, Women in Development, South East Asia Center for Research in Agriculture, Laguna, Philippines

Evidence has indicated that agriculture, in the sense of the use of domesticated plants and animals for the production of food, originated independently in several widely separated tropical and sub-tropical locations throughout the world. According to historians, this turning point took place some 12,000 years ago, but crop and livestock improvements were placed on a rational and systematic level only in the early 1900s. Through science and technology, agricultural productivity considerably increased in the first half of the twentieth century but, ironically, much less in the tropical and sub-tropical areas of the world which nurtured the beginnings of agriculture. However, it came to be recognized that these same areas hold the key to increasing the world food production so urgently needed then, now, and in the future. It was predicted that by 1985 the food deficits would reach as high as 85 million tons with at least 400 million people living on the edge of starvation.

World strategy on food and agriculture

With this grim backdrop, global agricultural research efforts started to be focused on crop and livestock improvement programmes throughout the Third World. Rice, the staple crop of Asia, which supports more than half of the world's population, became the first target of research attention with the establishment of the International Rice Research Institute (IRRI) in the Philippines in 1960. The International Maize and Wheat Improvement Centre in Mexico was later founded in 1967. Rice together with wheat make up more than 70% of the world's annual grain production. Rice improvement in Latin America took a big boost with the establishment of the International Center for Tropical Agriculture in Colombia in 1967. Cereal crops, being the mainstay of world nutrition, were from the

221

beginning at the centre of the stage in these international research efforts. Then improvement of other food energy sources, like legumes, root and tuber crops as well as livestock, started to be tackled as part of the overall strategy for the improvement of world food production. To do the work other international agricultural research centres were established in the tropics and sub-tropics.

Focus on rural women

What part do rural women play in food production? These are some of the facts about rural women in the Third World.

— Women have been credited by some historians of agriculture with being the first to domesticate crop plants, thereby initiating the art and science of farming. They were the first to gather seeds and to grow them as food, fodder, fibre and fuel. They have played and continue to play a key role in the conservation of basic life support systems such as land, water, flora and fauna. Dr. M. S. Swaminathan (1985), Director-General of IRRI, asserts that "without the total intellectual and physical participation of women, it will not be possible to popularize alternative systems of land management to shifting cultivation, arrest gene and soil erosion, promote the care of the soil and health of economic plants and farm animals".

— Of all the hours worked throughout the world, women contribute about two-thirds and much of this work is done by rural women. Women in rural areas grow at least 50% of the world's food, yet they are more likely to be overburdened and malnourished. They receive only one-tenth of world income and own less than 1% of world property.

— In Asia, except Singapore, Japan, and the Philippines, the number of women working in the agricultural sector is much higher than in any other sector (for example, services and industry).

— It is estimated that the 52% of Asian women engaged in farming are predominantly in subsistence production. In Africa, subsistence farming is almost entirely in the hands of women. In Nepal, 57% of subsistence agriculture is by women.

— Rural women work more hours per day than men because of their traditional duties (household work and child care) in addition to farm work. They are also the traditional food processors and the cooks.

— Rural women play a very significant role in rice farming, both as farmers and farm labour. Their roles, however, vary considerably in Bangladesh, India, Indonesia, Nepal, the Philippines, and Thailand, both within and between countries, according to ecological, cultural, religious, economic, social and institutional factors.

— Rural women may be grouped socio-economically into three categories. First, women who are poor, landless and come from marginal farm families, and who rely for their livelihood on employment in rich households. All members have to contribute to the family income to survive. Secondly, subsistence farm women, who generally provide substantial labour on the family farm and often engage in other income-generating activities. Thirdly, women from rich farm families, who rarely engage in field work, but may have supervisory or management roles.

— In Thailand, the Philippines, and some developing countries, women's customary control of finances gives them an important role in farm and household decision-making.

— The exclusion of rural women from science and agricultural technology is well documented. The following are cited as factors for this unfortunate situation: the perception of women's primary role at home and the stress of her domestic work; lack of access to education and training; lack of access to means of production; sociocultural barriers, the burden of daily tasks, and women's acceptance of the division of labour at home.

— The development of economies in urban areas has resulted in the urban migration of men for jobs in industry and services, leaving the rural women behind and adding to their work. However, this also opens up opportunities for them to learn and use technologies for the agricultural work left for them to do.

When a labour shortage arises due to male migration to the towns, the following positive effects of the new technologies on women arise, namely: increased employment for the landless and poor women; higher wage rates for women labourers; better contractual working conditions; less male competition; increased responsibility; introduction of equal wages for equal work. The negative effects could be: longer hours and more strenuous work; impaired health and lower nutritional status, not only of the women themselves, but also of their children.

In general, the effects of new technologies are reduced costs; more timely and efficient operations which will increase farm income, thereby benefiting the whole family; the increased income which can be invested in other enterprises, creating employment for the poor; reduced drudgery for farm women. Against these advantages, it must be accepted that some poor farm women would be displaced from their traditional employment and this would have to be overcome by creating alternative employment.

Reporting on the African front, Wiese (1985) laments that in spite of some achievements during the Decade of Women, which includes sensitizing planners and decision-makers to women's needs and problems, the prevailing situation for rural women indicates that in Africa, development has so far only meant an increase in functions associated with their roles without reaping benefits. She further observes that subsequent developments, such as the introduction of modern technology, have proved detrimental to rural women because *they were not included in training programmes.*

Three peaceful agricultural revolutions have swept India: the Green Revolution, which has increased rice and wheat yields since the early sixties; the White Revolution, which has turned traditional milk production "upside down"; and the Blue Revolution, which has modernized fish production. They roll on independently of each other, and "yet as a harmonious trinity, they cause women to lose their traditional central position in the subsistence and rural economy and push them to the sidelines of the new production technology. They have to work hard, but make very little money" (Wichterich, 1985).

The ILO (1985) underscores the urgency and need for fresh action on the plight of lonely women — "abandoned wives, widows, divorcees and single mothers who are struggling against overwhelming odds to bring up children and earn a living for the family".

The ILO study identifies the following mutually enforcing obstacles which complicate the uphill struggle of women who are family providers:

1. Outright or implicit exclusion from land ownership under many existing civil and inheritance codes, and in land reforms and resettlement programmes.
2. Discrimination in rural financial markets, inhibiting the participation of female borrowers in the formal or co-operative lending system, leaving them at the mercy of the "loan sharks".
3. Lack of access of innovations in agricultural methods.
4. Bias in most agricultural and rural extension programmes which are almost entirely directed at men, while women's productive and managerial roles are overlooked.

A redirection of development thinking in favour of the many millions of poor rural women is being urged. Remedial measures should be incorporated into policies to benefit them.

Conclusion

Rural women have been the "forgotten link in the development chain" at all levels. Science and technology education has its significant role to play in all development programmes. Reaching rural women through continuing education should be one of its priorities.

References

ILO (1985) The lonely women — a growing problem. *Development and Cooperation*, No. 2/1985, March–April.

Wichterich, Christa (1985) Progress in India but not for women *Development and Cooperation*, No. 2/1985, March–April.

Wiese, Eva-Maria (1985) Women in rural development. *Development and Cooperation*, No. 2/1985, March–April.

28

Nutrition and Agricultural Education Based on Biological Principles

L. HORST GRIMME

University of Bremen, Federal Republic of Germany

Contributions of science and technology

Science and technology have contributed a lot to food production (agriculture), food processing and food distribution. Agriculture has moved towards being an agro-industrial system of high productivity. It involves the use of high-yielding varieties of a restricted number of crop plants (maize, wheat and rice), large amounts of chemical fertilizers, increased irrigation and high inputs of pesticides. The highest productivity, measured in output, is based on Western world technologies, which are large-scale, mechanized, mono-cropping, capital-intensive, energy-intensive and skill-intensive. The food industry has used scientific knowledge and the techniques of automated food processing to enable increasing numbers of people in heavily populated areas to be supplied with more food at cheaper prices. Preparation methods (physical and thermal modification of food, separation and extraction) and preservation methods (by heat, cold, modified atmosphere, chemical modification, fermentation, dehydration) are used to produce a wide array of food.

Science and technology have also led to the possibility of food production from non-conventional sources, such as micro-organisms (bacteria, yeasts and algae), which can be grown on industrial wastes (like molasses). Chemical conversion of carbohydrates, such as cellulose to starch and sugars, and the spinning of plant protein into fibres, simulating beef, have made it possible to produce fabricated foods.

With the reductionism in the definition of food as "nutritive material absorbed or taken into the body of an organism, which serves for purposes of growth, work or repair and for the maintenance of vital processes", the development towards synthetic food components (amino acids) and the

227

processing of molecular constituents into mixtures for different purposes (soups, desserts, etc.) has wide applications.

Food marketing is governed by the needs of consumers for food which can be taken home and eaten (convenience food) or which is ready-to-eat (fast food). To make this kind of food acceptable, and even attractive, science and technology have provided the basis to overcome nutritional losses of food by fortification (nutrification), a concept heavily related to the understanding that food is a mixture of macro- and micro-nutrients, which can be improved (fortified) by the addition of constituents (vitamins, trace elements, etc.). Acceptability and attractiveness have been increased by the addition of artificial flavour and colour additives, preservatives, sweeteners, taste intensifiers and other food additives. Science has provided the basis for regarding such food additives as "ingredients generally recognized as safe" by defining models for evaluation of toxicological safety.

Concerns about progress

Concerns of the consumer are related to the deteriorative changes of processed food, which might be hazardous to health, and to safety of foods with regard to additives or residues. Some believe that they can be relieved of such concerns by being provided with foods which are available in the unmodified natural state, free from chemicals (fertilizers, pesticides and environmental residues) and free from food additives.

There are, however, dichotomies in consumer preferences, which show that consumers have become confused and hold diametrically opposing views on many issues concerning food. "They desire natural foods, raised without agrochemicals, BUT all oppose paying higher prices. Some desire definitive ingredient listing on the label, BUT all oppose chemical sounding names on the label. Some desire nutritional values listed on the label, BUT are annoyed by inability to understand nutritional labelling" (Melnick, 1979).

Even the specialist has trouble assessing how today's continual changes in industrial food production and processing affect the availability and quantities of individual nutrients. The choices which consumers make continue to change the character of food supply and could vitally affect the nutrition status. Educational advertising campaigns and adequate labelling are essential if consumers are to understand whether a diet is balanced in both calorific and nutrient content.

Controversy has also surrounded the new technologies in agriculture. Criticisms include that high yields are achieved only by massive applications of fertilizer, pesticides and irrigation; that cereals gradually replace legumes and thus impoverish the national diets; the new cereals benefit large farmers more than smallholders; and that rural employment is getting reduced. It is claimed that sustained agriculture must meet two requirements: (1) it must produce high and stable yields, and (2) it must preserve the resource base for endless generations, safeguarding soil, water, energy and genes.

Research, training and education

International conferences have urged the need for training of scientific and technical personnel in the systematic preservation of genetic material which is vital in the continuing progress in breeding. Special attention is needed to secure seeds from wild species, from historic land-races, and from plants which have evolved in natural centres of genetic diversity. Many of these irreplaceable genetic resources, with their unknown potential for use in breeding, are in danger of extinction.

The recent emergence of the system of international agriculture research centres dedicated to the needs of developing countries does not obviate the need for strong, competent national programmes. Especially in most developing countries, agricultural research systems suffer from inadequate facilities and scientific and technical staff, which requires international support for scientific and technical training in the developing countries themselves, as well as overseas training.

Agriculture, food processing and nutrition are not usually subjects in school curricula, but at least nutrition education has become an expanding area with the aim to improve nutrition-related skills of health care and to change nutritional behaviours. Some countries (Canada, Netherlands, Norway, UK, USA, etc.) have national nutrition education policies, and education in nutrition has assumed increasing importance due to the fact that empirical knowledge on food fails to keep up with the rapid development in the food supplying industry. Such nutrition and food policies help consumers improve nutrition practices. In The Netherlands, the Primary Education Act of 1985 makes it compulsory to teach "healthy living", including nutrition at all levels of the education system.

Macdonald (1983) commented on misleading information, concepts and advice concerning nutrition by "non" nutritionists: the "nonsense of dietary fibre", the "meaningless terms 'natural', 'organic' and 'health food' ". He claims that everyone should know "nutritional facts". Certainly from a scientist's point of view, nutrition should be taught by sound facts. But neither is nutrition a pure science (not even a subsection of biological science), nor can nutrition education be restricted to technical information about nutrition. The priorities of education should be to promote understanding of the interrelations between agricultural production, food science and technology, and nutrition; of the food chain governing the processes of life in the biosphere, and of the human role in this chain; and how to judge the quality of chosen food.

Nutrition education and biological principles

The teaching of biology in all schools and universities requires a structural approach, in which different levels of organization are involved. These different levels include individual organisms, populations and ecosystems. It is very easy to include aspects of diet, food processing and agriculture in a basic biology course:

Level	Topic
Individual	Diet
Population	Food production
	Food distribution
	Food consumption
Eco-system	Agricultural resources
	Management
	Development

This general approach along organizational levels may be linked to a functional approach using biological principles, known to all biology teachers, such as

— the principle of individuality and variability,
— the principle of development and evolution,
— the principle of communication and behaviour,
— the principle of cycling and recycling processes.

The application of such principles, amongst others, to the topic of nutrition will have useful educational links. For example, using the principle of individuality and variability, the teacher could collect all the individual preferences of food amongst members of a particular class and explore the physical and emotional similarities and differences, establishing respect for the intrinsic value of each individual. Daily intakes of food can be recommended and the broad limits in which these are relevant, when they are applicable to the wide spectrum of variable needs and preferences. The principle of individuality is of great value in strengthening self-confidence and to establish a self determined and conscious eating behaviour.

The principle of continuous individual development of evolution offers the chance to introduce a wide range of themes in nutrition from breast-feeding to special diets for the elderly. It also gives an opportunity to discuss the influences on children of refined sugar products with life-long consequences.

The discussion can also implicate levels of population and their co-evolution with food-resources, showing for example how different are enzyme patterns, which cause intolerance to certain food and drink components (alcohol dehydrogenance is missing in some Asian populations; lactose causes intolerance in some African populations). This principle is also important for ecosystems. Industrial inputs of chemicals have created great problems by diminishing non-agricultural species in agro-ecosystems on the one side and by creating pesticide-resistant pests and herbicide-resistant weeds on the other.

The setting of nutrition in an ecological context enables teachers to introduce topics in the interface of agriculture, food processing and nutrition. This can be done by using four themes:

1. All living organisms must eat.
2. Man is a link in food chains.
3. Man's food must reflect high natural complexity.
4. Food quality is an outcome of well-established agricultural practices.

29

Aspects of Education Related to Food and Agriculture in Developing Countries

THAVORN VAJRABHAYA
Chulalongkorn University, Thailand

A knowledge of technological advancement in food production, food processing and nutrition may be greatly beneficial to some, but it may have a negative effect on others if the social structure and economic situation, among other things, are not suitable for such development. Precautions should be taken against the direct transfer of modern technology to an actual situation. In the past, due to lack of academics in developing countries, direct transfer of technology was the only way to make rapid progress in food and agricultural technology. But now each country has built up scientific manpower of its own in many fields.

To illustrate the above, too often a book on how to grow plants introduces the use of chemical fertilizers too soon. Likewise, many teachers speaking to the general public or teaching an elementary course explain prematurely about pesticides without giving enough basic knowledge about plant life and the environment. This kind of teaching leads people to believe that whenever they grow plants they must invest heavily in such things without their being aware that plants can grow without them. Some books describe a remarkable increase in yield as a result of the application of chemical fertilizer or the use of a new method of irrigation without showing a cost/benefit analysis. It needs to be realized that a routine use of pesticide not only upsets the balance of the pest and predator, but it is also hazardous to the health of the user and the consumer. Mechanization is efficient, it saves time and labour, but it may create social problems by leaving the labour force idle, which in turn affects the socio-economic climate.

Transfer of technology from developed to developing countries has certainly been a short cut to development in the past, but on many occasions this has created problems. Now development has gone a long way in some countries and a skilled manpower is building up in many different occupations. This is therefore the time for a revision of syllabuses to meet local needs and several factors should be taken into consideration:

— a review of the link between basic sciences and technology;
— a serious consideration of the use of the social sciences (economics, psychology and sociology) in association with science and technology education;
— the use of more local examples instead of the typical textbook facts and figures derived from developed countries.

Too much emphasis placed on the application of technology without consideration of basic science can encourage the over-use of chemical fertilizer, which not only wastes money, but can cause damage to soil structure which, in turn, results in lower yield in subsequent croppings.

Looking at the other side, teaching plant nutrition by citing work in hydroponics can give students a clearer picture of the mineral requirements of the plant. Unfortunately, such experiments in hydroponics were made under rigid environmental controls, which cannot be applied directly to farms. This is an example of a very valuable scientific finding, which leads to an understanding of plant nutrition, but has no direct application in many countries.

Teaching on the use of fertilizer often refers only to a very small fraction of basic science. The same applies to other branches of plant and animal biology. The importance of the link between the technology and the basic science must be stressed and a proper balance developed between the two when drafting new syllabuses. Students need a better picture of plant and animal life before the technology of agriculture is introduced.

As a further example, in the teaching of pest control by the use of the technology of chemical pesticides, students must be given the choice of subtle and effective methods of pest regulation by biological and physical means. Ideally, more pest-resistant or pest-tolerant strains of plants and animals should gradually replace the ones being cultivated at present, and this would help reduce the use of toxic chemicals harmful to humans and other living things. Dissemination of such knowledge through education will not only reduce the cost of production in the future, but will also help to solve the pollution problem.

Other advances in science and technology, such as the development of biotechnology and genetic engineering, should be introduced to broaden the view of the technology to come. However, care must be taken not to mislead people to believe that new technologies will make conventional ones obsolete overnight, and the consequences of using such new technologies must be foreseen and revealed.

There are other dangers over the transfer of technology from a developed to a developing country. Differences in the environment, the economic situation, the ability to the users and other social factors may not make the transfer appropriate. Sophisticated machines that work efficiently and can replace labour by using a few well-trained operators are not suitable for developing countries. Most are densely populated and require industries that utilize a large labour force. Introducing highly advanced technologies not only increases the foreign trade deficit, but leaves them with surplus labour, both of which are serious problems in developing countries.

Another warning concerns the dangers of advertisements, which are becoming a more and more significant factor. If people are not given a good educational background, they are easily misled by various forms of advertisement, and farmers seem to be highly vulnerable.

The importance of new syllabuses including basic science has been stressed as an important background to studying food and agriculture and learning of new technologies. However, those at school have little experience in food production or food processing. Thus, an alternative and probably more effective means of education may be in the form of continuing or informal education and could be a profitable investment for the government.

30

Unesco and Nutrition Education

The Unesco Division of Science, Technology and Vocational Education has for a long time made valuable contributions to science teaching. In recent years they have given much attention to nutrition education and have published a series of monographs as part of their Nutrition Education Programme. For example, issue 10 is a 140-page monograph full of easy to make teaching aids; and issue 11, "New Developments in Nutrition Education", edited by Sheila Turner and Richard Ingle, is a 240-page monograph based on contributions made to a conference on this theme in July 1983.

In addition to the series of monographs, it is possible to recommend very strongly a Unesco resource pack specially prepared for use in developing countries, as outlined below.

Unesco resource pack
for nutrition teaching–learning

Volume I   — Unesco sourcebook for classroom nutrition teaching–learning.
Volume II — Unesco sourcebook for non-formal out-of-school nutrition teaching–learning.
Volume III— Unesco sourcebook for training in nutrition teaching methods
Volume IV— Easy-to-make teaching aids
Volume V — World-wide directory of nutrition teaching-learning resources.

Further details on the Unesco Nutrition Education Programme and on the availability of the above resources can be obtained from:

Dr. Susan Van der Vynckt
Nutrition Education Programme,
Division of Science, Technical and Vocational Education,
Unesco,
75007 Paris,
France

Index